WHEN BROTHERS
DWELL TOGETHER

W H E N
BROTHERS
D W E L L
TOGETHER

The Preeminence of

Younger Siblings

in the Hebrew Bible

Frederick E. Greenspahn

New York   Oxford
OXFORD UNIVERSITY PRESS
1994

Oxford University Press

Oxford   New York   Toronto
Delhi   Bombay   Calcutta   Madras   Karachi
Kuala Lumpur   Singapore   Hong Kong   Tokyo
Nairobi   Dar es Salaam   Cape Town
Melbourne   Auckland   Madrid

and associated companies in
Berlin   Ibadan

Published by Oxford University Press, Inc.
200 Madison Avenue, New York, New York 10016

Oxford is a registered trademark of Oxford University Press, Inc.

Library of Congress Cataloging-in-Publication Data

Greenspahn, Frederick E., 1946–
When brothers dwell together :
the preeminence of younger siblings
in the Hebrew Bible /
Frederick E. Greenspahn.
p.   cm.
Includes bibliographical references and indexes.
ISBN 0-19-508253-2
1. Brothers in the Bible.
2. Sisters in the Bible.
3. First-born children in the Bible.
4. Bible. O.T.—Criticism, interpretation, etc.
I. Title.
BS579.B7G73   1994   221.8′306875—dc20   93-28112

2 4 6 8 9 7 5 3 1

Printed in the United States of America
on acid-free paper

for Rachel and Daniel

Contents

Abbreviations

Transliteration of biblical Hebrew generally follows the guidelines of the *Journal of Biblical Literature* 107 (1988) 582–83, while that of postbiblical Hebrew follows the *AJSreview* 6 (1981) 209–10.

AB   Anchor Bible

ABL   *Assyrian and Babylonian Letters Belonging to the Kouyonjik Collections of the British Museum*, ed. R. F. Harper (Chicago: University of Chicago, 1892–1914)

AfO   *Archiv für Orientforschung*

AnOr   Analecta Orientalia

AOAT   Alter Orient und Altes Testament

ARM   Archives Royales de Mari

ATD   Das Alte Testament Deutsch

AV   Authorized Version of the Bible

b.   Babylonian Talmud

BKAT   Biblischer Kommentar: Altes Testament

BZAW   Beihefte zur *Zeitschrift für die alttestamentliche Wissenschaft*

BZNW   Beihefte zur *Zeitschrift für die neutestamentliche Wissenschaft*

CT	Cuneiform Texts from Babylonian Tablets in the British Museum
ET	English translation
HKAT	Handkommentar zum Alten Testament
HSS	Harvard Semitic Series
ICC	International Critical Commentary
KAT	Kommentar zum Alten Testament
LCL	Loeb Classical Library
LXX^L	Lucianic recension of the Septuagint
m.	Mishnah
MRS	Mission de Ras Shamra
MT	Masoretic Text
NAB	New American Bible
ND	Nimrud (Kalhu) tablets
NIV	New International Version of the Bible
NJV	*Tanakh, A New Translation of the Holy Scriptures According to the Traditional Text* (Philadelphia: Jewish Publication Society of America, 1985)
n.s.	new series
OTL	Old Testament Library
o.s.	old series
Pap.	papyrus
PG	*Patrologiae, cursus completus, series Graeca,* ed. J. P. Mignè (Paris: 1857–66)

PL *Patrologiae, cursus completus, series Latina*, ed. J. P. Mignè (Paris: 1844–64)

Q   Qumran text
    1QH – Hodayot (Thanksgiving Hymns) from Qumran cave 1
    4QDibHam – Diverei Hame'orot (Words of Heavenly Lights) from Qumran cave 4
    4QSam^a – first copy of Samuel from Qumran cave 4
    11QPs^a – first copy of Psalms from Qumran cave 11

RS Ras Shamra tablets

RSV Revised Standard Version of the Bible

SBOE Sacred Books of the East, ed. F. Max Müller

StOr Studia Orientalia

STVC *Sumerian Texts of Varied Contents*, ed. Edward Chiera (Chicago: University of Chicago Press, 1934)

t. Tosefta

TCL Textes cunéiformes du Louvre

TRS *Textes Religieux Sumériens du Louvre*, ed. H. de Genouillac (TCL 15–16; Paris: P. Geuthner, 1930)

UAR *Urkunden des alten Reichs*, ed. K. Sethe (Leipzig: J. C. Hinrichs, 1903)

VAS Vorderasiatische Schriftdenkmäler

y. Jerusalem (Palestinian) Talmud

YBC Yale University Babylonian Collection

YOS Yale Oriental Series, Babylonian Texts

WHEN BROTHERS
DWELL TOGETHER

Introduction

Family relations play a central role in biblical literature, with sibling interaction the focus in many of its tales. Almost every major character in the Bible has at least one brother or sister who contributes to the story's development in a material way. Princes kill their brothers to protect claims to the throne; mothers scheme in order to ensure a preferred son's succession; sisters become rivals in determining marital relations. If mother-child relationships typify sustenance and those between fathers and sons epitomize the transmission of authority, it is in sibling interaction that biblical authors develop some of their most memorable plots.

Such plots are hardly unique to ancient Israel. Throughout the world siblings provide a focal point for stories. Hansel and Gretel, Castor and Pollux, and the three little pigs merely exemplify this subject's widespread appeal. However, as these examples demonstrate, the relationship is often conceived as harmonious. That connotation can also be traced back to antiquity, when fraternal imagery was used to designate allies in international treaties.[1] Similar overtones persist in our own culture, with its interest in "fraternity" and "brotherly love."

It is not difficult to discern the basis for such imagery. There are many similarities between brothers, who share parents and are usually close in age. A particularly apt example of this is provided by twins, whose biological commonality offers the maximal identity possible between

[1] See, for example, J. M, Munn-Rankin, "Diplomacy in Western Asia in the Early Second Millennium B.C.," *Iraq* 18 (1956) 76–84; such language persists, as in Henry R. Luce's assertion that "America must be the elder brother of the nations in the brotherhood of man" ("America's War and America's Peace," *Life* 12:7 [February 16, 1942] p. 91).

distinct human beings. The classical example of this genre is the Greek depiction of the Dioscuri, Castor and Polydeuces, the latter more familiar to us as Pollux.[2] Although the offspring of different fathers, they had been conceived by Leda in a single night. Indeed, their harmony became legend: "Of all brothers they were the most affectionate, not striving in rivalry for the leadership nor acting without previous consultations."[3] So intense was their unity that in the face of Castor's death Polydeuces rejected Zeus's offer of immortality ("Bid me also die, O King, with this my brother"[4]). To this day, they continue in heavenly alternation.

Such tales of sibling harmony are not lacking in the Bible. Aside from brothers who do not act at all (the offspring of some of Israel's kings, for example), Noah's sons Shem and Japheth together covered their father after another brother told them that he lay naked in the tent (Gen 9: 20–27); Lot's two daughters cooperated by sleeping with their father on successive nights in order to produce heirs (Gen 19: 30–38); and Simeon and Levi jointly avenged their sister's rape (Genesis 34).[5] Yet the enumeration of these examples demonstrates both the paucity and the triviality of the Bible's stories about siblings who work together. None of these harmonious siblings is a major character, nor are the incidents of central importance to the biblical narrative. Simeon and Levi's is the only real "adventure," their one-chapter escapade an isolated example of what true brotherhood can be. There is simply no Castor and Pollux in the Hebrew Bible. Instead, its treatment of this relationship centers on stories of rivalry and conflict. This begins with Cain and Abel, the Bible's first human offspring. There is also conflict before birth for the two sets of biblical twins, Jacob-Esau and Perez-Zerah.[6] It is no wonder that sibling rivalry is considered virtually coexistent with humankind, as if to say that brothers have never been able to get along. In this context, the famous observation, "how good and pleasant it is when brothers dwell together" (Ps 133:1) takes on an almost wistful tone.

Sibling conflict is hardly unique to the literature of ancient Israel. It can be found in such familiar tales as those of Cinderella and her wicked stepsisters or of Oedipus' sons Eteocles and Polynices. An African proverb

---

[2] See Apollodorus, *The Library* 3.10–11 (LCL vol. 2, pp. 22–33).

[3] Hyginus, *Poetica Astronomica* 2.22 (in Mary Grant, *The Myths of Hyginus* [Lawrence, KS: University of Kansas Publications, 1960] p. 212).

[4] Pindar, *Nemean Odes* 10.76–77 (LCL pp. 422–25).

[5] Absalom also avenged his sister's rape, in this case by their half-brother Amnon (2 Samuel 13).

[6] Cain and Abel are not presented as twins, despite various claims to the contrary (e.g., Bruce Vawter, *On Genesis, A New Reading*, p. 92, on the basis of the phrase *wattōsep laledet* in Gen 4:2).

warns, "They hate like brothers,"[7] and Mesopotamian tradition looks forward to a golden age "when the younger brother . . . respects(?) his older brother."[8] What sets the Bible apart is not the theme but the frequency with which it appears; there is scarcely a family not wracked by such conflict and rivalry.

Equally remarkable is the fact that the overwhelming majority of biblical heroes who emerge triumphant in these tales are younger offspring. From Abel, whose offering God preferred, through Solomon, whom David selected as his successor, virtually every major figure in the Bible is said to have had older brothers or sisters. In this, Israelite tradition appears to defy statistical probability, the popular expectation that primogeniture was normative in antiquity, and the notion that firstborns are the ones most likely to be overachievers.

Several hypotheses have been offered to account for the striking predominance of younger siblings in biblical literature. Some have thought it a historical relic, preserving the memory of a time when youngest sons did receive preferential treatment. Others consider it a form of protest, challenging a specific Israelite practice, such as the sacrifice of firstborn sons, or a broader social convention, such as the favoritism familiar in our own culture.

Because these theories interpret this literary theme in light of some presumed social practice which it is said to follow or reject, our own interpretation of this phenomenon must begin by considering the nature of actual Israelite practice. This is not a simple undertaking. Although the Bible is necessarily our primary source, it is a limited text that cannot be assumed to be entirely reliable. Evidence must, therefore, be sought from other ancient Near Eastern sources as well as materials from around the world and throughout history, drawing on the resources of such fields as law, anthropology, folklore, and linguistics. In fact, a careful reading of such material will show that ancient Israelite practice was far more fluid than is usually allowed, with fathers apparently free to give whatever preferences there might be to the son of their choice. Even the terminology for designating this favored offspring, most notably the Hebrew word *běkōr*, is more ambiguous than the conventional translation "firstborn" suggests.

It is this social reality, rather than a system of automatic preference for firstborns, that underlies several of the biblical accounts. Thus God

---

[7] Cited by Edith G. Neisser (*The Eldest Child* [New York: Harper & Brothers, 1957] p. 13).

[8] STVC 66 and 67, TRS 15, 11th KI-RU-GÚ in Thorkild Jacobsen, *Before Philosophy* (Baltimore, MD: Penguin Books, 1966) p. 217.

was free to choose Abel's sacrifice over Cain's, Jacob could place his right hand over Ephraim rather than Manasseh, and David was entitled to appoint Solomon rather than some older son. This also explains the widespread metaphorical use of associated terminology when the Bible designates the people Israel as God's chosen child (*bĕkōr*), an image which may have originated in the Northern kingdom before it was adopted in the South and applied to the Jerusalem king.

The relationship between these tales and Israel's social structure is still not adequate to explain the overwhelming number of younger siblings who emerge triumphant, often in stories that do not involve either family inheritance or royal succession. Moreover, a substantial number of the Bible's younger children achieve prominence without having to displace older brothers or sisters. For example, neither Moses nor David encountered serious opposition from their older siblings. Likewise, Rachel is simply said to have been more beautiful than Leah, and Michal is just more interesting than Merab.

This theme of success without conflict conforms to a well-known folklore pattern in which younger offspring emerge triumphant in their various endeavors. Several examples of this motif are known in ancient Near Eastern literature. The unexpected nature of the success described in these accounts often seems to be the result of some sort of superhuman force, and the heroes' youth suggests their innocence and vulnerability. In light of these connotations, it may be no accident that so many of the figures characterized in this way were usurpers. The motif of youth justifies their success by contrasting their inner virtues with the shortcomings of those they replaced. Moreover, because most of the biblical heroes who are presented as younger children do not seem to have been uniquely meritorious, the presence of this motif strengthens the Bible's suggestion that their success was the result of divine assistance.

In this regard, what sets the Bible apart from other literatures is the intense concentration of this theme within its relatively few pages, where not only David and Solomon are presented as younger sons, but also Isaac and Jacob and Joseph and Moses and Samuel and on and on. Careful study will show that these stories do not simply repeat a common motif, but that each has its own agenda and some actually have several. The apparent emphasis on the emergence of younger siblings in the Bible is thus the result of these stories' present juxtaposition. Collectively, they imply that the success of Israel's ancestors was neither easy nor expected, making Israel's status both surprising and suspect.

Throughout, Israel's heroes are not presented as somehow better suited than their rivals. The aptitudes they possess, whether David's skill against Goliath or Jacob's cleverness, almost invariably include elements of self-denigration, calling into question whatever merit they seem to impute. Jacob is a cheat and an exploiter, as Jeremiah recognized in his pun-filled warning, "Never trust a brother, for every brother cheats" (*'āqôb ya'qōb*, 9:3). Nor are David's successes solely the result of his ability. His victory over Goliath came despite his having to rely on a slingshot, not because of it. Other younger sons, such as Solomon and Isaac, are largely passive, and even Moses and Samuel, whose virtues no one would deny, did not earn their positions. Evidence of their skills becomes apparent only as they emerge into positions of prominence. Although the reliability of familiar and popular indicators of ability are denied by various biblical authors, it is not the burden of this motif to present Israel's leaders as those of true worth, but to demonstrate that their success had come from God.

Several features shared by many of these accounts—their concentration within the "J" stratum of Genesis, their focus on a blessing, and their emphasis on the importance of paternal designation—suggest a possible connection with the accession of Solomon, himself a younger son whose acquisition of the throne appears to have been both complex and controversial. That is not to say that these stories were necessarily written or collected during Solomon's lifetime. The theme did, however, acquire a power of its own, which persisted into early Judaism and Christianity, coloring the relationship between these two postbiblical traditions. Even within the Bible, it resonates well beyond the families of Genesis and Kings, extending into the accounts of creation, the covenant, kingship, and the end-time. Implied uncertainty as to Israel's worth must, therefore, be broadened in order to accommodate this theme's implications for Israel's understanding of God and the world.

Before turning to the details of these issues, a comment is in order about the male orientation that pervades so much of the language used throughout this study, beginning with the title, which has been taken from the book of Deuteronomy (25:5). As should be clear from the examples already cited, this is no modern imposition but an accurate reflection of virtually all the biblical tales in which this theme appears. The few exceptions (Rachel and Leah or Michal and Merab) merely confirm the Bible's androcentric focus, for the narratives that do include females invariably function as adjuncts to those dealing with males in one way or another. Thus Rachel and Leah echo Jacob's relation with Esau, and Michal and Merab epitomize the conflict between David and Saul.

It would also be inappropriate to proceed without mentioning the numerous colleagues and friends whose assistance has contributed to the preparation of this work. They have responded to specific inquiries and been generous in their willingness to debate and discuss issues which may not have always interested them. Although none of them is responsible for the conclusions I have drawn from our conversations, I am pleased to acknowledge gifts of time and expertise that have played a major role in the preparation of this volume from Robert Alden, Tamara Eskenazi, Everett Fox,[9] Michael Fox, Paul Hoskisson, Stanley Insler, Kent Jackson, David Jobling, Paul Kobelski, James Kugel, Jon Levenson, Sieglinde Lug, Dennis MacDonald, Peter Machinist, Herbert Paper, Kent Richards, Gary Rendsburg, Stephen Ricks, Jeremiah Unterman, John Welch, David Wright, and Bruce Zuckerman. It is a pleasure to express my special gratitude to Nahum M. Sarna for both his wisdom in counseling that this project be postponed until there was ample time for it to be treated thoroughly and for providing guidance and support long after the passing of whatever obligations may have once existed. Finally, this book is dedicated to my own first and second born, whose relations have grown beyond those described in these pages, thus making their father doubly blessed.

[9] After this manuscript had been sent to the publisher, I had the opportunity to hear Everett Fox's paper "Stalking the Younger Brother: Some Models for Understanding a Biblical Motif," which will appear in a forthcoming issue of the *Journal for the Study of the Old Testament*. Unfortunately, it came to my attention too late for its insights, which seem to support many of the observations made here, to be incorporated into the body of the text.

1

Firstborn of All Creation

All seven of the original Mercury astronauts were the oldest children in their families, as are a disporportionately large number of college students and professors, poets and presidents.[1] This concentration of firstborns among high achievers has been recognized for some time. Over a century ago, the British scientist Francis Galton observed a preponderance of first-borns among his colleagues.[2] Since then, similar findings have accumulated for a wide range of occupations and accomplishments.

Being firstborn is not always advantageous. Besides their dispropor-tionate representation among American presidents, eldest siblings are also overrepresented among strippers and criminals[3] and, as Galton was

---

[1] Stanley Schachter, "Birth Order, Eminence and Higher Education," *American Socio-logical Review* 28 (1963) 764; Irving D. Harris, *The Promised Seed, A Comparative Study of Eminent First and Later Sons* (New York: Free Press of Glencoe, 1964) p. 17; Louis Stewart, "The Politics of Birth Order," *Proceedings of the Seventy-eighth Annual Convention of the American Psychological Association* (1970) vol. 5, p. 365. Richard Zweigenhaft reports similar findings for members of Congress ("Birth Order, Approval-Seeking and Membership in Congress," *Journal of Individual Psychology* 31 [1975] 206–9). *Newsweek* notes that two of the Mercury astronauts were only children and twenty-one of the twenty-three Americans who had been in space by 1969 were firstborns ("First Best?" *Newsweek* 73:1 [January 6, 1969] 37).

[2] *English Men of Science, Their Nature and Their Nurture* (London: Macmillan & Co., 1874) pp. 34–35.

[3] James K. Skipper, Jr., and Charles M. McCaghy, "Stripteasers: The Anatomy and Career Contingencies of a Deviant Occupation," *Social Problems* 17 (1970) 395; Havelock Ellis, *A Study of British Genius* (new edition; Boston: Houghton Mifflin, 1926) p. 104.

already aware, among the mentally disadvantaged. They are also especially susceptible to prenatal disorders.[4]

Few are inclined to dismiss these facts as mere coincidence. Most often they are explained as the result of a configuration of traits, a personality type deemed characteristic of firstborns. Typical is one author's description of such individuals as "perfectionistic, reliable, conscientious, list maker, well organized, critical, serious, scholarly . . . goal oriented, achiever, self-sacrificing, people pleaser, conservative, supporter of law and order, believer in authority and ritual, legalistic, loyal, self-reliant."[5]

Usually, this "firstborn personality" is traced to the unique experiences firstborns encounter as they grow up. In Galton's words:

> elder sons have, on the whole, decided advantages of nurture over the younger sons. They are more likely to become possessed of independent means, and therefore able to follow the pursuits that have most attraction to their tastes; they are treated more as companions by their parents, and have earlier responsibility, both of which would develop independence of character; probably, also, the first-born of families not well-to-do in the world would generally have more attention in his infancy, more breathing space, and better nourishment.[6]

Writing in this century, psychologist Alfred Adler developed a parallel interpretation. Like Galton, he believed that an older child initially enjoys

---

[4] *English Men of Science*, p. 35; see also William Caudill and Carmi Schooler, "Symptom Patterns and Background Characteristics of Japanese Psychiatric Patients" in *Mental Health Research in Asia and the Pacific*, ed. William Caudill and Tsung-yi Lin (Honolulu, HI: East-West Center Press, 1969) p. 114, and Brush Cushna, Mitchell Green, and Bill C. F. Snyder, "First Born and Last Born Children in a Child Development Clinic," *Journal of Individual Psychology* 20 (1964) 180–81. Charles B. Willis contends that firstborns are on average less intelligent than subsequent children ("The Effects of Primogeniture on Intellectual Capacity," *Journal of Abnormal and Social Psychology* 18 [1923–24] 377). Awareness of firstborns' physical vulnerability is apparent already in the Babylonian Theodicy's observation that "the first calf is lowly, the later offspring is twice as big. A first child is born a weakling, but the second child is called a heroic warrior (*littu būršu rēštû šapilma ligimûša arkû maṣi šittinšu lillu māru panā ᵓallad lᵉᵓûm qardu ša šanî nibissu*) (lines 260–63, W. G. Lambert, *Babylonian Wisdom Literature* [Oxford: Clarendon Press, 1960] pp. 86–87). Brian Sutton-Smith and B.G. Rosenberg point out that this could serve to firstborns' statistical advantage if it were to result in survivors' being more highly selected than their later-born counterparts (*The Sibling* [New York: Holt, Rinehart and Winston, 1970] p. 15); however, Corrado Gini suggests these frailties may be a function of small family size rather than birth order per se ("Superiority of the Eldest," *The Journal of Heredity* 6 [1915] 37).

[5] Kevin Leman, *The Birth Order Book, Why You Are the Way You Are* (Old Tappan, NJ: Fleming H. Revell, Co., 1984) p. 11 (see also p. 39); a more scholarly survey of the research is presented by William D. Altus, "Birth Order and Its Sequelae," *Science* 151 (1966) 44–49.

[6] *English Men of Science*, pp. 34–35.

the "advantage of an excellent position for the development of his psychic life" because of the undivided parental attention in which firstborns bask. However, he thought that the arrival of siblings later breeds a sense of resentment in older brothers or sisters who must share the limelight they had grown accustomed to monopolizing. This leads to what Adler called a feeling of "dethronement" in contrast to the sense of inferiority fostered by the relative neglect accorded younger childern.[7]

Alongside the endless stream of studies correlating birth order with an ever-increasing number of personality traits are several recent reports taking issue with the widespread perception that firstborns tend to be high achievers. These generally give empirical support to the obvious fact that not all firstborns conform to the postulated "type" and that many prominent and successful individuals are not eldest children. In one commentator's words, "one would be hard put even to guess whether such first sons as Newton, Kant, and Shakespeare had greater or lesser genius than such later sons as Descartes, Hume, and Dostoevski."[8] More fundamentally, these skeptics claim to have found a flaw in the reasoning of the various psychological theories and suggest other plausible reasons why firstborns are overrepresented in so many different groups. For example, first-time parents are younger and usually less economically secure than when later siblings arrive. First children also grow up, at least for a time, in smaller families. These, or similar factors, may play a more immediate role than ordinal position in evoking the characteristics observed in such individuals.[9]

This uncertainty as to whether and how being firstborn actually affects personality development ultimately makes the widespread belief in its impact all the more remarkable. However one chooses to explain the monumental amount of accumulated data as to firstborns' personality and accomplishments, the theory of their psychological uniqueness itself remains a significant cultural fact. So pervasive is this view that one popular author actually sketched out three unidentified personality types, confident that his audience would recognize which belongs to the firstborn,

---

[7] *Understanding Human Nature* (Garden City, NY: Garden City Publishing Co., 1927) p. 152; see also "Characteristics of the First, Second, Third Child," *Children* 3:5 (May 1928) pp. 14 and 52.

[8] Irving D. Harris, *The Promised Seed*, p. 17; a tabular presentation of Harris's findings can be found on p. 8 of Brian Sutton-Smith and B. G. Rosenberg, *The Sibling*.

[9] For a detailed presentation of the vast number of studies on this subject, culminating in the conclusion that "birth order and sibship size do not have a strong impact on personality" (p. 248), see Cécile Ernest and Jules Angst, *Birth Order, Its Influence on Personality* (Berlin: Springer-Verlag, 1983).

which to the middle, and which to the youngest child, and thus find his more detailed, if largely anecdotal, descriptions credible.[10]

Sociologists have found that birth order does affect how we esteem individuals. For example, firstborn children are more likely than their younger sisters or brothers to be named after family members.[11] Such honor is no isolated prejudice, but has been traced to "the beginning of recorded time" and found "in most known societies."[12] Indeed, one survey of several, unrelated cultures reported that

> the birth of a first child of either sex is more likely than the birth of other children to increase parent status, stabilize parent marriage, and provide a parental teknonym. Firstborns are more likely to receive more elaborate birth ceremonies and, in childhood, to have more authority over siblings and to receive more respect from siblings. In adulthood firstborn daughters are likely to receive more respect from siblings than other daughters, and firstborn sons, in comparison to other sons, are likely to have more authority over siblings, more control of property, more power or influence over others, to be more respected by siblings and to head a kin group.[13]

Age and status have been correlated since antiquity. The oldest son of the ancient Persian king Darius is reported to have justified his claim to his father's throne on the basis "that it was *everywhere* customary (*nomizomenon eiē pros pantōn anthrōpōn*) that the eldest should rule," and the Alexandrian Jewish philosopher Philo observed that "the man of worth is elder and first, and so must he be called; but younger and last is every fool who pursues the ways which belong to rebellious youth and stands lower in the list."[14] Many cultures, including that of ancient Israel, have vested power in a group called "the elders," although membership is not necessarily a function of age.[15] Our own term "senator," which is

---

[10] Kevin Leman, *The Birth Order Book*, p. 11; this assumption was confirmed by audience reaction to Leman's description on the Phil Donahue show (transcript no. 06036 [Cincinnati, OH: Multimedia Entertainment Inc., 1986] p. 1).

[11] Alice S. Rossi, "Naming Children in Middle-Class Families," *American Sociological Review* 30 (1965) 504.

[12] Edith G. Neisser, *The Eldest Child* (New York: Harper & Brothers, 1957) p. 1; cf. Nahmanides at Gen 27:15.

[13] Paul C. Rosenblatt and Elizabeth L. Skoogberg, "Birth Order in Cross-Cultural Perspective," *Developmental Psychology* 10 (1974) 48.

[14] Herodotus 7.2–3 (LCL vol. 3, pp. 300–302), cf. 5.42, 6.5 (LCL vol. 3, pp. 44–45, 196–97); and Philo, *On Abraham* 274 (§46, LCL vol. 6, pp. 132–33).

[15] For the biblical evidence, see Hanoch Reviv, *Mosad ha-Zeqenim be-Yisra'el* (Jerusalem: Magnes Press, 1983). This usage is preserved in the office of *presbyter*, which provides the ultimate origin for the English term "priest."

reserved for members of the legislature's "*upper* chamber," derives from the same Latin root as both "senior" and "senile."

In light of this widespread cultural bias, it is remarkable to discover how many of the Bible's leading figures were not firstborn. Indeed, the list of younger siblings who are ascribed positions of prominence reads like a "Who's Who" of biblical literature: After Abel's death, Adam's line did not continue through the surviving son Cain but through Seth, a newly born son explicitly described as having replaced his murdered brother. Later, the patriarchal blessing passed through Abraham's second son Isaac, even though the birth of Ishmael, his older brother, is presented in a way that should have ensured his complete legitimacy. Isaac's younger son Jacob managed to supplant his older brother Esau and, despite his cousin's machinations, married Rachel, the younger of two sisters. Rachel became the mother of another younger child, Jacob's preferred son Joseph, who in turn fathered the specially blessed younger son Ephraim. Among the later figures of Moses, Samuel, David, and Solomon, not one was first-born. Even the prophet Ezekiel's portrayal of Israel's divided kingdom as two sisters identifies the chosen nation of Judah as the younger sister (23:4).[16]

It is difficult to accept this remarkable chain of events as the result of pure coincidence. Several theories have been offered to explain it. Some have seen it as pure fiction, a narrative device incorporated into the text to make a literary or theological point. In one version of this approach, these stories are connected with folklore, where younger siblings often play featured roles. More often, the ascendance of younger offspring is understood to reflect various realities from Israelite culture. Some interpreters, for example, consider it a protest against specific practices, such as the sacrifice of firstborns, or a theological polemic against the preference given oldest children.

We will look closely at each of these theories to see what light they can shed on this impressively consistent pattern. Before assuming that it requires a literary interpretation, however, we must first consider the

---

[16] Contrast Jer 3:6–10, where Israel and Judah are portrayed as sisters without reference to their relative ages. Gen 10:21 may suggest that Shem should be added to this list (see note 138 in chapter 2 below). Joseph Jacobs would include Abraham as well, since he appears to be contemporary with his nephew Lot (*Studies in Biblical Archaeology* [London: David Nutt, 1894] p. 51). However, Abraham is consistently listed first among his own brothers (e.g., Gen 11:26), although such evidence is not without problems of its own (see below pp. 64–66). This ambiguity persisted in rabbinic tradition where *Genesis Rabbah* 38:14 considers him to be Terah's oldest son, but *b. Sanhedrin* 69b recognizes that he may be a younger brother.

possibility that these tales preserve an accurate recollection of ancient Israelite custom.

It was Joseph Jacobs who asserted that these stories cannot be dismissed as coincidental, but should be treated as accurate descriptions of Israel's earliest social practice, from a time when it was customary for youngest children to be treated preferentially. In his view, this system of ultimogeniture did not endure, but came to be replaced by the practice of primogeniture (election of the eldest child) when Israel abandoned her nomadic lifestyle to settle in Canaan.[17]

Although this view is still occasionally invoked, it encounters serious problems.[18] Some of these have to do with the fact that several specific biblical instances do not fit Jacobs's scheme very well. For example, Solomon's accession to the throne, a dramatic example of a younger son's success in the Bible, took place long after the settlement which Jacobs thought responsible for the transition to primogeniture, although one might claim that royal succession could have preserved archaic norms. Even more germane is scholarly doubt as to whether Israel's settlement can be characterized in the way Jacobs assumes.[19] Even if his view of the settlement were correct, ultimogeniture is most often associated with settled cultures rather than nomadic ones, typically providing a mechanism for the transmission of property in societies where children receive land at the time of their marriage. Because youngest sons are usually the last to marry and, therefore, the least likely to have built up significant holdings by the time of their father's death, allowing them to receive whatever is left of the paternal estate ensures their security under circumstances where they might otherwise be left impoverished.[20] In addition, most of the biblical stories are not concerned with the transmission of land, as ultimogeniture most commonly provides, but with the transfer of status, whether in the form of kingship or a father's blessing.

Beyond these specific weaknesses, there is a broader methodological problem with Jacobs's approach. Although younger siblings enjoy remark-

---

[17] Joseph Jacobs, *Studies in Biblical Archaeology*, pp. 46–62.

[18] Nisan Rubin points out the theoretical difficulty with ultimogeniture of being certain which child will ultimately be one's youngest ("*Le-Mashmaʿuto ha-Ḥevratit shel ha-Bekhor ba-Miqraʾ*," *Beth Mikra* 33 [1987/88] 158).

[19] For an alternative view, see Norman K. Gottwald, *The Tribes of Yahweh, A Sociology of the Religion of Liberated Israel, 1250–1050* B.C.E. (Maryknoll, NY: Orbis Books, 1979) pp. 448–59.

[20] Henry Sumner Maine, *Lectures on the Early History of Institutions* (London: John Murray, 1875) pp. 222–23, where a Welsh law stipulating that a man's sons may divide his estate only after "the youngest son has had the paternal dwelling-house, eight acres of land and certain tools and utensils" is cited. Several cultures with similar practices are listed in Robert H. Lowie, *Social Organization* (New York: Rinehart and Co., 1948) p. 151.

able and extensive preeminence in the Bible, nowhere is their ascendance to positions of authority and prestige given either legal or social sanction. To the contrary, their success is consistently presented as anomalous and needing explanation, which the Bible sets out to provide in some of its most memorable tales. David's promise that he would be succeeded by Bathsheba's son (1 Kings 1:17), Reuben's dalliance with his father's concubine (Gen 35:22), Sarah's demand that Hagar and her newly born child be expelled (Gen 21:10), God's insistence that Samuel look beyond the physical stature of Jesse's sons (1 Sam 16:7), Joseph's failure to convince Jacob to place his right hand over Manasseh rather than Ephraim (Gen 48:17–19), Zerah's withdrawing his hand after it had emerged from his mother's womb (Gen 38:27–30), and Esau's repeated loss of priority as a result of duress and deception (Genesis 25–27)—all are intended to justify what the biblical authors plainly recognized as unexpected turns of events.

The presumption that senority would prevail sometimes reaches explicit expression, as when Joseph brought his sons to be blessed by their grandfather Jacob (Israel), putting the older "Ephraim...at Israel's left and Manasseh...at Israel's right" (Gen 48:13) and then objecting when Jacob crossed his hands before blessing them: "No, my father, for *this* is the *bĕkōr*; put your right hand on his head..." (v. 18). Given the higher status widely accorded the right side over the left, a view which the Bible shares,[21] it is evident that Joseph assumed that his older son should receive the better blessing. Centuries later, this same assumption led David's oldest surviving son Adonijah to take steps to gain control over his dying father's kingdom and, according to Chronicles, the Judean king Jehoshaphat to appoint Jehoram to be his successor "because he was the *bĕkōr*" (2 Chron 21:3). In a similar vein, Laban had thought that his older daughter should be married before her sister, explaining, "it is not customary in our place to marry off the younger before the older" (Gen 29:26).

The outcome of such stories is presented as being *un*expected. The brithright was clearly Reuben's to lose and Esau's to sell. By seeking to justify the apparent discrepancy between practice and principle, they suggest that privilege normally rested with older offspring. To deny that is to turn Jacob into an honest man, ignoring precisely the story's message.

Joseph Jacobs was not unaware of this discrepancy. His point was not to defend every detail of the biblical narrative. Rather, he claimed

---

[21] See H.-J. Fabry and A. Soggin, "*Yāmîn*" in *Theological Dictionary of the Old Testament*, ed. J. Botterweck and H. Ringgren (Grand Rapids, MI: W. B. Eerdmans, 1974–   ) vol. 6, p. 100, to which the connotation of such words as "sinister," "gauche," and "right" should be compared.

that these stories were intended to account for the incongruity created by the recognition that the heroes of Israel's most hallowed traditions had achieved authority under a system no longer in force or even remembered at the time these tales were told. In this respect, his theory resembles the more recent, now discarded view that the famous wife-sister stories in Genesis are attempts to rationalize an archaic and forgotten custom whereby special wives were honored with the title of "sister."[22] Both seek to justify morally uncomfortable accounts by treating them as late rationalizations of what had come to be unfamiliar customs. In so doing, they seem to salvage the historicity of the biblical account by accepting some "kernel" of truth without respect for the details presented, assuming that the actual historical events were quite different from what the Bible reports. In this, they paradoxically sacrifice the reliability of its plot in order to protect an underlying premise. As a result, the biblical account is treated as a garbled misunderstanding. The virtue of its heroes is protected by denying the reliability of our only source.

In fact, there is no evidence for ultimogeniture in either the Bible or any other ancient Near Eastern text. Instead, studies of surviving documents have consistently found attitudes and practices similar to those of more familiar times and places.

The well-known Mesopotamian legal codes unfortunately provide less information about matters of inheritance that one might wish. Only the Middle Assyrian Laws are explicit in allowing a double portion of *qaqqaru* property and the first choice for an extra share of *eqil šiluḫli* to a man's "big son" (dumu . gal).[23] An unpublished Egyptian code from the third pre-Christian century at Hermopolis is also reported to stipulate, "If a man dies, leaving lands, gardens, temple offices(?) and slaves; if he had children and he did not assign shares to them while alive, it is his eldest son who takes possession of the property of his father."[24]

Because of the limited information these ancient codes provide about inheritance, the best evidence for preferential treatment must be inferred from the records of actual legal transactions. Texts from Egypt's Old Kingdom describe firstborns as their "father's heir" and "master of all

---

[22] Cf. E. A. Speiser, "The Wife-Sister Motif in the Patriarchal Narratives" in *Biblical and Other Studies*, ed. Alexander Altmann (Cambridge, MA: Harvard University Press, 1963), especially p. 27, which should be read in light of Samuel Greengus, "Sisterhood Adoption and the 'Wife-Sister' in Genesis," *Hebrew Union College Annual* 46 (1975) 5–31.

[23] B§1. For a recent discussion of these terms' meaning, see J. A. Brinkman, "A Note on the Middle Assyrian Laws," *Revue d'Assyriologie* 79 (1985) 88–89.

[24] Girgis Mattha, "Rights and Duties of the Eldest Son According to the Native Egyptian Laws of the Third Century B.C.," *Bulletin of the Faculty of Arts*, University of Cairo 12:2 (December 1950) 115.

his things."[25] Unequal division of estates is also known from numerous Mesopotamian texts, which accord individual heirs various forms of preference. Often, the "biggest son" (d u m u . g a l or *māru rabû*) received first choice or was given a special portion, called the s í b . t a or *elâtu*. In some cases this advantage seems to have constituted two shares; elsewhere, other extra allocations can be inferred.[26]

Further evidence for this kind of preference can be inferred from its denial in several ancient documents. For example, an Old Babylonian letter asserts that "the institution of younger and older offspring does not exist is Sippar" (*aplūtum ṣeḫertum u rabītum ina Sippar ul ibašši*).[27] The phrasing suggests that Sippar was unusual in this regard. If primogeniture was not followed there, the statement shows that it was known and that deviations from this norm were considered grounds for comment. Several documents from the Nuzi archives also state, "They shall divide equally, with no older or younger among them" (*kīma mitḫāriš izuzzū rabû [GAL] u ṣeḫru [TUR] ina libbīšunu yānu*),[28] and, after identifying the offspring involved, an adoption tablet from Ugarit stipulates, "There is neither older nor younger between them" (*yānu rabû yānu ṣeḫru ina birīšunu*).[29]

In antiquity as today, one would not ordinarily deny a totally unfamiliar custom, or the list of practices not followed, whether at Sippar or Nuzi or Ugarit, would be many times longer than it is. By phrasing these statements in the negative ("there is not . . ."), these documents reflect an awareness that standard procedure, whether in their own communities or elsewhere, was quite different from what they impose.

The Hebrew Bible also preserves evidence of preferential treatment. Although it does not include a detailed exposition of Israelite inheritance

---

[25] Kurt Sethe, "Ein Prozessurteil aus dem alten Reich," *Zeitschrift für Ägyptische Sprache* 61 (1926) 69, which cites another son as saying of his mother, "I am her oldest son, her heir."

[26] The evidence is conveniently surveyed by Gershon Brin, "*Shetei Sugeyot be-Dinei Yerushah ba-Tequfah ha-Miqra'it—Meḥqar Hashva'ati*," *Dinei Yisra'el* 6 (1975) 232–43. For the identity of the Akkadian and Sumerian terms, see Benno Landsberger, "Die Serie *ana ittišu*" 6.I.1, *Materialien zum sumerischen Lexikon* (Rome: Pontifical Biblical Institute, 1937) vol. 1, p. 75. A similar preference is evident in Strabo's description of pre-Islamic Arabs (*Geography* 16.4.25; LCL vol. 7, p. 364).

[27] F. R. Kraus, *Briefe aus dem British Museum* (Leiden: E. J. Brill. 1964) p. 70 no. 92, lines 16–17.

[28] HSS 19:44, lines 13–14 (Jonathan S. Paradise, "Nuzi Inheritance Practices" [University of Pennsylvania, Ph.D. dissertation, 1972] p. 129); see also HSS 19:23 lines 5–6 and 19:17, lines 12–13 (ibid., pp. 68 and 158).

[29] RS 21.230, line 5, published as no. 81 in *Ugaritica* V (MRS 16; Paris: Imprimerie nationale and Paul Geuthner, 1968) p. 173.

regulations, the book of Deuteronomy does state that a father should "give the *bĕkōr . . . pî šĕnayîm*" (Deut 21:17), a privilege echoed in other, nonlegal passages.[30] The exact meaning of this idiomatic phrase is not entirely certain. Some have understood the deuteronomic law as reserving two-thirds of an estate for the favored son, on the basis of a prophetic warning that "*pî šĕnayîm* of [the land] will be cut off and die while one third (*šĕlišît*) will remain in it" (Zech 13:8); other considerations suggest that phrase means "twice as much" (as other heirs), in other words, "two shares."[31] In either case, the son designated *bĕkōr* received more than his brothers.

Further evidence that firstborns did play a leading role, and thus a challenge to Jacobs's theory of Israelite ultimogeniture, can be derived from the biblical version of a widely used theological metaphor, with which many cultures describe their leading gods as firstborns. Such epithets were used by Indian tradition to speak of Indra and by the Greeks and Romans for Heracles, Pan, and Fortuna.[32]

This pattern also existed in the ancient Near East. The Egyptians used similar terms for both Horus and Osiris,[33] and Mesopotamian

---

[30] Thus Elisha requested a double portion of Elijah's spirit (2 Kings 2:9; note his reference to Elijah as "my father" in v. 12), which Ben Sirah regarded as having been fulfilled in his doubling the number of signs performed (Sirah 48:12). Cf. also Gen 48:22, if *šĕkem 'aḥad 'al-'aḥeyka* implies an extra portion as it has often, though not always, been understood.

[31] The latter view is supported by the usage in Sirah 12:5 and 18:32 as well as the reference to Elisha (note 30 above) and is the interpretation reflected in such early works as Josephus' *Antiquities* (4.8.23 §249 [LCL vol. 4, pp. 594–95]), Philo's *Special Laws* (2.25 §133 [LCL vol. 7, pp. 386–87]), rabbinic law (*b. Bava Batra* 122b–123a, cf. *Sifre* Deuteronomy *Ki Teṣey* §217 [ed. Finkelstein, p. 250]), and various ancient translations of Deut 21:17. For a general overview of the philological issues, see Frithiof Rundgren, "Parallelen zu Akk. *šinēpūm* '2/3,'" *Journal of Cuneiform Studies* 9 (1955) 29 and Eryl W. Davies, "The Meaning of *Pî Šᵉnayim* in Deuteronomy XXI 17," *Vetus Testamentum* 36 (1986) 341–47.

[32] Rg Veda 1.32.4 (Ralph T. H. Griffith, *The Hymns of the Ṛgveda* [Varanasi-1, India: The Chowkhamba Sanskrit Series Office, 1971] vol. 1, p. 43); see Orphic hymns 10, 12, 25, 30, and 52 in Guilelmus Quandt, *Orphei Hymni* (Berlin: Weidmann, 1962) pp. 6, 10, 13, 21, 24, and 37; Livy 29.36.8 and 43.13.5 (LCL vol. 8, p. 348 and vol. 13, p. 46); Cicero, *De Legibus* 2.11.28 (LCL pp. 404–5); C. Julius Hyginus (in *The Myths of Hyginus*, ed. Mary Grant [Lawrence, KS: University of Kansas Publications, 1960] p. 47) and Lactantius, *Divine Institutes* 1.5 (*PL* vol. 6, p. 130). The words used are usually *prōtogonan* and *primogenitus*. The Greek term *prōtotokos* appears to have originated with the Septuagint, which generally uses it as the translation equivalent for the Hebrew *bĕkōr*.

[33] Pyramid Text §§301, 466, 1259, 1538, 1608, and 1814 (utterances 256, 303, 532, 578, 588, and 649 in R.D. Faulkner, *The Ancient Egyptian Pyramid Texts* [Oxford: Clarendon Press, 1969, reprinted Oak Park, IL: Bolchazy-Carducci, 1985] pp. 66, 92, 200, 234, 241, and 265). Daniel G. Brinton provides a similar usage among the Aztecs (*The Myths of the New World, A Treatise on the Symbolism and Mythology of the Red Race of America* [3d ed., 1876; reprinted New York: Haskell House, 1968] p. 169).

mythology identified numerous deities as the *aplu* or *māru rēštu* (lit. "chief heir" or "son") of one or another god.[34] Likewise, Ishtar is called "the first of the gods" (*rēštīti ilāni*) and Sin "the greatest among his divine brothers" (*rabûm ina ilī aḫḫīšu*).[35] These phrases use imagery borrowed from the legal realm of inheritance to elevate individual gods above other members of the pantheon, who are conceived as their siblings.

Among the titles used this way is the Akkadian term *bukru*.[36] Thus far, *bukru* has been found only in poetic contexts, unlike its Hebrew cognate (*bĕkōr*), which designates the privileged heir in the Bible's legal passages dealing with inheritance and succession.[37] However, its place within the realm of inheritance law is assured by lexical tablets that equate it with such terms as *ašarēdu* and *rabû*.[38]

Strangely, the Hebrew Bible never uses such terms to describe Israel's God. However, the book of Job may echo this convention when Bildad mentions the wicked one's fate at the hands of the *bĕkōr māwet* (18:13). If the latter word is taken as a proper, rather than a common noun ("death"), the phrase would allude to the firstborn of Mot, the Canaanite god of death.[39] This same mythological pattern may also be preserved

[34] See Cecil J. Mullo Weir, *A Lexicon of Accadian Prayers in the Rituals of Expiation* (London: Humphrey Milford, 1934) p. 284, and Knut L. Tallqvist, *Akkadische Götterepitheta* (StOr 7; Helsinki: Societas Orientalis Fennica, 1938) pp. 122–23, as well as pp. 11, 35–36, and 169 for *rabû* ("great"), *ašarēdu* ("foremost"), and *rēštu* ("first"). For an analogous usage in Sumerian, see Adam Falkenstein, "Sumerische religiose Texte," *Zeitschrift für Assyriologie* n.s. 22 = 56 (1964) 59; note also the Ugaritic usage cited by Cyrus Gordon (*Ugaritic Textbook* [AnOr 38; Rome: Pontifical Biblical Institute, 1965] p. 482).

[35] Leonard W. King and E. A. Wallis Budge, *Annals of the Kings of Assyria* (London: British Museum, 1902) p. 29 (see also pp. 206 and 254); Georges Dossin, "L'inscription de fondation de Iaḫdun-Lim, roi de Mari," *Syria* 32 (1955) 12.

[36] Knut L. Tallqvist, *Akkadische Götterepitheta*, pp. 66–67, and *The Assyrian Dictionary of the Oriental Institute of the University of Chicago*, ed. A. Leo Oppenheim et al. (Chicago: Oriental Institute, 1964–   ) vol. 2 (B), pp. 309–10.

[37] F. R. Kraus, "Erbrechtliche Terminologie im alten Mesopotamien" in *Essays on Oriental Laws of Succession* (Leiden: E. J. Brill, 1969) p. 26.

[38] Benno Landsberger, "Das Sa Vocabular" M 1–9, *Materialien zum Sumerischen Lexikon* (Rome: Pontifical Biblical Institute, 1955) vol. 3, p. 64; for supportive evidence from Ebla, see the bilingual lists where that language's cognate to the Akkadian term is glossed with the Sumerian d u m u . s a g (Giovanni Pettinato, *Testi Lessicali Bilingui della Biblioteca L. 2769* [Materiali Epigrafici di Ebla 4; Naples: Istituto Universitario Orientale di Napoli, 1982] nos. 4–6, 20, and 24 [pp. 9, 47, 52]).

[39] Nahum M. Sarna, "The Mythological Background of Job 18," *Journal of Biblical Literature* 82 (1963) 316–18. According to John B. Burns, the allusion is to the Mesopotamian deity Namtar ("The Identity of Death's First-Born [Job xviii 13]," *Vetus Testamentum* 37 [1987] 362). Lienhard Delekat takes it more broadly as meaning "leprosy" ("Erstgeburt" in *Biblisch-historisches Handwörterbuch*, ed. B. Reicke and L. Rost [Göttingen: Vandenhoeck & Ruprecht, 1962] vol. 1, p. 434). The usage may be echoed in two New Testament references to Jesus as "firstborn from the dead" (*prōtotokos ek tōn nekrōn*), although their primary

in later Christian and Jewish pejorative use of the phrase "firstborn of Satan."[40]

The fact that such epithets are not used for God in the Hebrew Bible is surprising. This can hardly be ascribed to any reluctance about comparing God with other deities, since such statements are abundant there.[41] A more likely explanation is the nature of biblical theology. For besides elevating one god within the pantheon of his peers, speaking of him as "chief son" also locates him as chronologically secondary to some other deity, conceived as his father. In other words, the image is bidimensional. Not only does it impute superiority over other members of the same class, but it also allows for the possibility that the deity described was preceded by another, possibly once superior, being. It may even hint at that older god's eventual displacement by his up-and-coming offspring. Even if biblical theology might have tolerated ascribing brothers to God, it certainly could not allow Him a father.

Although the language of a divine firstborn was not, therefore, suitable for Israel's God, it does appear in the Bible, but in a somewhat unusual way. In the course of ordering Moses to bring Israel out from Egyptian slavery, God tells him to inform Pharaoh, "Israel is My son, My *bĕkōr*" (Exod 4:22). This phrase invokes the wider range of associations derived from that term's natural inheritance setting. Israel appears to be both subordinate and special to God. In this respect, the image joins many other descriptions of that relationship, epitomized in Deuteronomy's remarkable collocation:

> The Lord has affirmed today that you are a treasured people (*'am sĕgullâ*)...making you the highest (*'elyôn*) of all the nations which He made, for fame, renown, and honor, so you will be a holy people (*'am qādōš*) to the Lord, your God.... (26:18–19)

In addition to conveying Israel's elevated status, the use of inheritance language may also call to mind the *bĕkōr*'s entitlement to a special portion

---

reference is to the expectation that his resurrection would be the first of many (Colossians 1:18 and Revelation 1:5, cf. 1 Corinthians 15:20–23); note also *rb tmtt* in Cyrus Gordon, *Ugaritic Textbook*, no. 2059, lines 16 and 22.

[40] *Y. Yevamot* 1:6 (3a), *b. Yevamot* 16a, and Polycarp's "Epistle to the Philippians" 7:1 (*PG* vol. 5, p. 1012), where the phrase was directed to Marcion according to other Church traditions (Irenaeus, *Contra Haereses* 3:3.4 [*PG* vol. 7, p. 853]; Eusebius, *Historia Ecclesiastica* 4.14.7 [*PG* vol. 20, p. 340], and Jerome, *Liber de Virus Illustribus* 17 [*PL* vol. 23, p. 667]).

[41] Cf. C. J. Labuschagne, *The Incomparability of Yahweh in the Old Testament* (Leiden: E. J. Brill, 1965); for an interesting development in the use of such terminology within Jewish tradition, see Frederick E. Greenspahn, "Abraham ibn Ezra and the Origin of Some Medieval Grammatical Terms," *Jewish Quarterly Review* 76 (1986) 217–27.

of his father's estate. Since biblical authors often refer to the whole earth as belonging to God (Lev 25:23, Ps 24:1, etc.), this image may reasonably be understood as implying that He intends a special territorial portion for His chosen child. This conclusion is supported by the Bible's frequent use of the term "inheritance" (*naḥălâ*) with reference to the land of Canaan.[42]

Because Israel's depiction as God's *běkōr* is interwoven with exodus themes, some have thought that it developed in order to serve the literary needs of that story, specifically justifying God's killing the Egyptian *běkōrôt* and thereby setting the stage for His claim on Israel's firstborn.[43] Understood in this way, the image would function aetiologically, they suggest, laying the thematic groundwork for Israel's practice of redeeming her firstborn from priestly service.

There are several reasons for being skeptical about this view. To be sure, firstborn children are assigned special responsibilities for their (deceased) parents, particularly with regard to burial and maintenance of family ancestor cults, in many cultures.[44] In the words of Hindu tradition, the oldest son "is born for duty, upon whom [the father] bestows the debt [of ancestor worship] and through whom [the father] obtains immortality. They say that the other [sons] are born of love."[45] A similar attitude can be detected in an ancient Egyptian's statement that, as his mother's "oldest son and heir, I buried her in the necropolis" and in the belief that the cult of Osiris was maintained by Horus, "his firstborn son, his heir."[46] However, these responsibilities are not always limited to firstborns. For example, the Ugaritic King Danel laments not having "a son in his house, a scion in the midst of his palace to set up a stele for his divine ancestors,

---

[42] The biblical citations are listed by Arthur M. Brown ("The Concept of Inheritance in the Old Testament " [Columbia University, Ph.D. dissertation, 1965] pp. 181–209), who notes the connection to inheritance on pp. 303–6. Jer 3:19 explicitly links the fatherhood of God to Israel's possession of the land; cf. *Midrash Psalms* 5:1, where this imagery is reversed and God presented as Israel's *naḥălâ*.

[43] E.g., Martin Noth, *Exodus, A Commentary* (OTL; Philadelphia: Westminster Press, 1962) p. 47. The symmetry is made explicit in Exod 4:23. According to Mordecai Gilula, this tradition may have an Egyptian origin ("The Smiting of the First-Born—An Egyptian Myth?" *Tel Aviv* 4 [1977] 94–95).

[44] See Meyer Fortes, "The First Born," *The Journal of Child Psychology and Psychiatry and Allied Disciplines* 15 (1974) 84, 88–89.

[45] Laws of Manu 9:107, as graciously translated by Stanley Insler (personal correspondence).

[46] Pyramid Text §301 and 1538 (utterances 256 and 578 in R. D. Faulkner, *The Ancient Egyptian Pyramid Texts*, pp. 66 and 234) and UAR I 164.31, cited by Erwin Seidl, *Einführung in die ägyptische Rechtsgeschichte bis zum Ende des neuen Reiches* (2d ed., Glückstadt: J. J. Augustin, 1951) p. 59; see also Kairo S7139, lines 31–32, as cited by Kurt Sethe, "Ein Prozessurteil aus dem alten Reich," *Zeitschrift für Ägyptische Sprache* 61 (1926) 69.

a family shrine in the sanctuary" (*bnh bbt šrš bqrb hklh nṣb skn ʾilʾibh bqdš ztr ʿmh lʾarṣ mšṣʾu qṭrh lʿpr ḏmr ʾaṭrh*).[47]

In Israel, there is no evidence that firstborns had ever exercised priestly responsibilities. Although the rabbis did infer that firstborns had once served in this capacity, the Bible says only that the Levites were chosen as substitutes for them (Num 3:12–13, 40–45, 8:15–16), not that firstborns had ever actually been priests.[48] Nor is there any evidence that Israel's priesthood was ever restricted to firstborns. Aaron may have been the oldest male in his family, but Levi's first three offspring, Gershon, Kohath, and Merari, all fathered important priestly lines, as did Kohath's first, second, and fourth sons, Amram, Izhar, and Uzziel.[49] Other priestly groups are presented as collateral lines, with no indication that one was more highly regarded than another.[50] In a story that is widely seen as legitimating certain elements of the Israelite priesthood, the death of Aaron's sons Nadab and Abihu is reported as having led to their being replaced by their brothers Eleazar and Ithamar.[51] Whatever the purpose of this account—some have seen it as reflecting the discomfort of later generations with the fact that these lines were not the oldest[52]—the text accords equal status first to Nadab *and* Abihu, then to Eleazar *and* Ithamar. Later, David's sons are said to have become priests,[53] casting doubt on both that positon's hereditary nature as well as the criteria by which any one individual achieved a higher status than others.

---

[47] *Corpus des tablettes en cunéiformes alphabétiques*, ed. Andrée Herdner (Paris: Imprimerie nationale, Librarie Orientaliste Paul Geuthner, 1963) 17:1.27–29. See Yitzhak Avishur, "The 'Duties of the Son' in the 'Story of Aqhat' and Ezekiel's Prophecy on Idolatry," *Ugarit-Forschungen* 17 (1986) 49–60. John F. Healy regards these as a son's obligations to his living father ("The *Pietas* of an Ideal Son at Ugarit," *Ugarit-Forschungen* 11 [1979] 353–54).

[48] Cf. *m. Zevaḥim* 14:4, *Targum Onqelos* Exod 24:5, and *Numbers Rabbah* 4:8; for the biblical data, see Aelred Cody, *A History of the Old Testament Priesthood* (Rome: Pontifical Biblical Institute, 1969).

[49] Exod 6:6–15, Num 3:19.

[50] E. Bammel has pointed to evidence of fraternal succession in the Herodian priesthood ("Die Bruderfolge im Hochpriestertum der herodianisch-römischen Zeit," *Zeitschrift des Deutschen Palästina-Vereins* 70 [1954] 147–48), and J. R. Bartlett has speculated that Jerusalem priests were appointed ("Zadok and His Successors at Jerusalem," *Journal for Theological Studies* n.s. 19 [1968] 1–18).

[51] Leviticus 10. A surprisingly persistent view links Nadab and Abihu with the sons of Jeroboam; e.g., Moses Aberbach and Leivy Smoler, "Aaron, Jeroboam, and the Golden Calves," *Journal of Biblical Literature* 86 (1967) 129–40.

[52] John C. H. Laughlin, "The 'Strange Fire' of Nadab and Abihu," *Journal of Biblical Literature* 95 (1976) 562–63.

[53] 2 Sam 8:18, but see the parallel 1 Chron 18:17 and the discussion by Gordon J. Wenham, "Were David's Sons Priests?" *Zeitschrift für die Alttestamentliche Wissenschaft* 87 (1975) 79–82.

More important than their inability to provide an entirely convincing origin for the Exodus reference to Israel as God's *běkōr*, the plague tradition and the redemption of firstborns from priestly service are also absent from several other passages where this image occurs. For example, Amos spoke of those living in Samaria as "notables from the foremost of nations" (*rēʾšît haggôyîm*, 6:1), an image echoed over a century later in Jeremiah's depiction of Israel as the "best of [God's] produce" (*rēʾšît těbûʾātōh*, 2:3). He also reports God as saying, "I have become Israel's father, and Ephraim is my *běkōr*" (31:8).

The variety of settings in which this image occurs, extending well beyond references to the exodus, suggests that there was a long-standing Israelite tradition of using "firstborn" and "firstfruit" terminology to convey the people's sense of being God's favorite. Amos's usage is particularly revealing in this regard, since he is especially given to citing conventional beliefs, which are then rhetorically transformed for his own purposes. His sarcastic tone in describing the Northern Kingdom's view of itself supports the likelihood that the concept was not his invention, as does the presence of the same phrase in Numbers 24:20, where it is applied to Amalek.[54]

There are two possible sources for this theological metaphor apart from the exodus setting where it is now found. One is the deeply rooted description of God as Israel's father. The antiquity of this image is supported by its widespread presence in various Semitic religious traditions.[55] Biblical authors, of course, sought to avoid the problematic overtones that might follow from taking the metaphor too literally, as demonstrated by Jeremiah's use of adoption language (God "became [*hāyîtî*] Israel's father").[56] However, the theological implications stay very much the same; though not God's actual child, something only pagan cultures could assert, Israel had been taken as His own. The prophet Hosea connects

---

[54] Whether the image reflects power, antiquity, or virtue is unclear in both this passage and Amos 6:1.

[55] The evidence is conveniently collected in W. Marchel, *Abba, Père! La Prière du Christ et des Chrétiens* (rev. ed., Rome: Pontifical Biblical Institute, 1971) pp. 29–41. Examples from Mesopotamian personal religion are found as early as neo-Sumerian times (Hermann Vorländer, *Mein Gott, Die Vorstellung vom persönlichen Gott im Alten Orient und im Alten Testament* [AOAT 23; Kevelaer: Verlag Butzon & Bercker; Neukirchen-Vluyn: Neukirchener Verlag, 1975] pp. 16–29).

[56] Werner Schlisske suggests that this usage was derived from Hosea (*Gottessöhne und Gottessohn im alten Testament, Phasen der Entmythisierung im alten Testament* [Stuttgart: W. Kohlhammer, 1973] pp. 134 and 147). For biblical usage of adoption imagery, see Arthur M. Brown, "The Concept of Inheritance in the Old Testament," pp. 309–18.

this image with the exodus in his statement, "I called to My son from Egypt" (11:1).[57]

Alternatively, the description of Israel as God's *bĕkōr* could be understood within the context of West Semitic terminology, which spoke of members of the heavenly court as *bĕnê 'ēlîm* (lit. "the gods' sons"), a usage also found in the Bible. To speak of leading deities as divine first-borns in the way that other cultures do places them within this larger pantheon. By describing Israel in these terms, biblical authors could similarly imply her elevation above the inhabitants of heaven, thereby granting Israel a kind of quasi-divine status.[58]

However one explains the metaphor's conceptual background, it is present in the Bible, albeit not with reference to God. Moreover, the title God's *bĕkōr* incorporates several of the central components of biblical theology, embodying Israel's relationship with God, her neighbors, and her land.

Particularly striking is the frequency with which this kind of imagery is used for the Northern Kingdom. It is those in Samaria to whom Amos refers as the "foremost of nations," and Ephraim which Jeremiah describes as God's *bĕkōr*. Elsewhere, the Septuagint justifies Israel's claim to superiority over Judah, which in the Hebrew tradition is based on their having ten portions (i.e., tribes) in David, as deriving from their view of themselves as *prōtotokos* ("firstborn," 2 Sam 19:44).[59] In this regard, one might recall that it is Reuben, the ancestor of one northern tribe, whom Genesis considers to have been Jacob's *bĕkōr*, the eldest of his sons (35:23, 46:8, 49:3, cf. 29:32). Although these narratives refer to familial relations, they are widely recognized as having tribal connotations. Nor is it without interest that according to 1 Chronicles this status was taken from Reuben and given to Joseph, another northern tribe (5:1). The image's northern orientation is, finally, reinforced by its connection with the exodus

---

[57] Although Martin Buss considers the Exodus reference to Israel as God's *bĕkōr* to be dependent on Hosea (*The Prophetic Word of Hosea, A Morphological Study* [BZAW 111; Berlin: Alfred Töpelmann, 1969], p. 111), the prophet never describes Israel as God's firstborn, while the image of her as His child, which Ernest W. Nicholson has found in all the pentateuchal sources (*God and His People, Covenant and Theology in the Old Testament* [Oxford: Clarendon Press, 1986] p. 86), occurs already in Deuteronomy 32 (vv. 5 and 19). A similar image was used by the ancient Sabeans and Qatabanians; see A. F. L. Beeston, "Kingship in Ancient South Arabia," *Journal of the Economic and Social History of the Orient* 15 (1972) 267.

[58] See already *'Avot de-Rabbi Natan* B 44 (ed. S. Schechter, p. 124; cf. *b. Shabbat* 31a) as well as Werner Schlisske, *Gottessöhne und Gottessohn im alten Testament*, pp. 183–87; contrast the Extracts of Theodotus 27:3 (*PG* vol. 9, p. 673), where the angels are identified as *prōtoktistoi* ("first begotten").

[59] Cf. P. Kyle McCarter, Jr., *II Samuel* (AB; Garden City, NY: Doubleday, 1984) p. 419.

tradition, which may have originated among northern tribes, particularly those associated with the family of Joseph.[60] Even though God's description of Israel as "My *bĕkōr*" (Exod 4:22) is generally considered part of the Pentateuch's "J" source, to which many scholars assign a southern origin,[61] the image could have been absorbed by Judah along with the exodus tradition as a whole.

Surprisingly, this metaphor, which was very much alive during the intertestamental period,[62] does not occur in rabbinic texts, which apparently found it an unattractive way to describe Israel's relationship with God. However, it did survive in the early Christian community's description of itself as "the assembly of the first-born" (*ekklēsia prōtotokōn*, Hebrews 12:23),[63] "a kind of first fruits (*aparchēn*) among [God's] creatures" (James 1:18).

Nor was the image entirely rejected by Jewish theology, but came to be used for several of the supernatural entities granted growing metaphysical stature during the postbiblical period. One midrash speaks of the messiah as God's firstborn,[64] a depiction that can be found in Jewish tradition as late as the seventeenth century when Shabbatai Zevi identified himself as God's firstborn in a letter originally written in Hebrew and now preserved in Greek, Armenian, and Italian translations.[65]

More typical is Philo's use of these terms for the *logos* (*prōtogonon huion*), which can be traced back to the Bible's understanding of wisdom

---

[60] See John Bright, *A History of Israel* (3d ed.; Philadelphia: Westminster Press, 1981) p. 140.

[61] H. Cazelles assigns the passage to E, which is widely regarded as having a Northern origin ("Premiers-nés dans l'ancien testament," *Dictionnaire de la Bible*, Supplément vol. 8 [Paris: Librairie Letouzey et Ané, 1972], p. 486).

[62] Sirah 36:12 (see also the Peshitta and the margin of Hebrew manuscript B at 44:22), 4 Ezra 6:58, Psalms of Solomon 18:4, and 4QDib Ham 3:6 (Maurice Baillet, "Un recueil liturgique de Qumrân Grotte 4: 'Les paroles des luminaires'," *Revue Biblique* 68 [1961] 202).

[63] This persists in Mormon tradition, where Joseph Smith referred to "the general assembly and the church of the first born" (*The Doctrine and Convenants of the Church of Jesus Christ of Latter-Day Saints* 107:19 [Salt Lake City: Deseret News Co., 1880] p. 385).

[64] *Exodus Rabbah* 19:7, where Exodus 4:22 is juxtaposed with Jacob's (= Israel) acquisition of the *bĕkōrâ*. Jacob himself is called God's *bĕkōr* in *Numbers Rabbah* 6:2, *Mechilta Shirta* 10 (ed. H. S. Horovitz, p. 150, line 17), and perhaps Jubilees 2:20. In the Prayer of Joseph, he identifies himself as "the firstborn of every living thing (*prōtogonos pantos zōou*) to whom God gives life" (*PG* vol. 14, p. 169, cf. Jonathan Z. Smith, "The Prayer of Joseph" in *Religions in Antiquity, Essays in Memory of Erwin Ramsdell Goodenough*, ed. Jacob Neusner [Leiden: E. J. Brill, 1968] p. 256). *Testament (Assumption) of Moses* 1:14 implies a similar status for Moses. The designation of Israel's king as God's *bĕkōr* (see pp. 27–29 below) is also likely to have affected the messianic usage.

[65] Abraham Wasserstein, "*Gilguleha shel 'Iggeret Shabbeta'it be-Ha'ataqot she-'einam Benei Berit*," *Zion* 37 (1972) 239–40.

as having been present alongside God during the process of creation.[66] In a similar vein, the Latin translation of Ben Sirah speaks of Wisdom as "firstborn, before all creatures" (*primogenitum ante omnem creaturam*, 24:3[5]). Placing the origin of wisdom, or the *logos*, before creation entails metaphysical as well as chronological priority. For the rabbis, this status belonged to the Torah, which they said not only antedated the rest of the world, but had also participated in its creation.[67]

Given the multiplicity of theological concepts and entities which converge in this imagery—including father, son, messiah, logos, and Torah—it is not surprising that early Christian sources found this an appropriate way to speak of Jesus.[68] Contrasting him with the angels in a manner remarkably reminiscent of the way polytheistic myths speak of one god as superior to the others, the author of Hebrews identifies him as "the firstborn" (*prōtotokon*, 1:6) and Colossians as the "firstborn of all creation" (*prōtotokos pasēs ktiseōs*, 1:15).[69]

---

[66] See Prov 3:19–20, 8:22, and Sirah 1:4; cf. Job 40:19, where *bĕhēmôt* is described as *rēʾšît darkê-ʾēl*. Philo's statements are in "On Husbandry" 12.51 (LCL vol. 3, pp. 134–35); see also "Confusion of Tongues" 28.148, "On Dreams" 1.215, and "Questions and Answers on Genesis" 4.978 (LCL vol. 4, pp. 88–89; vol. 5, pp. 412–13; vol. 11, p. 381).

[67] *B. Pesaḥim* 54a, *b. Nedarim* 39b, *Sifre* Deuteronomy ʿ*Eqev* §37 (ed. L. Finkelstein, p. 70), *Song of Songs Rabbah* 5:11, and *Midrash Tanḥuma* (Buber) *Bereishit* §5 (p. 2b).

[68] Cf. Wilhelm Michaelis, "Die biblische Vorstellung von Christus als dem Erstgeborenen," *Zeitschrift für systematische Theologie* 23 (1954) 137–57. By way of contrast, Tatian speaks of the devil as firstborn (*prōtogonos*), "Oratio adversus Graecos" (*PG* vol. 6, p. 821). Luke 2:7 and some manuscripts of Matt 1:25 also describe Jesus as Mary's firstborn (*prōtotokon*), a designation that has troubled some Christians committed to the doctrine of her perpetual virginity (thus Jerome's comment, "*Primogenitus est non tantum postquem et alii, sed ante quem nullus*" ["De Perpetua Virginitate B. Mariae," *PL* vol. 23, p. 202]). That issue, which echoes in the comment of the philosopher Lucian, "if there is no other, you are not the first; if you are first, then there are others" (*Demonax* 29 [LCL vol. 1, pp. 160–61]), was resolved by the discovery of a pre-Christian tombstone of a Jewish woman who had died after bearing her *prōtotokon*, thus demonstrating that the term need not imply there having been any subsequent children (see Hans Lietzmann, "Jüdisch-griechische Inschriften aus Tell el Yehudieh," *Zeitschrift für die neutestamentliche Wissenschaft* 22 [1923] 283). For the history of the Greek word, see Wilhelm Michaelis, "Der Beitrag der Septuaginta zur Bedeutungsgeschichte von πρωτοτοκσ" in *Sprachgeschichte und Wortbedeutung, Festschrift Albert Debrunner* (Bern: Francke Verlag, 1954) pp. 313–16.

[69] The Hebrew equivalent is applied to Adam in *Numbers Rabbah* 4:8 (cf. *Testament of Abraham* A 11 and *Wisdom of Solomon* 7:1, 10:1) and rejected by *Life of Adam and Eve* 14:3, which considers the devil to have been prior (see note 68 above). J. B. Lightfoot claims to have found the same terminology applied to God by rabbinic sources (*Saint Paul's Epistles to the Colossians and to Philemon* [London: Macmillan and Co., 1904] p. 145). In his commentary to Isaiah, Jerome cites a Hebrew gospel as identifying Jesus as God's firstborn (*tu es filius meus primogenitus*) at the time of his baptism (Book IV at Isa 11:2, *PL* vol. 24, p. 145). The history of Colossians' interpretation is surveyed by Alfred Hockel, *Christus der Erstgeborene, zur Geschichte der Exegese von Kol 1,15* (Düsseldorf: Patmos-Verlag, 1967).

Paul's description of Jesus as the "firstborn of many brothers" (*prōtotokon en pollois adelphois,* Romans 8:29) suggests a somewhat different perspective. Rather than claiming priority over the world as a whole, the phrase puts him at the head of the church, which had adopted Israel's understanding of itself as God's children.[70] This use of firstborn imagery to indicate a leader's precedence over his own followers has ancient Near Eastern antecedents of its own, including some in Israel where the metaphor took an interesting turn.

Mesopotamian kings are often described as *rēštu* ("first") or *ašarēdu* ("foremost"),[71] and Ugaritic texts use the term *rb* ("great") in a similar way.[72] Language drawn from the realms of inheritance and theology thus found its way into politics. However, these phrases alone do not make it clear whether it was to his people or to other rulers that the king was considered superior. This ambiguity is resolved by the Akkadian epithet *ašarēd kal malkī* ("foremost among kings")[73]; but a different tone is apparent in southern Arabia. There chieftains are called the *bkr* of their kingdom or their tribe.[74] Such usage clearly emphasizes the ruler's preeminence within his own group. Still other rulers, however, particularly from Qataban, are identified as a god's *bkr*, an image best paralleled in Egypt, where some pharaohs are described as the gods' eldest son.[75] This terminology clearly derives from the familiar practice of describing rulers as the deity's sons, a characterization that has left its trace in the Bible.[76] There, however, the relationship is nuanced by the use of adoption phraseology, speaking of the king as having become God's son, so as to avoid any claim of an actual biological relation.

[70] See Romans 8:14, Galatians 3:26, and Ephesians 1:5. Romans 8:23 should be understood more sequentially.

[71] M.-J. Seux, *Épithètes Royales Akkadiennes et Sumériennes* (Paris: Letouzey et Ané, 1967) pp. 43–44 and 242.

[72] Cyrus Gordon, *Ugaritic Textbook* 118:13, 26 1018:2, 17; compare Ps 48:11 and Ezra 5:11.

[73] M.-J. Seux, *Épithètes Royales Akkadiennes et Sumériennes,* p. 44.

[74] For the texts, see A. P. B. Jamme, *Les listes onomastiques Sabéennes de Ṣirwâḥen ʾArḥab* (Washington, DC: Catholic University of America, 1966) pp. 50 and 54, A. G. Lundin, *Die Eponymenlisten von Saba (aus dem Stamme Ḥalīl)* (Vienna: Hermann Böhlaus Nachf. Kommissionsverlag der Österreichischen Akademie der Wissenschaften, 1965) pp. 42–43, and, perhaps, *Répertoire d'épigraphie sémitique* vol. 6 (ed. G. Ryckmans; Paris: Imprimerie nationale, 1933) no. 3946.

[75] *Répertoire d'épigraphie sémitique* vol. 6, nos. 3540 line 2 and 3880 lines 1–3; see also Henri Frankfort, *Kingship and the Gods, A Study of Ancient Near Eastern Religion as the Integration of Society and Nature* (Chicago: University of Chicago Press, 1948) p. 87.

[76] For example, 2 Sam 7:14 and Ps 2:7, cf. 1 Chron 22:10; see also C. R. North, "The Religious Aspects of the Hebrew Kingship," *Zeitschrift für die Alttestamentliche Wissenschaft* 9 (1932) 24–27.

It is this convention which provides the background for the Psalmist's statement that David "will cry out to [God], 'You are my Father'... and I will surely make him My *bĕkôr*" (*'ap 'ānī bekôr 'etnēhû*, 89:27–28). However, this passage asserts more than sonship when it elevates the king to a position of primacy among God's children. The identity of the implied children of God becomes explicit when the verse concludes that Israel's ruler will be "the highest of the earthly kings" (*'elyôn lĕmalkê 'āreṣ*), a phrase analogous to the Akkadian *ašarēd kal malkī*.[77] The term *'elyôn* ("highest"), which has an interesting history of its own, is familiar from Deuteronomy, where it is applied to the people of Israel.[78] Like the title *bĕkôr* and the notion of divine adoption, it is used for both Israel and her king.

This theological parallelism raises several interesting possibilities. If, as suggested above, the derivation of *bĕkôr* from the realm of inheritance entails a justification of Israel's possession of the promised land, then its application to the monarch could have similar overtones, in this case legitimating the Davidic empire.[79] More immediately relevant for our purposes, however, is the question of the relationship between these two usages. Specifically, one must ask which is more original—that pertaining to the king or to the people.

The fact that such epithets are widely applied to royalty could suggest that it was first used for Israel's ruler. Prophetic references to the people as God's *bĕkôr* would then be understood as a kind of "democratic" protest against royal theology.[80] However, the prophets, in whose writings many of these passages are found, did not see themselves as theological innovators but relied heavily on existing images and beliefs. Moreover, the reference to Israel as God's *bĕkôr* occurs in a part of Exodus conventionally ascribed to the oldest of Pentateuchal sources, which is usually understood as having preceded the earliest classical prophets. Finally, if

[77] Cf. E. Lipinski, *Le Poème Royal du Psaume LXXXIX 1–5, 20–38* (Paris: J. Gabalda, 1967) p. 68. Paul G. Mosca connects this phrase with Baal ("Ugarit and Daniel 7: A Missing Link," *Biblica* 67 [1986] 512).

[78] Deut 26:19 and 28:1. For the history of *'elyôn*, see Rémi Lack, "Le origines de *elyon*, le tres-haut, dans la tradition culturelle d'Israel," *Catholic Biblical Quarterly* 24 (1962) 44–64.

[79] Moshe Weinfeld, "The Covenant of Grant in the Old Testament and in the Ancient Near East," *Journal of the American Oriental Society* 90 (1970) 194.

[80] Thus, for example, Gershon Brin, "*Le-Toledot ha-Nusḥah 'Hu' Yiheyeh Li le-Ven va'ani 'Eheyeh Lo-' Av*" in *Ha-Miqra' ve-Toledot Yisra'el*, ed. B. Uffenheimer (Tel Aviv: Tel Aviv University, 1972) pp. 57–60, Werner Schlisske, *Gottessöhne und Gottessohn im alten Testament*, p. 114, and Vitus Huonder, *Israel Sohn Gottes, zur Deutung eines alttestamentlichen Themas in der jüdischen Exegese des Mittelalters* (Göttingen: Vandenhoeck & Ruprecht, 1975) p. 24.

the image did originate in the North as proposed above, it is difficult to imagine why Northern sources would have borrowed a Judean royal image, whereas the opposite process is more easily explained: originally used for the people as a whole, perhaps by Northern groups that saw the exodus as evidence of divine commitment, the title "God's *běkōr*" could have been adopted by the Davidic dynasty, albeit in a form which at least tacitly acknowledges that the ruler's status had not always been so lofty, in order to assert its theological legitimacy and perhaps even primacy.[81] Such a process is not without precedent. David brought the ark, the symbol of Moses' covenant between God and Israel, from its Northern center at Shiloh to his new capital at Jerusalem in order to adapt an earlier, popular tradition to his own needs (2 Samuel 6). Asserting that the king was God's progeny could have been another attempt to co-opt a Northern tradition, originally applied to the people as a whole, on behalf of the Judean monarchy.[82]

The favored status accorded elder offspring is thus not only a wide-ranging practice, which reaches from antiquity to contemporary social life, but also a productive literary and theological motif. In this, both the Bible and subsequent Jewish and Christian traditions reflect pervasive attitudes, found in the ancient Near East as well as throughout the world. Collectively, this makes it still more difficult to agree with those who have thought that younger children may once have held privileged positions in ancient Israel. Instead, both legal usage and theological imagery seem to rest on the more conventional view that it was firstborns who were treated favorably.

In that case, the remarkable chain of heroes whom the Bible presents as having been their families youngest children becomes all the more striking. Its apparent contrast to the prevailing norms strengthens the evident concern of the biblical accounts themselves to justify the ascendance of these figures. Clearly these stories do not simply report what took place in an automatic or even a "natural" way. Discerning their intent will, therefore, require close scrutiny of actual practices both generally and in Israel.

---

[81] So too Gerald Cooke, "The Israelite King as Son of God," *Zeitschrift für die Alttestamentliche Wissenschaft* 73 (1961) 216–17.

[82] Compare the application of a traditional Israelite covenantal formula to Solomon in 1 Chron 28:6.

2

An Unnatural Custom[1]

The prevalence of senority-based imagery in the Bible and its repeated efforts to justify deviations from that norm make it impossible to accept its reports of the success of younger siblings as simply the natural outcome of Israelite law or custom. At the same time, however, this theme cannot be studied in isolation from actual practice. In fact, several scholars have suggested that it is a literary or theological protest against the preferential treatment accorded firstborns in Israel, whether in the realm of ritual or of law.[2]

Sacrifice of Firstborns

An example of this kind of position is Arnold Ehrlich's view of these stories as a polemic against the sacrifice of firstborn sons. In his opinion, these tales oppose this Israelite practice by repeatedly emphasizing the undesirability of older offspring.[3]

---

[1] John Earle, quoted in Joan Thirsk, "Younger Sons in the Seventeenth Century," *History* n.s. 54 (1969) 361; Thomas Paine described primogeniture similarly in his pamphlet "Rights of Man" (*The Complete Works of Thomas Paine*, ed. Philip S. Foner [New York: The Citadel Press, 1945] vol. 1, p. 439).

[2] E.g., Herbert N. Schneidau (*Sacred Discontent, The Bible and Western Tradition* [Baton Rouge, LA: Louisiana State University Press, 1976] pp. 1–12 and 243), who takes this motif as an assertion of God's freedom from social convention; cf. *Midrash Tanḥuma* (Buber) *Terumah* 7 (p. 46b).

[3] Arnold B. Ehrlich, *Miqra' ki-Feshuṭo* at Gen 4:11 (reprinted New York: Ktav, 1969) vol. 1, p. 16.

Ehrlich's premise, that firstborns were regularly sacrificed in the biblical world, is by no means an unusual assumption. Typical is one author's observation that "immemorial custom in the Near East required that the first-born son should be sacrificed to God in order that the Deity would give the couple more children and grant the family prosperity."[4] Nor is this view limited to those professionally engaged in the study of antiquity. How far it has spread can be judged from a recent book that describes a modern opponent of abortion as tracing his objections to this contemporary practice back to the emotions first stirred by a photograph he remembers from an elementary school history text which showed a burial urn with a "caption saying that the Canaanites had practiced the sacrifice of the first-born male child."[5]

The charge that the Canaanites had engaged in human sacrifice is a long-standing belief. It originated among classical authors who accused the people of Carthage of offering their children in order to gain divine support.[6] The reliability of these accounts has been hotly debated by scholars. However, there is no reason for us to be detained by the dispute over whether human sacrifice was actually practiced in the ancient Near East or is merely "an ancient slander," as one scholar has called it.[7] For our purposes, all that matters is whether firstborns were singled out—in *any* way—and here the evidence is virtually unanimous. For despite their authors' perverse pleasure in describing the horrors of Carthaginian child sacrifice, classical accounts usually speak of its victims generically as "children."[8] When further qualifications are offered, it is almost invariably adjectives such as "best" or "favorite" which are used.[9] The only exception

[4] Rolland E. Wolfe in *The Interpreter's Bible* at Micah 6:7 (ed. G. A. Buttrick; New York; Abingdon Press, 1952) vol. 6, p. 939; see also Walther Eichrodt, *Theology of the Old Testament* (Philadelphia: Westminster Press, 1961) vol. 1, p. 148.

[5] Kristin Luker, *Abortion and the Politics of Motherhood* (Berkeley, CA: University of California Press, 1984) p. 132.

[6] The sources are collected in Paul G. Mosca, "Child Sacrifice in Canaanite and Israelite Religion, A Study in *Mulk* and מלך (Harvard University, Ph.D. dissertation, 1975) pp. 2–23.

[7] Sabatino Moscati, quoted by Roberto Suro, "A Neglected Civilization Gets Its Due in Venice," *New York Times* (March 15, 1988) p. C15.

[8] A possible exception from Ugarit (RS 24:26, line 14, published by Andrée Herdner, "Nouveaux Textes Alphabetiques de Ras Shamra—XXIVᵉ campagne, 1961" in *Ugaritica* VII [MRS 18; Paris: Librairie Orientaliste Paul Geuthner; Leiden: E. J. Brill, 1978] p. 36) involves textual reconstruction (see George C. Heider, *The Cult of Molek, A Reassessment* [Sheffield, England: JSOT Press, 1985] p. 144).

[9] *Kratistous* (Diodorus Siculus 20:14 [LCL vol. 10, pp. 178–79]), *philtatōn* (Porphyri, *De Abstinentia ab animalibus necandis* 2.56 [Cantabrigiae Guil: Morden, 1685] p. 94), and *ēgapēmenon* (Porphyri as quoted in Eusebius, *Praeparatio Evangelica* 4:16, §91 (*PG* vol. 21, p. 272) and Philo of Byblos as quoted in Eusebius, *Praeparatio Evangelica* 1:10, §44 and 4:16, §95 (*PG* vol. 21, pp. 85 and 273).

is an isolated report that Hannibal's wife had urged him to resist before his "firstborn and only son (*prima domus atque unica proles*) is seized."[10] However, there is no evidence for that being the explicit demand of Carthaginian custom, which she had initially characterized as requiring an annual offering of young children (*parvos imponere natos*), rather than the expected impact on her own family.[11]

Archaeologists have found child burial precincts in several Phoenician settlements around the Mediterranean. These raise further doubts as to whether firstborns were singled out for this treatment. Among the massive number of child burials from the best known of these at Carthage are many urns containing skeletons from several children of different ages. Assuming that these are the result of some ritual practice and that the skeletons in each urn came from a single family, they cannot all be first-born. This conclusion is supported by the fact that in those urns containing the bones of three children, the two younger ones, invariably infants of the same age, can be shown to have been twins, providing further evidence that birth order was not the cause of their fate.[12]

The Hebrew Bible is also concerned with human sacrifice, which it repeatedly condemns as a violation of God's will. However, virtually all of these passages conform to the pattern of classical sources in describing the slaughter of children in general rather than that of firstborns alone.[13]

The sole exceptions to this rule are statements by two biblical prophets mentioning the sacrifice of human firstborns in ancient Israel. Ezekiel condemns the practice as based on "wicked statutes" (*ḥuqqîm lōʾ ṭôbîm*, 20:25–26), and Micah does the same, albeit more inferentially, asking, "Is this what God wants?" (6:6–7). Both passages are dramatically rhetorical. Micah begins with conventional sacrifices (burnt offerings and year-old calves) before extending his examples first hyperbolically (thousands of rams and ten thousand rivers of oil) and then, perhaps, hypothetically

---

[10] Silius Italicus, *Punica* 4.785 (LCL vol. 1, pp. 226–27; for the juxtaposition of "firstborn" and "only," see pp. 62–63 below.

[11] Ibid., line 767 (LCL pp. 224–25). Herodotus does report that the Achaeans would sacrifice the eldest (*presbytatos*) of any family who entered the town hall (7.197, LCL vol. 3, pp. 512–15), and Plutarch cites Aristotle as telling that the Cretans had fulfilled a vow by sending their firstborn (*apárchēn*) to Delphi (*Lives*, "Theseus" 16:2 [LCL vol. 1, pp. 30–31]).

[12] Lawrence E. Stager and Samuel R. Wolff, "Child Sacrifice at Carthage: Religious Rite or Population Control?" *Biblical Archaeology Review* 10:1 (January-February 1984) 47–49; a survey of the archaeological evidence for child sacrifice is presented in Paul G. Mosca, "Child Sacrifice in Canaanite and Israelite Religion," pp. 38–55.

[13] E.g., Lev 18:21, 20:2–5, Deut 12:31, 18:9–10, 2 Kings 16:3, 21:6, Jer 7:31, 19:5, 32:35, Ezek 16:20–21, 20:31, 23:39, Ps 106:37–38. The sacrifice described in 1 Kings 16:34 includes both the *běkōr* and the *ṣāʿîr*.

(the fruit of my body).[14] The exaggerated tone of this speech, which opposes reliance on ritual alone, makes it a dubious basis from which to draw inferences as to actual Israelite custom.

Although Ezekiel's condemnation does appear to be directed against actual practices,[15] he considers the treatment of firstborns (*kŏl-peṭer rāḥam*) to be grounds for punishment, a perversion of God's expectations along with idol worship and desecration of the Sabbath. His point is not that this practice was normative, but that some people *thought* it was what God wanted.

The law that Ezekiel believed had been misunderstood and the likely source for modern notions that firstborns were regularly sacrificed in ancient Israel is the Bible's demand that all *bĕkōrôt* be given to God (Exod 22:28). Whether this dictum intends actual sacrifice or some more benign treatment has occasioned great disagreement.[16] The lack of evidence that all firstborns were sacrificed in other, far more bloodthirsty Near Eastern cultures makes it improbable that Israel differed in this regard. Moreover, biblical authors have far too much at stake in the contrast between God's treatment of Egyptian and Israelite firstborns for it to be credible that their fate had ever been the same.

Further reason for doubting that Israelite religion ever required the sacrifice of firstborns can be gleaned from the Bible itself, which provides various exemptions from the rule, whatever it means, that all *bĕkōrôt* be "given" to God. The most familiar of these is the requirement that they be redeemed and the Levites serve in their place.[17] As we have already seen, however, that need not mean that firstborns had once actually been set aside for God's service.[18] To the contrary, the text's point is to explain why that was *not* the case. The aetiological element seeks to justify the levitical priesthood and, perhaps, certain payments for the religious

---

[14] The Targum renders the parallel *bĕkōrî* as *bĕrî*, although some manuscripts have *bûkîr*.

[15] George C. Heider suggests that the prophet's focus on firstborns is based on pentateuchal phraseology ("A Further Turn on Ezekiel's Baroque Twist in Ezek 20:25-6," *Journal of Biblical Literature* 107 [1988] 723-24).

[16] See the debate between Moshe Weinfeld ("The Worship of Molech and of the Queen of Heaven and Its Background," *Ugarit-Forschungen* 4 [1972] 133-54 and "Burning Babies in Ancient Israel," *Ugarit-Forschungen* 10 [1978] 411-13) and Morton Smith ("A Note on Burning Babies," *Journal of the American Oriental Society* 95 [1975] 477-79).

[17] E.g., Exod 13:11-13 and 14:19. For the history of these provisions, see Walther Zimmerli, "Erstgeborene und Leviten: Ein Beitrag zur exilisch-nachexilischen Theologie" in *Near Eastern Studies in Honor of William Foxwell Albright*, ed. Hans Goedicke (Baltimore, MD: The Johns Hopkins University Press, 1971) pp. 459-69, and Gershon Brin, "*Dinei Bekhorot ba-Miqra*," *Tarbiz* 46 (1976-77) 1-7.

[18] See pp. 21-22 above.

establishment while explaining how Israelite children avoided the suffering inflicted on their Egyptian counterparts. As such, it reflects only the belief that *bĕkōrôt* were *supposed* to have served God, not that they had ever done so. The offering given to priests at the birth of a firstborn child may have originated as an expression of gratitude for the new status of parenthood rather than as a demonstration of the child's obligation. In any event, this commandment, too, is a slim reed on which to rest the theory of firstborns' religious importance.

The fact that firm evidence for this practice in ancient Israel does not emerge until the time of Ezekiel, and then in the form of a complaint that those so engaged had misunderstood God's intent, provides the most effective challenge to the view of this as an Israelite custom. The most realistic proponents of this position acknowledge the ambiguity of the evidence that it actually occurred with any regularity in antiquity by arguing that biblical language preserves only a reminiscence of earlier practice.[19] However, Ezekiel's exilic date conforms to the relative lateness of the Carthaginian evidence in suggesting that far from being a "primitive" practice, human sacrifice was actually a late and therefore decadent phenomenon.[20]

This conclusion is supported by the nature of the supposed practice itself. Even granting the psychology which underlies offering first things (whether plants or animals) and the understandable desire to share a portion of what one has with God,[21] slaughtering all firstborn children would be an expensive and dangerous practice for any society to demand, particularly in antiquity with its high infant mortality. More practical and appropriate alternatives are easily conceived, as in one individual's reported vow that, if granted ten sons, he would sacrifice the *tenth*.[22]

---

[19] Cf. Otto Kaiser, "Den Erstegeborenen deiner Söhne sollst du mir geben" in *Denkender Glaube, Festschrift Carl Heinz Ratschow* (Berlin: Walter de Gruyter, 1976) pp. 25–27 and 45–46, and Joseph Heinninger, "Premiers-nés, 1. La Primogéniture en Ethnologie," *Dictionnaire de la Bible*, Supplement 8 (Paris: Librairie Letouzey et Ané, 1982) p. 478.

[20] Cf. Joseph Henninger, "Über Menschenopfer bei den vor-islamischen Arabern" in *Akten des Vierundzwanzigsten internationalen Orientalisten-Kongresses München*, ed. Herbert Franke (Wiesbaden: Deutsche Morgenländische Gessellschaft, 1959) p. 246. J. Lust regards the statement in Ezekiel as an interpolation ("Ez., XX, 4–26 une Parodie de l'histoire religieuse d'Israel," *Ephemerides theologicae lovanienses* 43 [1967] 512–13).

[21] W. Schmidt, "Die Primitialopfer in der Urkultur" in *Corona Amicorum, Emil Bächler zum 80. Geburtstag 10. Februar 1948* (St. Gallen: Tschody-Verlag, 1948) p. 82; note the Bible's view that firstborn animals were sacrificed already in the time of Abel (Gen 4:4).

[22] Joseph Henninger, "Menschenopfer bei den Arabern," *Anthropos* 53 (1958) 747; note Julius Wellhausen's qualifications about this report in *Reste Arabischen Heidentums Gesammelt und Erläutert* (2d ed., Berlin: Georg Reimer, 1897) p. 116.

Requiring the death of all firstborns would be tantamount to societal suicide. For this reason, it is "absurd to suppose that there could have been in Israel or any other people, at any moment of their history, a consistent law compelling the suppression of the firstborn who are the hope of the race."[23]

The very limited nature of the evidence supporting firstborn sacrifice (one classical statement and two prophetic outbursts) is hardly sufficient to sustain Ehrlich's position that the Bible's focus on younger children was intended to combat this practice. That is not to say that Israelite firstborns never suffered at their parents' hands. Ezekiel's statement in particular cannot be dismissed as pure rhetoric. Centuries earlier, the Moabite king Mesha is said to have offered his *běkôr* son in an effort to win divine favor for a military venture against Israel (2 Kings 3:27). However, rather than demonstrating a regular practice with social support, these incidents conform to the classical accounts of Phoenician child sacrifice as having been limited to times of great emergency. Under these circumstances, there is no reason to think that the children's being *běkôr* was a legally or religiously stipulated precondition for their selection. That status is mentioned only to emphasize the gravity of their parents' situation, much as the Bible identifies Jephthah's daughter and Isaac (neither of whom is presented as *běkōr*) as their respective parents' only (*yāḥîd*) offspring in order to dramatize what was at stake in their respective situations.[24] The reference to Mesha's and Hannibal's sons being firstborn likewise points to the extraordinary nature of the circumstances rather than their fathers' adherence to accepted custom. Indeed, the drama of these texts would be undercut if firstborn sacrifice were to have been a regular occurrence.

A similar conclusion applies to the handful of Assyrian contracts from the ninth through the seventh pre-Christian centuries which stipulate that should one of the parties violate the agreement, then his "chief heir"

---

[23] Roland de Vaux, *Studies in Old Testament Sacrifice* (Cardiff: University of Wales Press) p. 71.

[24] Gen 22:2, 12, 16 and Judg 11:34. Regarding the appropriateness of describing Isaac in this way, see pp. 114–15 below. The fact that both of these passages clearly present the circumstances they describe as extraordinary undermines their relevance for determining regular Israelite practice. Although Genesis 22 has often been connected with firstborn sacrifice and Isaac is identified that way in various presentations of that story from antiquity (Jubilees 18:11, cf. *Genesis Rabbah* 55:5) to the modern day (e.g., Wilfred Owen, "The Parable of the Old Man and the Young" [line 4] in *The Complete Poems and Fragments*, ed. John Stallworthy [New York: W. W. Norton and Co., 1984] vol. 1, p. 166), Genesis never describes him in those terms although he was, technically, a *peṭer reḥem* (George Heider, *The Cult of Molek*, p. 276). For the correlation between *běkōr* and *yāḥîd*, see pp. 62–63 below.

(ibila . gal) will be burnt.[25] Although these, too, have been occasionally cited as demonstrating that firstborns were actually sacrificed, they really show the opposite—that this practice was neither regular nor religious. These contracts invoke the most horrible consequence, that the guilty party would lose his chief offspring, in order to discourage default. What they suggest is how high a premium was placed on such youngsters and how their deaths could be invoked only in the most dire of circumstances.

In sum, the available evidence does not justify the inference that first-borns, or any children for that matter, were actually killed on a regular basis, either in Israel or among her neighbors. Each reported instance is exceptional in its own way. The accounts of Mesha and of Abraham reflect only their protagonists' unusual fervor; the Assyrian contracts and the biblical story of Jephthah demonstrate only how grave they understood their situation to be. All attest to the high value placed on favored children by their respective families, but that is a tautological conclusion which would be psychologically understandable whether or not the circumstances were culturally mandated.

Inheritance

Even if oldest children were not regularly sacrificed in antiquity, some other form of special treatment could have been the target of biblical authors' repeated accounts about the success of younger offspring. Evidence has already been provided of how widely various forms of favoritism had spread. The most prominent of these relate to succession, whether in the legal or the political realm. It may have been this which biblical authors had in mind as they described the abilities and accomplishments of so many younger children.

Before examining biblical references to inheritance, it is important to realize that explicit evidence is not the only basis on which assertions of Israelite primogeniture usually rest. Many rely on a frequently unstated assumption that in the earliest stages of human culture oldest sons auto-matically succeeded to their fathers' position, with other systems having developed or deviated from that norm. This assumption is not unrelated to that which underlies the belief in the antiquity of firstborn sacrifice, which we have now seen to be almost exactly opposite from the truth. Analogously, one must be cautious of unsupported assumptions that primogeniture is a "law of nature."[26]

[25] See Karlheinz Deller's review of *Les Sacrifices de l'Ancien Testament* by R. de Vaux in *Orientalia* 34 (1965) 383–84.

[26] *Massachusetts Collected Historical Papers*, p. 168, cited by Evelyn Cecil Rockley, *Primogeniture, A Short History of Its Development in Various Countries and Its Historical*

The evidence of human practice, which is far more diverse than such views commonly allow, does not support that premise. As one anthropologist has put it, "Patterns of inheritance are...historically variable, and not laid down once and for all in some original germ plasm. They constitute adaptive responses to a variety of conditions."[27] Supporting the implications of this observation, one study of thirty-nine unrelated cultures from around the world found that in only one-third was the oldest child (male or female) granted more control over family wealth than other members.[28] Sometimes older offspring are totally excluded from inheriting their father's estate, most conspicuously when they are put in positions of authority for its disposition after his death.[29] More often, they are treated in the same way as other brothers or sisters.

Surveys of European social history have confirmed the existence of other systems, especially among Teutonic and Visigothic peoples.[30] Indeed, it is this which underlies a thirteenth-century German poet's characterization of primogeniture as a "foreign law" (*fremdieu zeche*) and "alien regulation" (*welhsch gerihte*).[31]

Nowhere has primogeniture been more visible than in England, where the throne passes automatically to the monarch's oldest surviving son, much like estates, which were once transmitted according to similar principles without division.[32] Yet even British practice has not been

---

Effects (London: John Murray, 1895) p. 76; a similar view is reflected in a 1713 Viennese memorandum cited by Paula S. Fichtner, *Protestantism and Primogeniture in Early Modern Germany* (New Haven, CT: Yale University Press, 1989) p. 81.

[27] Eric R. Wolf, "The Inheritance of Land Among Bavarian and Tyrolese Peasants," *Anthropologica* 12 (1970) 104; cf. Marc Bloch, *Feudal Society* (Chicago: University of Chicago Press, 1961) p. 203.

[28] Paul C. Rosenblatt and Elizabeth L. Skoogberg, "Birth Order in Cross-Cultural Perspective," *Developmental Psychology* 10 (1974) 53–54; thus E. Adamson Hoebel's comment that "the vast majority of societies adhere to neither of the set rules [primogeniture or ultimogeniture]" (*Anthropology, The Study of Man* [4th ed.; New York: McGraw-Hill, 1972] p. 360). A more systematic survey is presented in Jack Goody, *Death, Property, and the Ancestors, A Study of the Mortuary Customs of the Lodagaa of West Africa* (Stanford, CA: Stanford University Press, 1962) pp. 321–27.

[29] E.g., Hilda Kuper, "Kinship Among the Swazi" in *African Systems of Kinship and Marriage*, ed. A. R. Radcliffe-Brown and D. Forde (London: Oxford University Press, 1950) pp. 96–97; note also cultures that practice ultimogeniture (described on p. 14 above).

[30] E.g., Evelyn Cecil Rockley, *Primogeniture*. A map indicating the extent of European primogeniture can be found on p. 179 of Joan Thirsk, "The European Debate on Customs of Inheritance, 1500–1700" in *Family and Inheritance, Rural Society in Western Europe, 1200–1800*, ed. Jack Goody, Joan Thirsk, and E.P. Thompson (Cambridge: Cambridge University Press, 1976).

[31] Wolfram von Eschenbach, *Parzival*, 1.5.21 and 4.28 (ed. Karl Lachmann, 6th ed.; Berlin and Leipzig: Walter de Gruyter, 1926, reprinted 1964, p. 15).

[32] Although challenges to British primogeniture began in the sixteenth century, it was not fully repealed until 1925 (Joan Thirsk, "The European Debate on Customs of Inheritance" in *Family and Inheritance*, p. 177).

monolithic. In medieval Saxony a man's sons could choose the prime heir, whereas equal division, known as "gavelkind," was characteristic of Kent.[33] Fourteenth-century Nottingham was divided into English and French boroughs, with property in the latter descending automatically to the owner's oldest son while that in the former went to his youngest; as a result, ultimogeniture, or junior-right, has come to be known as "borough-English."[34]

As one legal authority has put it, "When [the law] decides that the whole land shall go to one son—he may be the eldest, he may be the youngest—and that his brothers shall have nothing, it is not thinking merely of the dead man and his sons."[35] Far from being rooted in hoary antiquity, British primogeniture was the product of historical circumstance, specifically medieval feudalism,[36] for which large fiefdoms were more productive than those that were small. By limiting inheritance to a single heir, primogeniture, which began in the eleventh century and developed with increasing rigidity over the next two hundred years, ensured that land parcels remained intact instead of being repeatedly divided over several generations. This would have been particularly important in a country such as Britain where land was limited. Restricting ownership served other needs of feudal rulers, who also needed to know who was responsible for such obligations as knightly service.

Blessed with a vast and seemingly unoccupied continent, England's American cousins consciously rejected this custom, which was recognized as perpetuating the concentration of wealth. Primogeniture was therefore completely abolished from America before the Revolution.[37] However, its legacy persists in our deep-seated certainty that it is conceptually, and thus historically, prior to other systems.

---

[33] The history of British inheritance practices is surveyed by Marc Bloch, *Feudal Society*, pp. 190–210. For gavelkind, see Charles I. Elton, *Origins of English History* (2d ed., London: Bernard Quaritch, 1890) p. 185 and Paul Vinogradoff, *Outlines of Historical Jurisprudence* (London: Oxford University Press, 1920) p. 276.

[34] Frederick Pollock and Frederic W. Maitland, *The History of English Law Before the Time of Edward I* (Boston: Little, Brown & Co., 1903) p. 279.

[35] Frederick Pollock and Frederic W. Maitland, *The History of English Law*, p. 262.

[36] Cf. Theodore F. T. Plucknett, *A Concise History of the Common Law* (5th ed., Boston: Little, Brown & Co., 1956) pp. 527–30, and Henry S. Maine, *Ancient Law* (10th ed., Boston: Beacon Press, 1963) pp. 222–25. Traces of prefeudal practice are presented by Charles I. Elton, *Origins of English History*, pp. 197–98.

[37] See C. Ray Keim, "Primogeniture and Entail in Colonial Virginia," *The William and Mary Quarterly* (3d series) 25 (1968) 545–86. The shifting policy of the American colonies can be seen by comparing the tables on pp. 32–33 and 64–65 (for 1720 and 1790 respectively) in Carole Shammas, Marylynn Salmon, and Michel Dahlin, *Inheritance in America from Colonial Times to the Present* (New Brunswick, NJ: Rutgers University Press, 1987).

More important than the variety of principles used to govern inheritance or their roots in particular cultural and historical circumstance is the fact that the concept of inheritance is itself culturally conditioned, presupposing individuals' right to control their holdings even after death. This notion of private property rests on a highly individualistic system of ownership, which is scarcely universal. In many cultures individuals are not believed to own things so much as to use them. Even where ownership is accepted, it is often vested in a group, which endures uninterrupted by the addition or loss of individual members over time.[38] In such societies, what little personal property people have—a garment or a favorite weapon—may be buried with them so as to be available after death.[39]

Where the concept of inheritance is more broadly accepted, the most widely attested pattern includes all eligible heirs, who may divide an estate or even share in it jointly. In fourth-century Athens, for example, the "law ordains that all the legitimate sons have an equal right to share in their father's property."[40] It is this which accounts for Hesiod's recommendation that one have an "only son ... so wealth will increase in the home; but if you leave a second son you should die old," for, as Aristotle warned, "if a number of sons are born and the land is correspondingly divided there will inevitably come to be many poor men."[41]

To be sure, even in such circumstances one individual must obviously be in charge of administering family property on the group's behalf or supervising its division.[42] However, there is no universal rule as to how

[38] Anthropologist Jack Goody associates this corporate view with African cultures, whereas Euroasian individualism results in appointive systems of inheritance ("Sideways or Downwards? Lateral and Vertical Succession, Inheritance and Descent in Africa and Eurasia," *Man* n.s. 5 [1970] 629). Philippe Aries connects European primogeniture with joint ownership's having become inconceivable (*Centuries of Childhood, A Social History of Family Life* [New York: Vintage Books, 1962] p. 371).

[39] See E.N. Faillaize, "Inheritance (Primitive and Savage)," *Encyclopaedia of Religion and Ethics*, ed. James Hastings (New York: Charles Scribner's Sons, 1908–27) vol. 7, p. 289, and also A.R. Radcliffe-Brown, *Structure and Function in Primitive Societies, Essays and Addresses* (London: Cohen & West Ltd., 1952) p. 32.

[40] Isaeus, "On the Estate of Philoctemon," 25 (LCL pp. 218–19).

[41] *Works and Days*, line 376 (LCL pp. 30–31) and Aristotle, *Politics* II.vi.13 (1270b; LCL pp. 140–41). For earlier practice, see David Asheri, "Laws of Inheritance, Distribution of Land and Political Constitutions in Ancient Greece," *Historia* 12 (1963) 6–7.

[42] E.g., Strabo, *Geography* 16.4.25 (LCL vol. 7, p. 364) and *The Laws of Manu* 9:105 (trans. G. Bühler, p. 346) where this is provided as an alternative to equal division by all sons; other examples are listed by E. Adamson Hoebel, "The Anthropology of Inheritance" in *Inheritance of Property and the Power of Testamentary Disposition*, ed. Edmond N. Cahn (The Social Meaning of Legal Concepts 1; New York: New York University School of Law, 1948) p. 19. It is this view which accounts for Rajkuman Sarvadhikari's counterintuitive correlation of primogeniture with a communitarian social structure, while considering systems of division individualistic (*The Principles of the Hindu Law of Inheritance* [2d ed., Madras: The Law Book Depot, 1922] p. 176).

that person should be selected, but many different systems, some of which specify the way this administrator should be chosen, others of which are quite vague. Often, the selection is left open, to be decided by various groups or individuals.[43] Where seemingly rigid principles are invoked, seniority is only one of many possibilities, and even that can be determined in a variety of ways—laterally or lineally, according to either matrilineal or patrilineal lines.[44]

It is this diversity which accounts for the surprising ambiguity of the term "firstborn" in many societies. Most obviously, females may be either included or ignored. Some cultures consider only children living at home, or those born to a particular wife, or judged competent.[45] Sometimes rulership is awarded to the first child (or son) born after the incumbent's accession.[46]

This same kind of diversity is found in the ancient Near Eastern environment from which Israel emerged. Although there is extensive evidence that oldest children were treated preferentially in ancient Egypt,

[43] For example, see Robert F. Gray and P. H. Gulliver, *The Family Estate in Africa, Studies in the Role of Property in Family Structure and Lineage Continuity* (Boston: Boston University Press, 1964) pp. 203 and 248; in southern Ghana, the entire family meets after a funeral to select the heir (Jack Goody, *Death, Property, and the Ancestors*, p. 346).

[44] Robert Lowie provides a general overview of the diverse possibilities: "The patrilineal Zulu recognize the eldest son as heir *par excellence*; among the bilinear Herero (Southwest Africa), who stress the mother's side for social, the father's for religious purposes, the eldest sister takes precedence of all other possible heirs to a man's stock; personal property is divided among the children; his sacred property, however, descends to the eldest sister's eldest son. The matrilineal Carrier (British Columbia) normally passed titles on to a sister's son or daughter; with the Haida all property went to a younger brother or, for lack of one, to the eldest sister's eldest son. A Hopi medicine bundle is similarly associated with the males of the matrilineage, but though theoretically a younger brother or the eldest sister's eldest son succeeds by preference, that sister's younger son or a younger sister's son may be chosen as the fitter incumbent. In other words, the Hopi are latitudinarians in practice, irrespective of theory. On the other hand, Tongans allowed titles to go only to the eldest-born. The Nootka (British Columbia) were equally fanatical about primogeniture, which implied superiority of rank and privilege. But they counted seniority not only by relative age, but by the relative ages of the parents. A grown man might call his ten-year-old girl cousin 'elder sister' if her father was older than his own; and that meant conceding to her a higher rank" (*Social Organization* [New York: Rinehart and Co., 1948] p. 150).

[45] For examples, see Robert H. Lowie, *Primitive Society* (New York: Horace Liveright, 1920) pp. 248, 253, and Jean Buxton, "The Mandari of the Southern Sudan" in *Tribes Without Rulers, Studies in African Segmentary Systems*, ed. John Middleton and David Tait (London: Routledge & Kegan Paul, 1958) p. 79.

[46] In the tenth century, Germany's Henry I was urged to leave his kingdom to a younger son who had been born in the royal palace (*quia natus esset in aula regali*) rather than to the older (*quia aetate esset maior et consilio providentior*), "Vita Mahthildis reginae" in *Monumenta Germaniae Historica*, ed. Georgius Heinricus Pertz (Hannover, 1841; reprinted New York: Kraus Reprint Group, 1963), Scriptorium vol. 4, p. 289; Herodotus ascribes Xerxes' succession to similar principles (7.3, LCL vol. 3, pp 300–302).

that seems not to have been legally required, but was the apparent result of allowing testamentary freedom in the fourth dynasty. The oldest discernible practice entailed dividing an estate into equal portions.[47]

Alongside indications that in parts of Mesopotamia property could be held in common,[48] most of the available evidence suggests that estates were usually divided. Plural forms of the words for "heir" are often used generically, suggesting that no one individual was preferred.[49] The Code of Hammurabi frequently refers to brothers' dividing an estate after their father's death (*warka abum ana šimtim ittalku inūma aḫū izuzzū*), a division that is once explicitly required to be equal (*mitḫāriš*).[50] Even the Middle Assyrian Laws, where certain individuals are given favorable treatment, assume that estates could be divided by the sons of the deceased.[51]

Numerous legal documents illustrate the implementation of these general principles. For example, an adoption tablet from the fifteenth century B.C.E. notes that "if Nashwi [the adopting father] should have a son of his own, then he shall divide equally (*mitḫāriš izuzzū*) with Wullu [the adoptee], but Nashwi's [natural] son shall receive Nashwi's gods."[52] In its reference to the family gods, this text demonstrates status distinctions alongside equal division of property. Other documents allow these same objects to be given to a secondary (*terdennu*) or even a tertiary son.[53]

---

[47] Ariste E. Théodoridés, "The Concept of Law in Ancient Egypt" in *The Legacy of Egypt*, ed. J. R. Harris (2d ed., Oxford: Clarendon Press, 1971) pp. 293 and 303; see also M.A. Moret, "Le privilège du fils aîné, en Egypte et en Mésopotamie au IIIe Millénaire," *Comptes Rendus de l'Académie des Inscriptions et Belles Lettres* (1933) 92–94.

[48] F. R. Kraus, "Von altmesopotamischen Erbrecht, Ein Vortrag" in *Essays on Oriental Laws of Succession* (Leiden: E. J. Brill, 1969) p. 7, and Stephen H. Bess, "Systems of Land Tenure in Ancient Israel" (University of Michigan, Ph.D. dissertation, 1963) pp. 59–62.

[49] See Adam Falkenstein, *Die neusumerischen Gerichtsurkunden* (Munich: Der Bayerischen Akademie der Wissenschaften, 1956–57) nos. 27, 32, 56, 82, and 99 (vol. 2, pp. 45, 53, 93, 135, and 161–62).

[50] 11.39–43 (§165, Godfrey R. Driver and John Miles, *The Babylonian Laws* [Oxford: Clarendon Press, 1955] p. 62); see also §166 (11.59–62), 167 (11.85–12.8), and 170 (12.48–55). A similar assumption underlies §24 of the Lipit-Ishtar Code (see Emile Szlechter, "Le Code de Lipit-Ištar (I)," *Revue d'Assyriologie* 51 [1957] 73) and *The Epic of Gilgamesh*, Assyrian recension 10:6.27 (ed. R. Campbell Thompson [Clarendon Press, 1930; reprinted New York: AMS Press, 1981] p. 59.

[51] A §29 (Godfrey R. Driver and John Miles, *The Assyrian Laws* [Oxford: Clarendon Press, 1935] pp. 398–99); cf. p. 16 above.

[52] C.J. Gadd, "Tablets from Kirkuk," *Revue d'Assyriologie* 23 (1926) 126, no. 51, lines 10–14. *The Assyrian Dictionary of the Oriental Institute of the University of Chicago* regards the reference to Nashwi's biological offspring as plurals (vol. 21 [Z], pp. 80–81). Other documents provide for the same property to be divided among Wullu's sons (nos. 5 and 6 in C.J. Gadd, "Tablets from Kirkuk," pp. 90–92).

[53] E.g., HSS 19:4 and 5, published in Jonathan Paradise, "Nuzi Inheritance Practices" (University of Pennsylvania, Ph.D. dissertation, 1972), pp. 94–97 (discussed on pp. 239–42);

Such provisions confirm our earlier observations that there was preferential treatment, whatever the nature of that advantage.[54] A similar inference can be drawn from several Nuzi texts in which provisions allowing all of a man's sons to receive portions of his estate are followed by the stipulation that each "receive according to his succession" (*attamannû kî šēpišu ileqqu*). Similar expressions are contained in documents from Egypt and Ugarit as well.[55] The fact that different heirs might be treated differently does not, however, demonstrate how that preference was assigned, much less that it was based on birth order. In fact, there are ample indications that this advantage may not have been automatic at all. Among these is a fourteenth-century Akkadian tablet from Ugarit which identifies one son as *rabû* (lit. "large") and another as *ṣeḫru* (lit. "small"), only to conclude that the estate "will be given to the one who has honored his mother Bidawa" (*mannumme ina libbišunu ša ukabbi[t]* ˹Bidawa [um]mašu ana šuwāti tanandin*).[56]

Testamentary freedom may also be apparent in the Code of Hammurabi, which allows a man to bestow certain kinds of property on "his heir who

---

however, see also Karlheinz Deller, "Die Hausgötter der Familie Šukrija S. Ḫuja" in *Studies on the Civilization and Culture of Nuzi in Honor of Ernest R. Lacheman,* ed. Martha A. Morrison and David I. Owen (Winona Lake, IN: Eisenbrauns, 1981) p. 55. Possession of the gods is a central issue in HSS 14:108 (presented by Paradise on pp. 90–91); their significance is discussed by Anne E. Draffkorn, *"Ilāni/Elohim,"* *Journal of Biblical Literature* 76 (1957) 216–18, Moshe Greenberg, "Another Look at Rachel's Theft of the Teraphim," *Journal of Biblical Literature* 81 (1962) 242, and Chaim M. Y. Gevaryahu, *"Le-Beirur Ṭivam shel ha-Terafim ba-Tanakh,"* *Beth Mikra* 7 (1963) 82. Interestingly, *Targum Pseudo-Jonathan* considers the biblical *terafim* to be the property of the *būkĕrā* (at Gen 31:19).

[54] See pp. 16–17 above.

[55] HSS 5:73, lines 15–17 (Jonathan Paradise, "Nuzi Inheritance Practices," p. 110); see also 19:5, line 37; 19:7, lines 27–28; 19:22, line 7; and 19:10, line 30 (ibid., pp. 97, 103, 123, 145), 5:21, line 10, and 73, lines 16–17 (in E. A. Speiser, "New Documents Relating to Family Laws," *Annual of the American Schools of Oriental Research* 10 [1928–29] 38–39, 51–52, and Paul Koschaker, "Drie Rechtsurkunden," *Zeitschrift für Assyriologie* n.s. 14–48 [1944] 192. For the rendering of gir, see the Chicago *Assyrian Dictionary,* vol. 1 (A)², p. 502. See also Gen 43:23, P. Berlin 9010 (line 3) as cited in Kurt Sethe, "Ein Prozessurteil aus dem alten Reich," *Zeitschrift für Ägyptische Sprache und Altertumskunde* 61 (1926) 71–72, and RS 17.38, line 6 (*rabūtu kīma rabūtišu*) in *Ugaritica* V (ed. J. Nougayrol et al., Paris: Imprimerie nationale and Paul Geuthner, 1968) p. 12.

[56] RS 8.145, lines 25–26 in F. Thureau-Dangin, "Trois Contrats de Ras-Sharma," *Syria* 18 (1937) 250; cf. H 71 (no. 19 in E. A. Speiser, "New Documents Relating to Family Law," *Annual of the American Schools of Oriental Research* 10 [1928–29] 49–50), John Huehnergard, "Five Tablets from the Vicinity of Emar," *Revue d'Assyriologie* 77 (1983) 15, and the Middle Kingdom text cited in Peter W. Pestman, *Marriage and Matrimonial Property in Ancient Egypt* (Leiden: E. J. Brill, 1961) p. 121. Several Nuzi documents allow widows to allocate their husbands' estate (Jonathan S. Paradise, "Nuzi Inheritance Practices," pp. 165–68).

[first] meets his eyes" (*ana aplīšu ša īnšu maḫru*). Although this phrase has sometimes been understood as referring to a firstborn (the son first seen by his father), it is usually interpreted as an idiomatic reference to personal preference (the son upon whom the father looks with favor).[57]

Disinheritance and adoption tablets demonstrate that there were other mechanisms for including or excluding selected individuals from an estate. The latter are particularly revealing in their suggestion that property holders had considerable freedom either to extend preferential status to adoptees or to reserve it for biological sons.[58] Documents defining how individual estates should be divided presuppose a similar kind of freedom.[59]

It is in light of these diverse lines of evidence of testamentary discretion that the numerous documents granting preferential treatment to individuals designated *rabû* must be considered.[60] Although commonly understood as showing that older sons were treated advantageously, the very existence of these texts suggests that preferential status may not have been automatic, in which case such documents would have been unnecessary. Their function appears to be to assign the status they are claimed to presuppose. For example, after indicating that Aliwum and Sinremeni were brothers, an Old Babylonian text identifies Aliwum as *rabû* and Sinremeni as *ṣeḫru*.[61] Such a document would not have been needed if it were universally recognized that older sons were automatically entitled to legal advantage by virtue of their age. In that case, Aliwum's rights would have been

---

[57] Code of Hammurabi §165; cf. the parallel provision in the Lipit Ishtar Code §31 (Miguel Civil, "New Sumerian Law Fragments" in *Studies in Honor of Benno Landsberger* [Chicago: University of Chicago Press, 1965] p. 3). Regarding the meaning of the cited phrase, see the Chicago *Assyrian Dictionary*, vol. 10[1] (M), p. 64 *s.v. maḫāru* 4b 2' b, and J. Klíma, *Untersuchungen zum altbabylonischen Erbrecht* (Prague: Orientalisches Institut, 1940) pp. 11–12. Additional examples of this phrase are provided by E.A. Speiser, "On the Alleged *namru* 'fair(-skinned),'" *Orientalia* 23 (1954) 235–36.

[58] For example, contrast the documents from Nuzi presented in E. A. Speiser, "New Documents Relating to Family Laws," *Annual of the American Schools of Oriental Research* 10 (1928–29) 30–35 (H 5:60, 67, and 7) with those cited by Emile Szlechter, "Des droits successoraux dérivés de l'adoption en droit babylonien," *Revue Internationale des Droits de l'antiquité* (3d series) 14 (1967) 92.

[59] The function of these *šimtu* documents is discussed in Josef Klíma, "Donationes mortis causa nach den akkadischen Rechtsurkunden aus Susa" in *Festschrift Johannes Friedrich*, ed. R. von Kienle et al. (Heidelberg: Carl Winter Universitätsverlag, 1959) pp. 230–40; their broader cultural background is described by A. Leo Oppenheim, *Ancient Mesopotamia, Portrait of a Dead Civilization* (rev. ed., Chicago: University of Chicago Press, 1977) pp. 201–5.

[60] See pp. 16–17 above.

[61] YBC 11174 no. 66 in S. D. Simmons, "Early Old Babylonian Tablets from Harma and Elsewhere (contd.)," *Journal of Cuneiform Studies* 14 (1960) 32.

protected by the presumably well-recognized fact of his seniority. The text's purpose, therefore, is not to prescribe what was legally guaranteed, but to ensure his advantage by designating him as *rabû*. Similar conclusions can be applied to those texts that stipulate which of several children in a family with different sets of parents is to be regarded as the preferred heir. For example, a marriage agreement found at Alalakh requires that even "if Iri-ḫalpa [the groom] has earlier sons [by another woman] and then [his wife] Naidu does, Naidu's will be the *rabû*" (*šumma Iriḫalpa ana pānim šuātu u arkīšu Naʾidu aplam ūlid Naʾiduma rabû*).[62] Similarly, Egyptian marriage contracts often indicate which wife's oldest child will be regarded as the husband's "oldest" (*pȝj-j šr ꜥ pȝj-t šr ꜥ*, "my oldest son is your oldest son").[63] From such documents we can learn that individual property owners had the flexibility to select their chief heir. Oldest sons may, in fact, have been the most common beneficiaries of this practice. Their relatively advanced age would have provided ample opportunity for them to situate themselves favorably, while the ancient (and not so ancient) bias in favor of seniority suggests that incumbents' freedom to choose their successors often worked to the advantage of older offspring. However, that would have been the result of parental choice rather than the inevitable outcome of a predetermined legal system.

If the available texts do not prove the force of automatic criteria, their language is nonetheless frequently cited as evidence that they were intended to circumvent an existing system of automatic succession. After all, it is not specific shares in an estate which these documents assign, but the status of "oldest son." So deeply was primogeniture rooted in these cultures, it is claimed, that this kind of legal fiction, whereby a father might designate a younger child as his firstborn, was the only way he could give preference to the child of his choice.[64] This interpretation is

---

[62] Donald J. Wiseman, *The Alalakh Tablets* (London: The British Institute of Archaeology at Anakara, 1953) p. 55, no. 92, lines 19–20. A similar premise underlies adoption tablets which indicate whether preference will be accorded the adoptee or a subsequently born biological son (e.g., B. Meissner, *Beiträge zum altbabylonischen Privatrecht* [Leipzig: J. C. Hinrichs'sche Buchhandlung, 1893] no. 95 [p. 75]; cf. no. 1 in Georges Boyer, *Textes juridiques* [ARM 8; Paris: Imprimerie Nationale, 1958] pp. 2–4 [lines 19–26]). Cf. Zigi's assurance that "if [his bride] bears sons, the [her] *rabu* son will be my *rabu* son" (*šumma Šuwarḫepa mârê ûllad u maršu rabû ša Šuwarḫepa kīmē māria rabî*, HSS 9:24, lines 10–12) in Cyrus H. Gordon, "Nuzi Tablets Relating to Women" in *Miscellanea Orientalia dedicata Antonio Deimel Annos LXX Complenti* (AnOr 12; Rome: Pontifical Biblical Institute, 1935) p. 171. The Chicago *Assyrian Dictionary* offers a different interpretation of the text in vol. 21 (Z), p. 140.

[63] For examples, see Erich Lüddeckens, *Ägyptische Eheverträge* (Wiesbaden: Otto Harrassowitz, 1960) pp. 24, 30, 40, 56, 76, and 107; the formula is discussed on pp. 279–83.

[64] Cf. John Skinner, *A Critical and Exegetical Commentary on Genesis* (ICC; New York: Charles Scribner's Sons, 1910) p. 362.

often said to be supported by the statements from Nuzi, Ugarit, and Sippar which seem to reject the use of age as a criterion for inheritance, since it is claimed that these should be understood as disavowing the otherwise prevalent practice of primogeniture.[65] However, a closer look at their wording raises an alternative possibility. Although they are commonly rendered, "There is no older nor younger among us" (*yānu rabû yānu ṣeḫru ina birīšunu*), the phrasing of that assertion is bizarre: Did they really not have older and younger children in Ugarit or in Nuzi? Legal documents can alter social facts, but they cannot deny biology. Arbitrarily choosing who will be the oldest son is quite different from claiming not to have one at all.

The terms that appear in these texts—the Akkadian word *rabû* and the Sumerian word gal—are not unusual or obscure. They are the ordinary words for "big," as is self-evident from the way they are applied to animals.[66] In social contexts, they most commonly refer to rank. This connotation can be seen in their use for official titles where age was obviously not a factor. Some of these are even mentioned in the Hebrew Bible.[67] Among these titles, a variety of texts mention a position of šeš. gal (lit. "big brother") as existing in the temple bureaucracy and scribal schools.[68] Although that phrase was surely borrowed from family life—holders of this status presumably functioned much as big brothers do in a household—its appropriateness derives from the correlation of rank and experience rather than age per se. In this respect, it resembles our own English phrase "Big Brother," with its Orwellian connotations.

---

[65] For texts, see p. 17 above.

[66] Examples in Wolfram von Soden, *Akkadisches Handwörterbuch* (Wiesbaden: Otto Harrasowitz, 1965–81) p. 936.

[67] 2 Kings 18:17, Jer 39:3, Jonah 1:6, Esther 1:8, Dan 1:30. For a list of such titles, see Wolfram von Soden, *Akkadisches Handwörterbuch*, p. 938. Similar usages can be found in other Northwest Semitic languages (see C.-F. Jean and J. Hoftijzer, *Dictionnaire des Inscriptions sémitiques de l'ouest* [Leiden: E. J. Brill, 1960] p. 271) and in Ugaritic (see Cyrus Gordon, *Ugaritic Textbook* [AnOr 38; Rome: Pontifical Biblical Insitute, 1965] p. 482).

[68] See Samuel N. Kramer, "Schooldays: A Sumerian Composition Relating to the Education of a Scribe," *Journal of the American Oriental Society* 69 (1949) 209, note 186, and Hayim Tadmor, "'*Ir ha-Miqdash ve-'Ir ha-Melukhah be-Bavel uve-'Ashur*" in *Milḥemet Qodesh u-Martyrologiah be-Toledot Yisra'el uve-Toledot ha-'Ammim* and *Ha'ir veha-Qehillah* (Jerusalem: The Historical Society of Israel, 1967) p. 181; a similar usage can be found in Lev 21:10 and 1 Chron 24:31. The respect due elder brothers is widely evident (e.g., Laws of Manu 2:25; Shurpu 2:35, 87–88, 4:57–58, and 8:59 [Erica Reiner, *Šurpu, A Collection of Sumerian and Akkadian Incantations* (AfO Beiheft 11; Graz: 1958) pp. 14–15, 26, 42]; "Hymn to Enlil," line 32 and TCL vol. 15, nos. 9 iii.2–3 and 16.93.1–3; cf. Adam Falkenstein, *Sumerische Götterlieder* [Heidelberg: Carl Winter Universitätsverlag, 1959] pp. 39 and 201); and TRS 93f line 1 (in J. J. A. van Dijk, *La Sagesse Suméro-Accadienne, Recherches sur les genres littéraires des Textes sapientiaux avec choix de Textes* [Leiden: E. J. Brill, 1953] p. 104).

Several individual rulers are singled out as *rabû*, a usage which has also left its mark on biblical terminology.[69] In Mesopotamia, this title was applied to various deities as well as to the high gods, who are collectively called *ilāni rabûte*, a phrase that evokes their power, not their age.[70] Together, these usages suggest that the fundamental meaning of gal and *rabû* is "great" rather than "older." Although some of those described with these words may in fact have been older and the terms themselves may in certain circumstances have been intended to indicate chronological priority, that is not their necessary or even their fundamental meaning. This accounts for the identification of Ashurbanipal, the Assyrian royal heir, as the *rabû* prince of the House of Succession (*mār šarre rabû ša bīt rīdûti*) despite other indications that he was a younger son.[71]

Although rarely phrased so bluntly, the conclusion that it is status, not age, to which such terms refer, is not particularly new. The documents on which we have drawn are well known, and the incongruities emphasized here have been problematic for everyone who has studied them. And so, although these terms are conventionally defined as meaning "oldest," scholars have often been forced to render them differently.[72] Nowhere has this been more common than in the case of an adoption tablet from Nuzi, which subordinates the adoptee to any naturally born children by stating, "If a son of my own is born, he shall be *rabû*.... Indeed, should [my] wife bear ten sons, they shall [all] be *rabû* (*lū* 10 *ašassu ša Akab-šenni mārēša ulladu rabû*).[73] In this context *rabû* can hardly mean "firstborn," as various translations of the document have, perhaps unconsciously, recognized.

Cuneiform tablets indicating which child is to be *rabû*, therefore, designate rank, not age, a stipulation that would have been unnecessary

---

[69] Ps 48:3 and Ezra 5:11; compare 2 Kings 18:19, 28 (= Isa 38:4, 13), Mal 1:3, Pss 47:3 and 95:3.

[70] For texts, see Knut L. Tallqvist, *Akkadische Götterepitheta* (StOr 7; Helsinki: Societas Orientalis Fennica, 1938) p. 14.

[71] Rassam Cylinder 1.1 (Maximillian Streck, *Assurbanipal und die letzten assyrischen Könige bis zum Untergange Niniveh's* [Leipzig: J. C. Hinrichs'sche Buchhandlung, 1916] vol. 2, p. 2). Similar terms are applied to his brother Shamash-shum-ukin, the evidence for which is collected by Donald. J. Wiseman, "The Vassal Treaties of Esarhaddon," *Iraq* 20 (1958) 6–7 and 84. The Old Babylonian statement *aplum rabûm kussâm iṣabbat* (the *rabû* son will take over the throne), quoted from YOS 10 31 ii 4 by the Chicago *Assyrian Dictionary*, vol. 1 (A)², p. 175, must be interpreted in this light.

[72] Jonathan Paradise ("Nuzi Inheritance Practices") is particularly consistent in rendering them as "chief heir" and the like.

[73] HSS 5:7 in E. A. Speiser, "I Know Not the Day of My Death," *Journal of Biblical Literature* 74 (1955) 255–56; see also the citations in the Chicago *Assyrian Dictionary*, vol. 1 (A)², p. 174.

in a society where primogeniture was automatic. The function of these documents is not to make younger children fictitiously older than their siblings, but to identify which offspring are to be treated preferentially. Presupposing a system of unequal distribution, they do not ratify what would have occurred anyway, but implement a father's decision as to which of his children should be favored (*rabû*). Communities where differential inheritance was not allowed would note the lack of *rabû* and *ṣeḥru* heirs in their midst, something quite different from not having older and younger children. These documents, therefore, mean exactly what they say—that in some places there really was no *rabû* and no *ṣeḥru*, so that no one person received more than any other. It is this kind of advantage which they reject on principle, not primogeniture.

Following a pattern of argument which is by now familiar, there are some who have seen the lack of evidence for primogeniture as evidence of its antiquity, suggesting that it had been discontinued by the time the surviving documents were written.[74] Such arguments from silence are vivid demonstrations of the important role theoretical presuppositions play in discussions of this issue.

To support their position, proponents muster evidence from Mesopotamian legal terminology. They claim that the Akkadian word *aplu*, which means "heir," was borrowed from the Sumerian language, in which the equivalent and patently cognate term i b i l a has been interpreted as a compound, which literally means "one who burns (b i l) the oil (i)," a ritual commonly connected with the family ancestor cult.[75] The correlation of ritual responsibility with matters of inheritance is supported by a Mesopotamian curse: "May (Ninurta) deprive him of an heir (i b i l a), a pourer of water."[76]

---

[74] Josef Klíma, *Untersuchungen zum altbabylonischen Erbrecht* (Prague: Orientalisches Institut, 1940), p. 2: primogeniture is widely considered to have been only a regional phenomenon (e.g., ibid., pp. 32–33). For a similar argument, see Isaac Mendelsohn, "On the Preferential Status of the Eldest Son," *Bulletin of the American Schools of Oriental Research* 156 (1959) 38–40.

[75] F. Thureau-Dangin, "Notes Assyriologiques," *Revue d'Assyriologie* 10 (1913) 97.

[76] Miranda Bayliss, "The Cult of Dead Kin in Assyrian and Babylonia," *Iraq* 35 (1973) 119. H. Pognon suggested that *aplu* is related to an Akkadian verb referring to making libations ("Lexicographie Assyrienne," *Revue d'Assyriologie* 9 [1912] 128); for water pouring, see also the Laws of Manu 9:186 (ed. G. Bühler, p. 366). Family rituals were also linked to succession in Greece (Isaeus, "On the Estate of Philoctemon" 2.51 [LCL pp. 232–33]), Rome (Cicero, "De Legibus" 2.19.48 [LCL pp. 430–31]), and Egypt (Pap. Bulaq X r. 10–11, cited by J. J. Janssen and P. W. Pestman, "Burial and Inheritance in the Community of the Necropolis Workmen at Thebes [Pap. Bulaq X and O. Petrie 16]," *Journal of the Economic and Social History of the Orient* 11 [1968] 10–11). Herbert C. Brichto has proposed that the fifth commandment may originally have referred to funerary rites ("Kin, Cult, Land and Afterlife—A Biblical Complex," *Hebrew Union College Annual* 44 [1973] 30–31).

Numerous uncertainties make this hypothesis a weak foundation for any theory as to the nature of ancient inheritance. The etymology of *aplu*/ibila is itself a matter of dispute. Some scholars believe that the Sumerian term was borrowed from Akkadian rather than the other way around, in which case its supposed Sumerian components are irrelevant for understanding the word's origin.[77] Nor is there any evidence that pouring oil was part of an ancestor cult, much less one in which oldest sons played the central role. Extant texts mention a variety of rituals and allocate responsibility for their performance to a wide range of different relatives, including women.[78] As for the word ibila, it means only "heir," as can be seen from its logographic representation by dumu . nita (lit. "successor son"). In fact, many early occurrences of both the Sumerian term and its Akkadian cognate are either plural or modified with such superlatives as *reštu, rabu,* and *ašarēdu,* which themselves designate the "first" or "greatest *aplu*" and thereby clearly demonstrate that the noun's meaning is less specific than "firstborn."[79]

Israelite Inheritance

There is little compelling evidence that it is either natural or typical for older offspring to receive preferential treatment in matters of inheritance, whether in general or among those cultures in whose midst Israel lived. Thus we must turn to the Bible as the primary source of information for determining Israelite practice in order to establish the context for its recurring interest in younger children.

[77] Benno Landsberger, "Schwierige akkadische Wörter," *Archiv für Orientforschung* 3 (1926) 169–70, and Adam Falkenstein, "Kontakte zwischen Sumerern und Akkadern auf Sprachlichem Gebiet" in *Aspects du Contact Sumero-Akkadien,* ed. Edmond Sollberger (IXe Rencontre assyriologique internationale, *Genava* n.s. 8; Geneva: Musée d'art et d'histoire Genève, 1960) p. 313. Landsberger compares the form *'āpîlōt* in Exod 9:32 (p. 170).

[78] See Miranda Bayliss, "The Cult of Dead Kin in Assyria and Babylonia," especially pp. 118–19, and Aaron Skaist, "The Ancestor Cult and Succession in Mesopotamia" in *Death in Mesopotamia* (XXVIe Rencontre assyriologique internationale) ed. Bendt Alster (Copenhagen: Akademisk Forlag, 1980) p. 124. Note that the curse cited on p. 47 above refers to the heir (ibila) as a pourer of water and that the Ugaritic story of Aqhat refers to rituals performed by a son, not a firstborn (*Corpus des tablettes en cunéiformes alphabétiques,* ed. Andrée Herdner, no. 17 i lines 27–29, quoted on page 21–22 above); for Egyptian practice, see the Old Kingdom letter cited by Rolf Tanner, "Untersuchungen zur ehe- und erbrechtlichen Stellung der Frau im pharonischen Agypten," *Klio* 49 (1967) 29.

[79] For examples, see the Chicago *Assyrian Dictionary,* vol. 1 (A)^2, pp. 174–75, as well as the Lagash documents published in Adam Falkenstein, *Die neusumerischen Gerichtsurkunden* (see note 49 above). In the absence of an ibila, two of these allow a man's property to go to his brother (nos. 80 and 183, vol. 2, pp. 132 and 292).

A preliminary indication that the biblical evidence may be less supportive of primogeniture than is commonly assumed can be found in the role which the Bible played during the centuries-long debate over British primogeniture. During that time, a host of objections were raised in an effort to overthrow what critics perceived as an unfair and unwise law. Some saw the diversity of human practice as demonstrating that primogeniture was neither universal nor natural. Others questioned the morality of a system that effectively disenfranchised a substantial proportion of the population and left younger children impoverished. Of singular relevance for our purposes, however, is an intriguing argument which combined elements from both the empirical and the moral approaches by claiming that primogeniture violated biblical teaching.[80] With this argument, opponents of primogeniture combined the Bible's moral authority with its testimony of actual Israelite practice. They certainly did not regard primogeniture as having been normative in ancient Israel, and we cannot, therefore, simply assume that it was.

As one would expect, Israel's inheritance customs fit well within the context of ancient Near Eastern practice, where there is little evidence that primogeniture was binding. For purposes of comparison, it is useful to consider the British form of this custom, which provided for the transmission of family estates to a single individual without division. One result of this practice was that younger offspring were left to make their own way, with social consequences that were, predictably, severe. Thus, many of those attracted to Britain's settlements in the New World are reported to have been younger sons; the colonies offered "worthy employement for many younger brothers and brave gentlemen now ruined...."[81] Other younger offspring were forced into monasteries or the military.[82] Left to

---

[80] Joan Thirsk, "The European Debate on Customs of Inheritance, 1500–1700," pp. 181 and 187, and Paula S. Fichtner, *Protestantism and Primogeniture*, p. 25. Although Georg Ludolf claimed this practice was Mosaic, German leaders seeking a biblical base were forced to rely on children's obligation to respect their parents' wishes (ibid., pp. 21 and 79).

[81] From a 1623 letter cited by Joan Thirsk, "Younger Sons in the Seventeenth Century," p. 368. As recently as 1879, a colony established in Tennessee's Cumberland Plateau comprised mostly the gentry's younger sons (Marguerite B. Hamer, "Thomas Hughes and His American Rugby," *North Carolina Historical Review* 5 [1928] 391). Bernard M. Aginsky and Te Rangi Hiroa offer a similar explanation for Maori migrations ("Interacting Forces in the Maori Family," *American Anthropologist* 42 [1940] 196); see also Herodotus 5.42 (LCL vol. 3, pp. 44–47) and the reported fate of the younger son Tangaroa (William W. Gill, *Myths and Songs from the South Pacific* [London: Henry S. King & Co., 1876] pp. 13–14).

[82] Cf. Falstaff's remark that his "whole charge consists of ancients, corporals, lieutenants gentlemen of companies, slaves as ragged as Lazarus in the painted cloth, where the glutton's dogs licked his sores; and such as, indeed, were never soldiers, but discarded unjust

their brothers' mercy, younger sons received, in the words of a seventeenth-century observer, only "that which the cat left on the malt heap."[83] Shakespeare gave voice to the implications of this practice too in the complaint he put into the mouth of one younger son:

> Shall I keep your hogs, and eat husks with them? What prodigal portion have I spent that I should come to such penury?...The courtesy of nations allows you my better, in that you are the first born; but...I have as much of my father in me as you.   (*As You Like It*, 1:1)

By contrast, the Bible offers no evidence for exclusive inheritance, whether by older sons or any other heir, in ancient Israel. Although it does mention several rootless individuals, there is no reason to think that they were impoverished younger sons, wandering through the interstices of an unconcerned society as happened in parts of medieval Europe.[84] Only one passage suggests otherwise, and a closer look at it will lead us in a quite different direction.

The book of Genesis records that towards the end of his life Abraham gave Isaac everything that was his (*kŏl 'ăšer lô*, Gen 25:5, cf. 24:36). Although this statement does include exclusivity, the phrasing "he gave" (*wayittēn*) and the fact that the transaction took place while Abraham was still alive suggest that it has to do with a gift rather than inheritance of any kind, much less one governed by automatic principles. In the next verse the same verb is used to refer to Abraham's gifts to the sons of his concubines, and it appears earlier with reference to the bread and water given Hagar before she was sent out into the desert (21:14). It is, therefore, reasonable to conclude that Isaac's good fortune was a sign of his father's favor rather than the inescapable consequence of ancient law.

Supporting this conclusion is the fact that all this is said to have taken place at the same time that Abraham's other sons were being sent away (Gen 25:6). The significance of this statement is best measured by considering the other occasions on which the Bible describes various siblings as

---

serving-men, younger sons to younger brothers, revolted tapsters, and ostlers tradefallen; the cankers of a calm world and a long peace" (William Shakespeare, *Henry IV*, Part I, 4:2).

[83] Thomas Wilson, *The State of England Anno Domini 1600*, cited by Joan Thirsk, "Younger Sons in the Seventeenth Century," p. 360.

[84] Contra Lawrence Stager, "The Archaeology of the Family in Ancient Israel," *Bulletin of the American Schools of Oriental Research* 260 (1985) 25–28. There is no evidence that the bands led by Jephthah and David (Judg 11:3 and 1 Sam 22:2) comprised younger sons, although Norman Gottwald's inference that Jephthah was an older son (*The Tribes of Yahweh, A Sociology of the Religion of Liberated Israel, 1250–1050 B.C.E.* [Maryknoll, NY: Orbis Books, 1979] pp. 286–87) is also unsupported.

having been so treated. Earlier, for example, Sarah had asked that Ishmael be expelled so that he not inherit alongside his half-brother Isaac (Gen 21:10), and Jephthah is reported to have been forced out of his household by his half-brothers, with the explanation, "You shall not inherit in our father's house" (Judg 11:2). There would have been no reason to remove such children from their households unless they had legal rights of their own. The texts make it clear that the purpose of these actions was to maximize the size of inheritance shares by reducing the number of heirs among whom the estate would be divided. Although the identification of those whom Abraham expelled as the offspring of concubines and the description of Jephthah as the son of a prostitute raise at least some questions about their legal rights, collectively these accounts make it quite clear that estates were not necessarily limited to a single heir.

This presumption is shared by virtually every biblical reference to inheritance.[85] For example, Job's estate was divided among all his children (Job 42:15). Although this is ascribed to testamentary discretion ("Their father gave them..." [*wayyittēn lāhem 'ăbîhem*]), the fact that his daughters are said to have been included "alongside their brothers" (*bĕtôk 'ăhêhem*) suggests that, even had Job chosen to exclude his daughters, the estate would still have been divided among his sons.

Even if we set the case of Job aside as irrelevant to Israelite practice, since Job was not considered an Israelite,[86] other texts devoted to Israelite figures presuppose a similar approach. It can even be discerned in the famous case of Zelophehad's daughters, who sought Moses' assistance in resolving the problems created by their not having brothers who could inherit the family property. Rather than singling out one of the sisters, Moses responded to their plight by decreeing that, in the absence of sons, *all* daughters should serve as substitute heirs.[87] Failing that, the text lists

[85] Elephantine documents suggest a similar practice; cf. A Cowley, *Aramaic Papyri of the Fifth Century B.C.*, nos. 9, 15, and 28 (Oxford: Clarendon Press, 1923) pp. 27–28, 45–46, and 103–5, and Emil G. Kraeling, *The Brooklyn Museum Aramaic Papyri, New Documents of the Fifth Century B.C. from the Jewish Colony at Elephantine*, nos. 3, 4, 9, 10, and 12 (New Haven, CT: Yale University Press, 1953) pp. 154–55, 168–69, 238–39, 249–50, and 272–73. Regarding Luke 12:13 and 15:12, see David Daube, "Inheritance in Two Lukan Pericopes," *Zeitschrift der Savigny-Stiftung für Rechtsgeschichte* (Romanistische Abteilung) 72 (1955) 326–34.

[86] So Samuel Loewenstamm, "*Yerushah*," *Encyclopedia Miqra'it* (Jerusalem: Bialik Institute, 1950–88) vol. 3, p. 791.

[87] Num 27:7 and 36:2; see also Josh 17:4, Jer 3:19, Prov 17:2, and Sirah 33:23. The singular usage in Num 27:8 is apparently generic (like the preceding *ben*) or constitutes a minimal condition. For a parallel situation, see 1 Chron 2:34–35; note also that Josephus describes the Essenes as sharing "like brothers" (*hōsper adelphois, Wars* 2.8.3 §122 [LCL vol. 2, pp. 370–71]).

other relatives who may receive an estate, again in the plural: "If he has
no daughter, you shall give his estate to his brothers, and if he has no
brothers, you shall give his estate to his father's brothers" (Num 27:9–10).
Even the division of Canaan, which the Bible presents as a matter of
inheritance by the descendants of Jacob's sons, follows the same pattern,
with each tribe receiving an allocation.[88] Biblical references to inheritance
are thus consistent in their expectation that all sons receive portions of
a father's estate. This is scarcely surprising in a culture such as Israel's,
where the family was the fundamental social unit and ample land was
available.

Among the clearest manifestations of this commitment to familial
solidarity is the custom of levirate marriage, which held a man responsible
for his brother's childless widow (Deut 25:5–10). This practice has sometimes been understood as intended to maintain the line of a family head
who died without natural heirs, and two stories associated with the practice
seem to suggest that its provisions were applied in accordance with the
brothers' age. Genesis 38 traces the fate of Tamar, whose father-in-law
Judah refused to give her his youngest son after his firstborn and middle
sons had both died while married to her. From this story one might infer
that the levirate requirements were invoked in order of seniority. A similar
impression is conveyed in the synoptic gospels' description of a Sadducean
challenge to Jesus' view of the resurrection, which presents the case of a
woman who had been widowed by an apparently oldest son and was then
married to each of his six younger brothers in succession.[89] However,
this interpretation must be treated cautiously. The absence of principles
of seniority in both Deuteronomy and parallel provisions from other Near
Eastern cultures opens the possibility that the sequence with which the
brothers are mentioned in these two accounts may be a literary feature
rather than a legal requirement.[90] The Genesis story is particularly suspect,

---

[88] The division's being "by lot" (Num 34:13–29, Josh 14:2) shows that none of the
portions was perceived as inherently preferable to any other. According to Judg 1:1–3, Judah
was among the first to take possession of its allocation, although that simply demonstrates
that tribe's merit (as confirmed by its unique success in that chapter); it does not entail its
allotment being larger or preferable to those of other tribes. The Joseph tribe appeals for
more land because of its size (Josh 17:14) and appears to be related to the fact that two
tribes were believed to be descended from it (Josh 14:4); see pp. 120–22 below, where
Genesis 48 and Ezek 47:13 are also treated. For a more general discussion of the use of
inheritance imagery to describe Israel's possession of the land, see Arthur M. Brown, "The
Concept of Inheritance in the Old Testament" (Columbia University, Ph.D. dissertation,
1965) pp. 162–210.

[89] Mark 12:20–22, Matthew 22:25–27, Luke 20:29–32.

[90] For another example of this configuration, see p. 98 below. Cf. the Hittite Laws
§193 (Johannes Friedrich, *Die Hethitischen Gesetze* no. 79a [Leiden: E. J. Brill, 1971]

since its description differs from Deuteronomy's stipulations in several ways, most notably by placing fundamental responsibility with the deceased's father rather than his brothers.

The belief that the levirate custom was an effort to perpetuate an otherwise doomed line of descent has ancient roots.[91] Its origin lies within Deuteronomy itself, which explains the regulation by mandating that the widow's first offspring by her brother-in-law "shall be accounted to his dead brother so that his name not be wiped out from Israel" (*yāqûm ʿal šēm ʾāḥîw hammēt wĕlōʾ yimmāḥeh šĕmô miyyiśrāʾēl*, 25:6). Whatever the sincerity of this explanation, it is not a wholly satisfying account for the social practice to which it refers. Whereas our contemporary preoccupation with individual mortality may give credence to the concern with perpetuating the deceased's name, in ancient Israel there would have been little of real consequence which was at stake. Since the law presupposes that the deceased had brothers but no offspring, there would have been no line whose survival was actually in jeopardy: the father's line would have continued through his surviving sons, whereas his now dead offspring had not yet established a family of his own.[92] The law's provisions would, therefore, have been unnecessary to ensure that the family's property remained within the family. The only "line" at risk was one that had barely begun. The custom cannot, therefore, be understood as an effort to maintain a family line. More likely, it was intended to protect childless widows from social isolation and economic abandonment.[93]

Whatever the law's purpose, birth order plays no role either in its application or in achieving its ends. There is no evidence that responsibility had to pass among the surviving brothers according to the order of their birth—Genesis 38 and the synoptic stories notwithstanding—nor are oldest sons the only ones whose death would occasion its procedures, as might have been the case in a culture where a firstborn's death raised unique legal or social problems.

---

pp. 84–85). The Mishna does explicitly assign this responsibility to the eldest surviving son (*m. Yevamot* 4:5); however, the Middle Assyrian Laws allow a man to assign his widowed daughter-in-law to any son of his choosing (A §43 [ed. G. R. Driver and John Miles, pp. 410–11]).

[91] So already Josephus, *Antiquities* 4.8.23 §254 (LCL vol. 4, pp. 596–99); see also Eryl Davies, "Inheritance Rights and the Hebrew Levirate Marriage," *Vetus Testamentum* 31 (1981) 140–42.

[92] In the book of Ruth, where a similar concern is mentioned (4:5, 10), there are no surviving males (cf. 1:1–5).

[93] Cf. Paul Koschaker, "Zum Levirat nach hethitischem Recht," *Revue Hittite et Asianique* 2 (1933) 89.

In fact, there is no need to speculate as to the law's real interests. The opening clause expressly limits its provisions to situations in which "brothers dwell together" (*kî-yēšĕbû 'ahîm yahdāw*, Deut 25:5). This phrasing, which occurs elsewhere in the Bible, suggests a shared household, perhaps a communal arrangement like the *consortium* of ancient Rome.[94] It is these circumstances which appear to be idealized in the Psalmist's oft-quoted statement, "How good and pleasant it is when brothers dwell together" (Ps 133:1). In any event, this phrase provides both the law's precondition and its *raison d'etre*. Intended to ensure that brothers committed to fraternal solidarity live up to their obligations, it applies to *all* brothers who live in such an arrangement, irrespective of their relative age. It, therefore, offers no evidence to demonstrate the status of firstborns as family leaders.[95]

Even granting the division of Israelite estates among all equivalent heirs, allocations need not have been equal. The use of favoritism-based imagery in the Bible and its numerous depictions of struggles for primacy and preeminence both clearly demonstrate that there were advantages to be had and only one brother who could have them.

The classic text for this, as for all of biblical inheritance, also comes from the book of Deuteronomy. The details of its phrasing merit careful consideration. Referring to a father with sons by two different wives, it states:

> ... if the *bĕkōr* son is from the less loved woman, then when he bequeaths his property to his children the father may not make the favored wife's son *bĕkōr* over the son of the wife he loves less, who is [already] *bĕkōr*. Instead, he must recognize the *bĕkōr*, the son of the less-loved wife, giving him two shares of all that is his. ...   (21:15–18)[96]

The language of this passage is unambiguous in its refutation of exclusive inheritance. The law allows something for each brother. All that is at stake is an extra portion, not the entire estate. At the same time, its

---

[94] David Daube, "*Consortium* in Roman and Hebrew Law," *Juridical Review* 62 (1950) 71–91. Johannes Pedersen understands this phrase, which also occurs in Gen 13:6 and 36:7, to mean "in the same town" (*Israel, Its Life and Culture* [London: Oxford University Press, 1926] I–II, p. 508).

[95] A. F. Puukko, "Die Leviratsehe in den altorientalischen Gesetzen," *Archiv Orientâlni* 17 (1949) 296.

[96] For the translation "less loved," see David Qimhi at v. 15; the connection between *'ahab* and inheritance is noted by H. Z. Szubin and Bezalel Porten, "Testamentary Succession at Elephantine," *Bulletin of the American Schools of Oriental Research* 252 (1983) 37. Abraham ibn Ezra understands *yakkîr* as entailing a formal declaration (comment at Gen 29:31). Regarding the meaning of *pî šĕnayim*, see p. 18 above.

reference to the *běkōr* confirms the existence of preferential treatment, although there is no evidence that family leadership, which often appears as exclusive inheritance,[97] was included among its provisions.

Remarkably, the Bible contains no proof that preferred sons, whether younger or older, were given control over their fathers' households. Both Isaac and Jacob led only their own families. Isaac never achieved dominance over his brother, despite the efforts of Sarah. Instead, Ishmael's departure effectively precluded his falling under his brother's authority. Although Esau remained with his family after losing both the birthright and the blessing, the now-favored Jacob had to flee. When he returned years later, Esau left to pursue his own affairs (Gen 36:6). If Esau's fate and that of Ishmael recall those impoverished younger sons under British primogeniture, it is a consequence of their way of life not its cause, and certainly not the result of their having been left without resources. The Bible provides no evidence that either one did poorly.[98]

In fact, actual leadership and inheritance are not the real focus of these stories at all. As they repeatedly make clear, what is at stake in the patriarchal tales is neither property nor office, but the transmission of a blessing—"mere words...unaccompanied even by a slightest token of material possession."[99] It is this which resolves the nettlesome legal problem of how the Bible could tolerate Jacob's keeping a blessing he had fraudulently obtained. Scholars have inferred from this account that deathbed declarations must have been irrevocable in ancient Israel.[100] But few societies sanction transactions accomplished in that way.[101]

---

[97] See p. 39 above.

[98] Of some relevance may be Niels Lemche's observation that extended families are rare in nomadic societies (*Early Israel, Anthropological and Historical Studies on the Israelite Society Before the Monarchy* [Supplement to *Vetus Testamentum* 37; Leiden: E. J. Brill, 1985] p. 112).

[99] Raphael Patai, *Sex and Family in the Bible and the Middle East* (Garden City, NY: Doubleday & Co., 1959) p. 220; cf. Nahmanides at Gen 25:34 and Alfred Adler's comment that the competition between Jacob and Esau was "not so much for power, but for the semblance of power" (*Understanding Human Nature*, [Garden City, NY: Garden City Publishing Co., 1927] p. 154). Solomon, Ahaziah (2 Chron 22:1), and the priests Eleazar and Ithamar (Leviticus 10) are the only younger sons whom the Bible describes as having succeeded to actual positions.

[100] E. A. Speiser, "I Know Not the Day of My Death," *Journal of Biblical Literature* 74 (1955) 252–56.

[101] Moshe Greenberg makes a similar observation about the supposed legal implications of Rachel's possession of her family's gods, which she had stolen from Laban's home ("Another Look at Rachel's Theft of the Teraphim," *Journal of Biblical Literature* 81 [1962] 244); see also John van Seters, *Abraham in History and Tradition* (New Haven, CT: Yale University Press, 1975) p. 95.

The Bible has its own ways of communicating disapproval of Jacob's behavior.[102] However, fraud need not be a concern, since it is not a legal proceeding that these stories describe nor, for the most part, the transfer of property. As is clearly stated, their focus is a blessing, a theme that dominates the book of Genesis. Esau's statement, "Have you only one blessing?" (Gen 27:38) is not a legal fact, but the pained cry of a cheated youth. As his rhetorical tone makes clear, the implied response is negative: fathers are not limited to a single blessing in the way they might have only one house or their family a single patriarch.[103] Nor was Esau alone in expecting that Isaac could bless him, too. There is nothing in Jacob and Rebecca's words or deeds to suggest that they thought Esau's blessing was Isaac's only one. Their urgency resulted from their belief that Isaac was about to die. It was not his only blessing that they wanted for Jacob, but the *best* one, which they presumed that he intended to bestow upon Esau. In this, they were both correct and ultimately successful. But Esau was not excluded. After telling him, "Your brother came deceitfully and took *your* blessing" (v. 35), Isaac does have another, which he proceeds to bestow upon Esau.

Nowhere in this story is there any reference to Isaac's property or, for that matter, leadership. Israelite sons may have succeeded to their fathers' positions or been assigned their estates, but that is not what these narratives are about. Esau was not disinherited, nor Jacob granted *patria potestas*. What was at stake was destiny, not property.[104] The story has to do with a blessing, precisely as the Bible says—no less, but also not more. In fact, being blessed offers the patriarchs little identifiable benefit. Judging from the biblical account, its only advantage seems to have been the assurance that their descendants would be numerous and powerful. Even what little dominance it does allow is most often said to be over groups other than their own, and that only in some distant future. Being favored with the blessing—a theological category rather than a legal one—means being an ancestor of Israel, marking the line through which the people traced their descent and justifying the thread of the biblical account. Ultimately these tales are about which son (or daughter) will be followed by the continuing narrative. Essentially retrospective, they explain for later generations how God had determined those through whom *the* line would continue. Whether primogeniture prevailed in ancient

---

[102] See pp. 128–131 below.

[103] So already *Midrash Tanḥuma* (Buber) *Toledot* 23.

[104] Thomas L. Thompson, *The Historicity of the Patriarchal Narratives, The Quest for the Historical Abraham* (BZAW 133; Berlin: Walter de Gruyter, 1974) p. 293.

Israel or not has little to do with the thrust of these stories, whose focus is religious rather than legal.

Although the deuteronomic law is concerned with matters of inheritance, it is no more supportive of primogeniture than the stories in Genesis. Moreover, a careful reading of its phrasing will show that the way this passage is commonly interpreted is substantially broader than the text itself requires.

Frequently described as instituting or confirming an existing system of primogeniture, the deuteronomic law itself says nothing of the sort. It simply prohibits fathers from giving the offspring of a better-loved wife preference over those of another woman. However, its phrasing permits many other kinds of favoritism. For example, wicked sons could be disinherited, as 1 Chronicles reports happened to Reuben (5:1), or a favorite son chosen from among those of a single wife, as were Isaac and Joseph.[105] A preferred son could even be elevated or part of an ancestral estate given away as a gift prior to death. All that Deuteronomy prohibits is basing favoritism in matters of inheritance on the testator's affection for a particular woman.

Evidence that this actually occurred can be found in many societies, including ancient Israel.[106] The Bible explains Abraham's willingness to tolerate the expulsion of Hagar's son Ishmael as having been motivated by his concern for Sarah, just as David's selection of Solomon owes much to his interest in pleasing Bathsheba. Likewise, Joseph was the son of Jacob's beloved Rachel, and 2 Chronicles implies that similar motives played a part in Rehoboam's selection of Abijah to be his successor (11:21–22).

Some have thought that Deuteronomy's regulation was written in response to these cases,[107] but there is little evidence to support this position. Like the levirate law, Deuteronomy's treatment of inheritance is better understood as reflecting that book's general interest in protecting the weak and the vulnerable.[108] Just as its other provisions safeguarded

[105] Obadiah Sforno at Deut 21:16.

[106] See note 43 in this chapter.

[107] To Calum Carmichael, the phrasing suggests it was a reaction to the case of Rachel and Leah (*The Laws of Deuteronomy* [Ithaca, NY: Cornell University Press, 1974] p. 61), despite their having the same mother; Reuven Yaron considers David's elevation of Solomon a more likely background (*Gifts in Contemplation of Death in Jewish and Roman Law* [Oxford: Clarendon Press, 1960] p. 10). Robert M. Cover comments that "every legal order must conceive of itself in one way or another as emerging out of that which is itself unlawful" ("Nomos and Narrative," *Harvard Law Review* 97 [1983] 23, see also pp. 20–21).

[108] J. van der Ploeg, "Studies in Hebrew Law III," *Catholic Biblical Quarterly* 13 (1951) 35; see also Moshe Weinfeld, *Deuteronomy and the Deuteronomic School* (Oxford: Clarendon Press, 1972) p. 291.

widows, orphans, and strangers, this law protects an unloved mother by limiting her husband's power to deny her son the status of *bĕkōr*.

As with the levirate law, the circumstantial clause with which this provision begins provides further insight into its breadth. The opening statement, "when [a father] bequeaths [his property] to his children" (*bĕyôm hanḥîlô 'et bānāyw*), occurs elsewhere in the Bible.[109] Not only does it set this provision within a system in which estates could be divided among several heirs, but it also demonstrates the role of paternal discretion in determining how that would be done. Several familiar narratives provide further evidence of this practice. Sarah's request that Abraham expel Ishmael and Hagar presupposes that he had the power to do so. Jacob's deception of his father Isaac assumes that the blessing was Isaac's to give, as does Jacob's later behavior in choosing how to bless his grandchildren Ephraim and Manasseh.

Besides being free to divide their estates (*hinḥîl*) however they might choose, Israelite fathers could also apparently assign leadership to whichever son they preferred. David designated Solomon to be his successor, and Jacob blessed his fourth son Judah with the assurance that, "Your brothers shall praise you...your father's sons bow down before you" (Gen 49:8). The biblical evidence, therefore, does not support either primogeniture or ultimogeniture as automatic and invariable, but only a father's right to choose. The fact that, once made, a father's action could not be reversed, even if its effect was unintended, simply confirms the ceremony's authority.

Deuteronomy restricts a man's freedom to designate his *bĕkōr* (*ybkr*)[110] in a way which suggests that favoritism had previously played a role in the bestowal of that status. At the same time, the regulation implicitly allows that practice to continue, but only within certain limits. From this, we can infer that the status of *bĕkōr* was transferable. Support for this conclusion can be found in the story of Esau's having sold the *bĕkōrâ* to Jacob. Although the biblical interpretation of Jacob's name as meaning "supplanter" (Gen 27:36) surely entails some criticism of his having exploited his brother's suffering, there is not even an intimation that Jacob or Rebecca had violated Israelite law, but only that they had taken fullest advantage of its ambiguities. Jacob's son Reuben is also said to have lost

---

[109] In addition to Ezek 46:18 and Prov 13:22, note the reference to appointing an heir in Hebrews 1:2 (*hon ethēken klēronomon pantōn*).

[110] This denominative nuance underlies the usage in Lev 27:26 and has been proposed for Lachish letter II (*Kanaanäische und aramäische Inschriften*, ed. H. Donner and W. Röllig [Wiesbaden: Otto Harrasowitz, 1966–69] no. 192, lines 5–6); cf. Hans-Peter Müller, "Notizen zu althebräischen Inschriften I," *Ugarit-Forschungen* 2 [1970] 235), although the reading there is uncertain.

the *bĕkōrâ* (1 Chron 5:1), and the tradition that Elisha, who once called his mentor "my father, my father" (2 Kings 2:12), requested a double portion of Elijah's spirit (v. 9) may reflect the same procedure.[111] Ugaritic literature provides further evidence from outside of Israel that this status could be assigned in its report that King KRT was assured that his youngest (*ṣġrtk*) would be made *bkr*.[112] Likewise, the Psalmist states that God made David His *bĕkōr* (*'ap-'ānî bĕkōr 'etnēhû*, Ps 89:28), and Ben Sirah asserts that He so "named Israel" (*kinnîtihā*, 36:12).[113]

From such statements it is apparent that the position of *bĕkōr* was an assigned, not an automatic status, even if eldest sons were most likely to achieve its benefits. Deuteronomy 21 need not, therefore, be understood as an effort to eliminate a legal loophole whereby certain children were fictitiously designated firstborn in order to circumvent the rigidities of primogeniture, but simply as amending accepted procedure by limiting the criteria according to which the selection of a *bĕkōr* could be made.

bĕkōr

The fact that someone could be made *bĕkōr* makes no sense if that word means "firstborn" in a literal way, since that would be a biologically and not a socially determined status. Whatever their merits, Jacob and Joseph

---

[111] This request was fulfilled according to the Hebrew text of Sirah 48:12 (see note 30, chapter 1).

[112] *Corpus des tablettes en cunéiformes alphabétiques*, ed. Andrée Herdner, no. 15 iii.16. Note, however, J. C. L. Gibson's translation of the phrase *ṣġrthn abkrn* as "I will give the firstborn's blessing (even) to the youngest of them" (*Canaanite Myths and Legends* [2d ed.; Edinburgh: T. & T. Clark, 1978] p. 92). Although the juxtaposition of *bkr* and *ṣ'r* is familiar from the Bible, the absence of a parallel stich and the presence of the common root *brk* in the next line suggest that our text may not be in order. The root *bkr* occurs elsewhere in Ugaritic only as a noun (*Corpus des tablettes en cunéiformes alphabétiques* no. 14 iii.144; see also the fragmentary RS 15.134, line 9 in *Le Palais Royal d'Ugarit* vol. 2 [Textes en cunéiformes alphabétiques des archives est, ouest, et centrales, ed. Charles Virolleaud; MRS 7; Paris: Imprimerie Nationale, Librairie C. Klincksieck, 1957] p. 5, and the conjectural reading for line 14 of RS 24:26 described in note 8 of chapter 2 above). *Corpus des tablettes en cunéiformes alphabétiques* no. 13, line 28 is also problematic; many scholars prefer the reading *kbkb* ["stars," cf. ibid. p. 58, n. 3]).

[113] For the reverse process, see Jer 49:15. Later texts that belong to this category include 4QDibHam 3.5–6 *ky' qrth [l]yśr'l bny bkwry* (Maurice Baillet, "Un recueil liturgique de Qumrân, Grotte 4: 'Le paroles luminaires,'" *Revue Biblique* 68 [1961] 202) and *Exodus Rabbah* 19:7 which understands Exod 4:22 as meaning that Jacob had been made God's *bĕkōr*. Other references to Israel's being *bĕkōr* can be found in *Deuteronomy Rabbah, Shofeṭim* 7 and line 8 of a poem found in the Cairo Geniza and attributed to as-Samau'al ibn 'Adijā (Joachim W. Hirschberg, *Der Dīwān des as-Samau'al ibn 'Ādijā* [Polska Akademja Umiejetnósci Prace Komisji Orientalistyizney; Cracow: Polskiej Akademji Umiejetn'sci, 1931] p. 33). One medieval Jewish exegete explained the apparent incongruity by asserting that Israel was the first nation which God had planned to create (Hezekiah ben Manoah, *Sefer Ḥazzequni* [Vilna: Romm Brothers, 1875] p. 31b).

had not been born first, and no legal procedure could change that fact. However, the title "firstborn" is often socially rather than chronologically assigned and can be based on a wide range of possible criteria.[114]

The term's metaphorical use in the Bible demonstrates that it carried similar connotations in ancient Israel. After all, the point of these passages is not that Israel and David were older than others nor that their throne was more ancient than those of other kings. Rather, God had designated them to be His "chief heir," much as a Mesopotamian parent could select the *māru rabû*. This is clear from the way in which the phrase *'elyôn lĕmalĕkê 'āreṣ* ("the highest of the earthly kings," Ps 89:28) is used to parallel the term *bĕkōr*.[115] To say that "Israel is My son, my *bĕkōr*" (Exod 4:22) is thus theologically analogous to Deuteronomy's assertion that they had been "made higher (*'elyôn*) than all the nations" (26:19). Such statements make no claim as to the people's antiquity. What they assert is divine preference, not age.

Bĕkōr should, therefore, be understood in a way that is less rigid than the conventional rendering "firstborn" normally implies, even though there are some contexts in which that meaning may be suitable. The most notable of these is the Chronicler's obscure statement that Hosah appointed his son Shimri chief (*rō'š*) because there was no *bĕkōr* (*kî lō'-hāyâ bĕkôr*, 1 Chron 26:10).[116] Like those Akkadian texts which deny the existence of a *rabû*, the phrasing of this comment is strange in its implication that there was no *bĕkōr* in a family that did have sons, regardless of whether that term be understood in terms of age or rank. The Peshitta clearly senses the problem of this assertion when it explains that Hosah's eldest child (*brh qšyšh*) had died before the time to which this statement refers. The rabbis' difficulty with the biblical report that *every* Egyptian household had been affected by the slaying of the *bekōrôt* reflects a similarly rigid

---

[114] See note 44 in this chapter. Compare Polynesian usage, which allows a usurper to become *ariki* (lit. "firstborn"); Aarne A. Koskinen, *ARIKI, The First-Born, An Analysis of a Polynesian Chieftain Title* (FF Communications 181; Helsinki: Suomalainen Tiedeakatemia, Academia Scientiarum Fennica, 1960) p. 14 (for the word's etymology, see pp. 8–9). Nigerian tradition regards the first twin to emerge as the younger, who was sent to acknowledge his brother's superiority (Arthur G. Leonard, *The Lower Niger and Its Tribes* [London: Macmillan, 1906] p. 462); cf. James G. Frazer's reference to the south Chinese Lolo's custom of calling the second son the eldest (*Folk-Lore in the Old Testament, Studies in Comparative Religion, Legend, and Law* [London: Macmillan and Co., 1919] 1.531). Nisan Rubin points out that loss of its original function may have led this status, which was once socially determined, to have become more rigid and biologically determined ("*Le-Mashma'uto ha-Ḥevratit shel ha-Bekhor ba-Miqra*'," *Beth Mikra* 33 [1987/88] 155–56).

[115] See p. 28 above.

[116] Cf. the report in 2 Chron 11:22 that Abijah was elevated to *rō'š*, not *bĕkōr*.

interpretation of *bĕkōr*.[117] However, this understanding of the term, which became normative in postbiblical Hebrew, is generally rejected with regard to 1 Chronicles 26:10. Instead, most interpreters consider the Hebrew text to be corrupt, emending it to fit the Septuagint and Targum's assertion that Shimri was not *the bĕkōr*. Not only is this reading syntactically smoother, but it also accords with the relatively flexible system of inheritance and succession apparent elsewhere in the Bible while avoiding the present implication that a family with children could have had no *bĕkōr* at all.[118] In any event, that interpretation is unnecessary for understanding most of the term's occurrences, and some, such as Isaiah's metaphoric reference to the poorest as the "*bĕkôrê* of the poor" (*dallîm*) (14:30),[119] plainly take the status of *bĕkōr* as relative.

The likelihood that *bĕkōr* and its cognates in other, related languages can have a meaning that is less rigid than that implied by the translation "firstborn" is supported by various Mesopotamian sources which suggest that individual deities could have several *bukrū*. An Old Babylonian text, for example, describes the moon god Sin as having "no rivals among Enlil's *bukru*" (*Sin ina bukur Enlil šānini la išu*), and Tiamat is said to have elevated Kingu above her *bukrū* (*bukriša*), which apparently included the entire assembly of gods.[120] Elsewhere, the Akkadian term is modified with a variety of superlative adjectives, including *rēštu* (best), *rabû* (greatest), and *ašarēdu* (foremost). One lexical tablet even equates *bukru* with *māru*, and the Targum uses the Aramaic cognate *bûkrāʾ* to render several biblical occurrences of *naʿar* (lit. "youth").[121] A similar connotation

---

[117] *Mechilta R. Shimon Bar Yohai, Boʾ* (ed. J. N. Epstein and E. Z. Melamed, p. 29). This would accord with the more rigid meaning of *bĕkōr* attested in later usage (cf. *m. Bava Batra* 8:5, which provides the rabbinic interpretation of Deut 21:15–17, *b. Bava Batra* 127a–b, and Nahmanides at Deut 21:16). Gershon Brin also cites a tradition that younger sons were called *bĕkōr* after the death of their older brothers ("*Maʿamado shel ha-Bekhor be-Reshimot ha-Yaḥas*," *Beth Mikra* 24 [1978/79] p. 256, note 5).

[118] See pp. 58–59 above for a father's authority to appoint his *bĕkōr*.

[119] The text's reliability has been questioned; see Hans Wildberger, *Jesaja* (BKAT; Neukirchen-Vluyn: Neukirchener Verlag, 1978) pp. 573–74. A similar connotation is discernible in the description of South Arabian rulers as their tribe's *bkr* in the sources listed in note 74 of Chapter 1.

[120] CT 15, no. 5 II 4, cited in the Chicago *Assyrian Dictionary*, vol. 2(B), p. 309 and Enuma Elish 1.146–47 (= 2.33–34 = 3.37–38, 95–96; René Labat, *Le Poème Babylonien de la Création* [Paris: Adrien-Maisonneuve, 1935] pp. 92, 100, 112, 116); see also 1.56 and 4.20 (ibid., pp. 82 and 122). Although separate sources need not be consistent among themselves, various texts do refer to different deities as a particular god's *bukru*; for example, see Knut L. Tallqvist, *Akkadische Götterepitheta*, pp. 66–67.

[121] *Malku = šarru* I.148 and Explicit *malku = šarru* I.181 (published by Anne D. Kilmer, "The First Tablet of *Malku = šarru* Together with its Explicit Version," *Journal of the American Oriental Society* 83 [1963] 427 and 436; see also line 208 on p. 437). *Bukru* is

may also be reflected in Micah's placing *běkōr* in parallel with the Hebrew "fruit of my womb" (*pěrî biṭnî*, 6:7).[122]

It has been suggested that this connotation of the Akkadian word is the relatively late product of a process of semantic development in which an originally specific term ("firstborn") slowly lost its distinctive meaning and came to be synonymous with *māru* ("son").[123] There is little concrete evidence to support this view. The broader connotation is not limited to later texts; it could, therefore, have been the more original meaning of a word that developed increasing specificity over time.[124] However, there are good reasons to doubt that the vague meaning "son" is original. Bilingual lists found among the recently discovered Ebla tablets gloss that language's cognate to this word with the Sumerian d u m u . s a g (literally, "head son"), demonstrating the root's connotation of superiority as early as the third millennium.[125]

That connotation is shared in Biblical Hebrew. Jacob obviously saw Esau's *běkōrâ* as advantageous, and the Chronicler considered Reuben's loss of his *běkōrâ* as a punishment. In the same chapter where Ephraim is identified as God's *běkōr* (Jer 31:8), Jeremiah speaks of him as a "precious son" (*ben yaqqîr*, v. 19), and Deutero-Zechariah remarks, in a messianic context, "They shall mourn for him as one mourns an only child (*yāḥîd*) and be embittered over him as one is embittered for a *běkōr*" (12:10). These terms are also juxtaposed in the Psalms of Solomon ("Your discipline for us [is] as [for] a firstborn [*bwkr*] son, an only child [*yḥydy*]" (18:4) and 4 Ezra ("We, Your people, whom You have called Your first-born,

---

juxtaposed with *binta* ("daughter") in lines 15–16 of the "Counsels of a Pessimist" in W. G. Lambert, *Babylonian Wisdom Literature* (Oxford: Clarendon Press, 1960) p. 108. *Targum Onqelos* and *Targum Pseudo-Jonathan* use this root to render *na'ar* at Exod 24:5, which is elsewhere translated *ṭalê* by *Pseudo-Jonathan* and *'ûlêmû* by both it and *Onqelos*; note also the use of *rabtā'* to render *běkîrâ* at Gen 19:31.

[122] Cf. the Septuagint at Prov 31:2.

[123] See Peter Machinist, "The Epic of Tukulti-Ninurta I, A Study in Middle Assyrian Literature" (Yale University, Ph.D. dissertation, 1978) p. 204, where this issue is discussed in great and illuminating detail.

[124] So apparently the Chicago *Assyrian Dictionary*, vol. 2(B), p. 310, although its preceding assertion that the root *bkr* frequently means "firstborn" in *other* Semitic languages is also too broad. An analogous process of semantic narrowing can be seen in the development of words meaning "virgin" in various languages (cf. M. Tsevat, "*bᵉthûlāh*," *Theological Dictionary of the Old Testament*, ed. G. Johannes Botterweck and Helmer Ringgren [Grand Rapids, MI: W. B. Eerdmans, 1974–   ] vol. 2, pp. 340–42).

[125] Giovanni Pettinato, *Testi Lessicali Bilingui della Biblioteca L. 2769* (Materiali Epigrafici di Ebla 4; Naples: Istituto Universitario Orientale di Napoli, 1982) nos. 4–6, 20, and 24 (pp. 9, 47, 52).

only-begotten, zealous for you [?] and most dear..." [*primogenitum unigenitum, aemulatorem, carissimum*], 6:58).[126]

Although these passages use *bĕkōr* in a way that can hardly be described as neutral, chronological priority is not the only possible basis for the superiority it conveys, which could as well be a function of status rather than sequence.[127] Further evidence that this was not a matter of birth order alone can be derived from the fact that only males are designated *bĕkōr*. In fact, unlike its Akkadian and Ugaritic cognates, the Hebrew word is attested only in the masculine, with a morphologically distinct term (*bĕkîrâ*) used for females in the Bible.[128] Some have tried to connect these forms, explaining the vocalization of the attested feminine as the result of vowel dissimilation.[129] Others have considered them synonymous, with *bĕkîrâ* replacing a hypothetical *bĕkōrâ* after the latter acquired its abstract connotation.

It is true that these separate words are sometimes used in ways that are semantically equivalent. For example, both are contrasted with words meaning "small" (*ṣā'îr* and *qāṭān*) in order to identify the older in a pair of same-sex siblings.[130] This relative connotation is apparent in the way Joseph's brothers are described by the book of Genesis as having been

---

[126] In Syriac, *bwkry' yhydy' qrby' whbyb'*; see also Psalms of Solomon 13:9. This rhetorical juxtaposition, which can be found in other traditions (the Indian god Bhisma is described as Santara's first and only son, cf. Max Mühl, "Der Mythos vom eingeborenen Sohn," *Archiv für Kulturgeschichte* 37 [1955] 5) and is preserved in subsequent Jewish and Christian traditions, was to create difficult theological problems for later Christianity; see note 68 in Chapter 1.

[127] Cf. Rashi at Deut 33:17, Nahmanides at Gen 19:31, and *Midrash Ḥem'at ha-Ḥemdah*, cited from a fourteenth-century manuscript by Menahem Kasher (*Torah Shelemah* [New York: Shulsinger Brothers, 1940] at Exod 4:22, vol. 8, p. 193, note ṭ §125).

[128] Contrast Akkadian *bukurtu* (examples in the Chicago *Assyrian Dictionary*, vol. 2 [B], p. 310), Mandaic (see E. S. Drower and R. Macuch, *A Mandaic Dictionary* [Oxford: Clarendon Press, 1963] pp. 55 and 65), and even rabbinic usage (*b. Berakhot* 6a). The description of Hurriya as *n'mt šph bkrk* (*Corpus des tablettes en cunéiformes alphabétiques*, ed. Andrée Herdner, no. 14, iii.144 = vi.290) is sometimes understood as "the fairest, your firstborn," although others have rendered it "the fairest offspring *of* your firstborn" (e.g., H. L. Ginsberg, *The Legend of King Keret, A Canaanite Epic of the Bronze Age* [*BASOR* Supplementary Studies nos. 2–3; New Haven, CT: ASOR, 1946] p. 17, and John Gray, *The KRT Text in the Literature of Ras Shamra, A Social Myth of Ancient Canaan* [2d ed., Leiden: E. J. Brill, 1964] p. 42). On the separateness of these terms, see also Gershon Brin, "*Ma'amado shel he-Bekhor bi-Reshimot ha-Yaḥas*," p. 256.

[129] H. Cazelles, "Premiers-né dans L'ancien Testament," *Dictionnaire de la Bible*, Supplement, vol. 8 (Paris: Librairie Letouzey et Ané, 1972) p. 483.

[130] Female examples are in Gen 19:31–38, 29:26, and 1 Sam 14:49; males in Gen 41:51–52, 48:18–19, Josh 6:26, and 1 Kings 16:34. The Bible never compares the ages of different-sex siblings.

seated in order of seniority (*habbĕkōr kibĕkōrātô wĕhaṣṣāʿîr kiṣĕʿīrātô*,
43:33).[131] A similar meaning can be found in Deuteronomy's law of levirate
marriage, which requires that "the *bĕkōr* [child] which [a childless widow]
bears [after having been taken by her brother-in-law] shall be accounted
to the name of his deceased brother" (25:6). However, these masculine
and feminine terms are not completely equivalent. *Bĕkîrâ* never means
"firstborn," as is most clear in the introduction of Merab as Saul's *bĕkîrâ*
(1 Sam 14:49) following a reference to several of his sons. In this context,
the term does not imply that she was the oldest of Saul's children, but
only that she was older than her sister Michal.[132] If *bĕkōr* and *bĕkîrâ* are
sometimes used equivalently, then that must be understood as having
resulted from a process of suppletion. This is supported by the absence
of a masculine form *bākîr* in biblical Hebrew, although one did develop
later along with feminine forms of *bĕkōr*.[133]

Unlike *bĕkîrâ*, the masculine *bĕkōr* is not limited to a relative sense
("bigger" or "older"). More often, it carries an absolute meaning that
the feminine never has. It does not, however, follow that the word's
meaning must be restricted to "firstborn," especially given the statistical
unlikeliness that all Israelite firstborns were male. In fact, there is
surprisingly little positive biblical evidence that those designated *bĕkōr*
were actually the firstborn in their families. Biblical narratives describe only
three such individuals—Esau, Reuben, and Er—as having been oldest
children.[134] Four others (Nebaioth, Eliphaz, Manasseh, and Yerahmeel)
are named first in lists of brothers, but there is no assurance that these
lists are arranged chronologically and some reason to suspect they are
not.[135] For example, although two different passages identify Nebaioth
as Ishmael's *bĕkōr*, neither includes any of the daughters other texts tell

---

[131] Cf. Gen 44:12 and 2 Chron 31:15.

[132] The lists of Saul's children in 1 Chron 8:33 and 9:39 include only males.

[133] See Avraham Even-Shoshan, *Ha-Millon he-Ḥadash* (Jerusalem: Kiryat Sepher, 1969) pp. 118–19.

[134] The birth narratives are in Gen 25:25, 29:31–32, and 38:3.

[135] Gen 25:13, 36:4, 10, 46:21, 1 Chron 1:35, 2:9 (but see vv. 18 and 42); see also the discussion on p. 76 below. Among Benjamin's offspring was Becher, whose name derives from this same root. He is listed second (Gen 46:21, 1 Chron 7:6), but Martin Noth relates the name to a root meaning "camel" (*Die Israelitischen Personennamen im Rahmen der gemeinsemitischen Namengebung* [Stuttgart: W. Kohlhammer, 1930] p. 230; see also the comments of Rudolf Hirzel cited in note 18 of chapter 4). The rabbis already recognized that there were other principles that governed the arrangement of such lists (*b. Bava Batra* 120a, *Numbers Rabbah* 6:2; cf. *Mechilta Boʾ* [ed. H. S. Horowitz, p. 1], Augustine, *City of God* 16.11 [LCL pp. 66–69], and Abraham ibn Ezra at Exod 2:2). Reliance on these texts has often been based on the assumption that *bĕkōr* means "firstborn." *Lĕtōlĕdōtām*, which

us Ishmael had.[136] Moses and Rachel also appear at the head of such lists despite explicit descriptions of them as younger siblings.[137] Shem, too, is always named first among Noah's sons, although his brother Japheth may have been considered older in at least one passage.[138]

The fluidity of genealogical traditions has been demonstrated in numerous studies. A good example of this is the inconsistent sequence in which the Bible enumerates Jacob's sons and the tribes of Israel.[139] The fact that females are regularly put at the end of those genealogical lists in which they are included[140] confirms the unreliability of these traditions as a source of information regarding their authors' understanding of birth order.

This conclusion is strengthened by the fact that several such lists mention only one offspring for each generation. Although these are often assumed to have been firstborns, there is no independent basis for that inference. From among the children of Adam and Eve, for example, it is Seth who is named in such passages (e.g., Gen 5:3–8), even though he is elsewhere identified as their third son, with no evidence that his older brother Cain had died in the interim.[141] To ascribe this to an alternate tradition in which Seth was considered the oldest son merely begs the

---

occurs in some lists, is sometimes rendered "according to the order of their birth," (e.g., RSV Gen 25:13); however, its meaning too is far from clear (cf. Gen 10:32, 1 Chron 7:4, 8:28, 9:34).

[136] Gen 28:9, 36:3; the lists of Ishmael's sons are in Gen 25:13 and 1 Chron 1:31.

[137] For Rachel, see Gen 31:4, 14 and Ruth 4:11. As the rabbis recognized, the arrangement in Gen 33:1 is according to reverse value ("'aḥaron, 'aḥaron ḥaviv" [*Genesis Rabbah* 67:8], cf. v. 2). For Moses, see Num 12:4, Micah 6:4, and numerous juxtapositions with Aaron (but see 1 Chron 5:29); regarding problems of their relative ages, see pp. 102–3 below.

[138] Gen 10:21 as understood by many ancient and some modern interpreters (e.g., NIV and Umberto Cassuto, *A Commentary on the Book of Genesis* [Jerusalem: Magnes Press, 1961–64] vol. 2, p. 218; see also *Genesis Rabbah* 26:3 and *Midrash Tanḥuma* [Buber] *Toledot* 23 [p. 142]). Most moderns accept the common sequence of names as reflecting birth order and understand 10:21 as describing Shem as Japheth's older brother. Although Ham is commonly listed in the middle position, Gen 9:24 identifies him as the youngest (but see *Genesis Rabbah* 36:17).

[139] See the convenient chart provided by Jack M. Sasson, "A Genealogical 'Convention' in Biblical Chronography?" *Zeitschrift für die Alttestamentliche Wissenschaft* 90 (1978) 180; for more general discussion, see Marshall D. Johnson, *The Purpose of the Biblical Genealogies, With Special Reference to the Setting of the Genealogies of Jesus* (Cambridge: University Press, 1969) pp. 5–16, and Robert R. Wilson, *Genealogy and History in the Biblical World* (New Haven, CT: Yale University Press, 1977) pp. 145–89.

[140] Gershon Brin, "*Ma'amado shel ha-Bekhor bi-Reshimot ha-Yaḥas,*" 255–56.

[141] See Gen 4:25 and 1 Chron 1:1; so too Sirah 49:16 and Luke 3:38. There is no biblical warrant for the claim that Seth had received the *bĕkōrâ*. Eleazar is the only one of Aaron's sons named in 1 Chron 6:35.

question by presuming that these passages are in fact lists of firstborns. A similar problem can be seen in the case of Arpachshad, who is the only one of Shem's sons mentioned in Genesis 11 (vv. 10–11), even though he is listed third in the preceding chapter's more extensive list (10:22).

After describing one sibling as *bĕkōr*, some lists identify the others as *šēnî* ("second"), *šĕlîšî* ("third"), etc. Surely here, one would think, there is ample evidence that *bĕkōr* does mean "first," and so it does. But it does not follow that these terms necessarily refer to the order of birth. Priority can be a matter of status as well as sequence. That possibility is strengthened by the fact that in some of the lists *bĕkōr* is replaced with the title *rō'š* (lit. "head") or followed by *mišneh* (lit. "secondary"), both of which typically reflect rank rather than order.[142]

The fact that polygamous households seem to have had only one *bĕkōr* suggests that the term is indicative of a child's relationship with his father rather than his mother.[143] It has, therefore, been proposed that *peṭer reḥem* (lit. "the *peṭer* of the womb") is the maternal equivalent of *bĕkōr*, which would strengthen the likelihood that the latter relates to birth order. Both rabbinic usage and the etymology of the root *pṭr* ("split") support this position. A *peṭer reḥem* thus appears to be the child who opens up (splits) his or her mother's womb, hence her firstborn.[144]

Without denying the maternal dimension of *peṭer reḥem*, it must be added that *bĕkōr* can be used this way as well. For example, it is applied to animals, where both maternal identity and the fact of an individual's being its mother's firstborn are more readily determined than paternal relationships.[145] The book of Exodus also refers to "the *bĕkōr* of the maidservant who is behind the mill" (*bĕkôr haššipḥâ 'ăšer 'aḥar hārēḥāyim*,

---

[142] Cyrus Gordon points out that Chronicles prefers *rō'š* where earlier texts used *bĕkōr* ("Fratriarchy in the Old Testament," *Journal of Biblical Literature* 54 [1935] 228; cf. also J. R. Bartlett, "The Use of the Word *rō'š* as a Title in the Old Testament," *Vetus Testamentum* 19 [1969] 1–10). Of at least etymological interest is the connection between cognates of *bĕkōr* and the Akkadian *rēštu* and Sumerian dumu . sag noted above (see notes 38 in chapter 1 and 125 in this chapter); on the other hand, 1 Chron 26:10 implies a clear distinction between the Hebrew terms (see pp. 60–61 above).

[143] Cf. Gen 35:23, Deut 21:15, and 2 Sam 3:2–3.

[144] See Johannes Hempel, "Eine Vorfrage zum Erstgeburtsopfer," *Zeitschrift für die Alttestamentliche Wissenschaft* 54 (1936) 312, and Gershon Brin, "*Ha-Bekhor be-Yisra'el be-Tequfat ha-Miqra*'" (Tel Aviv University, Ph.D. dissertation, 1971) pp. 24–26. For cognates, see Wolfram von Soden, *Akkadisches Handwörterbuch*, p. 849, and Edward Lane, *Arabic-English Lexicon* (London: Williams and Norgate, 1863–93) p. 2415; a possible Ugaritic form can be found in Cyrus Gordon, *Ugaritic Textbook*, no. 71, line 9.

[145] E.g., Gen 4:4, Exod 11:5, Lev 27:26, Num 8:17, and Deut 15:19.

11:5)[146] and 1 Chronicles speaks of the Calebite Hur as Ephratah's *bĕkôr* (2:50, 4:4).[147] Some passages even treat these terms as synonyms.[148] Complicating matters further is the nature of the birth process, which is such that one might speak of any newborn as having "split" its mother's womb.

A more likely paternal equivalent for *peṭer reḥem* than *bĕkôr* is *rē'šît 'ôn*. Frequently juxtaposed with *bĕkôr*,[149] its antecedents are consistently masculine. Since the word *'ôn* means "strength" or "power," the phrase as a whole must reflect the belief that firstborns benefit from their father's greater vigor at the time of conception, a concept not limited to ancient Israel.[150] However, this phrase too may be somewhat equivocal, since *rē'šît* can refer to qualitative superiority as well as sequential priority.[151] *Rē'šît 'ôn* could, therefore, mean "the best" rather than "the first of his

---

[146] Umberto Cassuto considers this to have been borrowed from Egyptian usage (*A Commentary on the Book of Exodus* [Jerusalem: Magnes Press, 1967] p. 133). When the context recurs in v. 29 of Exodus 12, the phrase is changed to "the *bĕkôr* of the prisoner in the dungeon" (*bĕkôr haššēbî 'ăšer bĕbêt habbôr*. Johannes Hempel's suggestion that only illegitimate children were described as *bĕkôr* on the basis of their mothers ("Eine Vorfrage zum Erstgeburtsopfer," p. 212) has the aura of special pleading. Walther Zimmerli suggests that the distinction between *bĕkôr* and *peṭer reḥem* was lost by time of P ("Erstgeborene und Leviten: Ein Beitrag zur exilisch-nachexilischen Theologie" in *Near Eastern Studies in Honor of William Foxwell Albright*, ed. Hans Goedicke [Baltimore, MD: The Johns Hopkins University Press] pp. 461–62).

[147] To these should be added the form *mabkîrâ* (Jer 4:31), which is conventionally understood as a woman bearing her first child (see also Deut 25:6, *m. Bekhorot* 1:3–4, 3:2, and 1QH 3:7). Women's firstborns are also mentioned in Josephus (*Life* 527 §76 [LCL pp. 156–57]; cf. 5 §1, LCL pp. 4–5), Luke 2:7, and Septuagint Prov 31:2. Similar usages can be found in rabbinic usage (*b. Bava Batra* 126b) and in Mandaic (E. S. Drower and R. Macuch, *A Mandaic Dictionary*, p. 55), to which should be compared documents in which a man acknowledges the oldest offspring of a particular wife as his heir (e.g., HSS 9:24 in Jonathan S. Paradise, "Nuzi Inheritance Practices," p. 260, and VAS 6 101:8 cited in the Chicago *Assyrian Dictionary*, vol. 10 [M], p. 311, as well as the Egyptian documents listed in note 63 in this chapter). For further discussion, see Gershon Brin, "*Bekhor le-'Em u-Vekhor le-'Av ba-Miqra'*" in *Sefer Ben-Zion Luria, Meḥqarim ba-Miqra' uve-Toledot Yisra'el* (Jerusalem: Kiryat Sefer, 1979) pp. 31–50.

[148] Exod 13:2, Num 3:12, 8:16 (cf. 18:15); note also the juxtaposition of *pṭr* and *rē'šit* in Prov 17:14.

[149] Gen 49:3, Deut 21:17, Pss 78:51, 105:36.

[150] Courtney S. Kenny, *The History of the Law of Primogeniture and its Effect on Landed Property* (Cambridge: J. Hall and Sons; London: Reeves and Turner, 1878) p. 14; cf. *Yalqut Ner ha-Sekhalim*, as cited by Menahem Kasher, *Torah Shelemah* (Jerusalem, 1938) vol. 7, p. 1780. For *'ôn*, see Isa 40:26, 29 and Job 40:16 as well as the derivative meaning "wealth" in Hos 12:9.

[151] E.g., 1 Sam 15:2 and perhaps Jer 49:35. Cf. Wolfram von Soden, *Akkadisches Handwörterbuch*, pp. 972–73 for Akkadian *rēštu*.

strength."[152] Conventional translations thus obscure the semantic ambiguity of all these terms.

Etymological considerations provide further reasons for interpreting *bĕkōr* broadly. For example, Hebrew and Arabic cognates of this word are used for plants, where temporal priority is inherently more problematic than with people or animals.[153] The fact that the Hebrew word commonly occurs in the plural suggests a more cautions rendering than the conventional translation "first fruits." Several texts show that one could choose a *rē'šît* ("best" or "first") from among these *bikkûrîm*, further strengthening this conclusion.[154]

Evidence for a more specific meaning can be derived from the way in which singular forms of this word are used. *Bikkûrâ* refers to a fruit which, though not expected before the summer, is most desirable when it does arrive.[155] Although this has sometimes been explained as late-blooming produce of the fig tree, the word is more appropriately understood as indicating its early fruit.[156]

Various languages use other derivatives of this root to designate animals. Especially common are words for camels. Although the evidence from Hebrew and Old South Arabic is not particularly helpful on this point, Jeremiah does speak of a *bikrâ* as being light (*qallâ*, 2:23)—certainly not an old camel.[157] Akkadian texts describe a *bakru* as sucking from its mother and list the related form *bakkaru* alongside several other baby animals.[158]

---

[152] Deut 21:17 would then conclude that the father "must acknowledge the son of the less-loved wife as chief heir [*bĕkōr*].... Since he is the best of his strength [*rē'šît 'ōnô*], the law of seniority [*bĕkōrâ*] operates in his behalf."

[153] Edward Lane, *Arabic-English Lexicon*, p. 241; for a possibly related usage in South Arabic, see A. F. L. Beeston et al., *Sabaic Dictionary* (Beirut: Libraire du Liban, 1982) p. 28.

[154] Exod 23:19, 34:26, Ezek 44:30.

[155] Isa 28:4, Jer 24:2, Micah 7:1; see also Hosea 9:10.

[156] See G. Dalman, *Arbeit und Sitte in Palästina* (Gütersloh: C. Bertelsmann, 1928) vol. 1:2, pp. 378–79; cf. Mark 11:13 and the references to *bakkîr* in *b. Sanhedrin* 18b and *Qohelet Rabbah* 11:6. For a similar nuance, compare the Punic *qdmt* (*Kanaanäische und aramäische Inschriften*, ed. H. Donner and W. Röllig, nos. 69, line 12, and 76, line A7).

[157] Female camels are also designated with this root in Akkadian (Paulus Rost, *Die Keilschrifttexte Tiglat-Pilesers III nach den Papierabklatschen und Originalen des Britischen Museum* [Leipzig: Edward Pfeiffer, 1893] vol. 1, p. 26, line 157, and Donald J. Wiseman, "A Fragmentary Inscription of Tiglath-Pileser III From Nimrud," *Iraq* 18 [1956] 126).

[158] The inscriptions are in Maximilian Streck, *Assurbanipal und die letzten Könige bis zum Untergange Niniveh's* (Leipzig: J. C. Hinrichs'sche Buchhandlung, 1916) 2.76 and 378 (Annals ix 65 and tablet ii.13), and D. W. Myhrman, "Die Labartu-Texte, Babylonische Beschwörungsformeln nebst Zauber-verfahren gegen die Dämonin Labartu," *Zeitschrift für Assyriologie* 16 (1902) 186; cf. the derived meaning cited by Jørgen Laessøe, "Reflexions on Modern and Ancient Oriental Water Works," *Journal of Cuneiform Studies* 7 (1953) 25. Not-

What these usages share is not an emphasis on being first or oldest, but the concept of "earliness" and "youth." That nuance is also apparent in Arabic and Aramaic verbal forms ("to do or arrive early") as well as those biblical texts which stress relative age more than absolute sequence.[159] The word *bĕkōr*, therefore, need not point directly to the fact that a particular offspring was the first to have been born so much as to its having been early. The connotation "firstborn" may sometimes be appropriate for such usages, but that is due to context more than etymology.

This analysis has profound implications for our understanding of Israel's system of inheritance. The semantic ambiguity of the title *bĕkōr*, which designates the beneficiary of whatever advantages that system had to offer, undercuts the utility of that term for demonstrating that the transmission of property and authority was based on automatic principles. Whereas neither etymology nor context proves that one became *bĕkōr* by virtue of birth, there are several texts that demonstrate that one could be appointed *bĕkōr* by one's father, even if that opportunity was limited to males.

Succession

Anthropologists distinguish the transmission of status (succession) from that of property (inheritance). Because offices cannot be divided as easily as land and positions of authority must be clearly assigned to a particular individual, succession allows less room for the kinds of sharing and

---

ing that these occurrences are limited to neo-Assyrian texts dealing with Arabia, Armes Salonen regards then as loan words from Arabic (*Hippologica Accadica* [Helsinki: Suomalainen Tiedeakatemia, 1956] p. 89; cf. Edward Lane, *Arabic-English Lexicon*, p. 240). Ibn Barun also links the biblical term with Arabic (Pinchas Wechter, *Ibn Barun's Arabic Works on Hebrew Grammar and Lexicography* [Philadelphia: Dropsie College, 1964], p. 75, see also pp. 141–42). Additional cognates are found in Ethiopic and South Arabic (E. Littmann and Maria Höfner, *Wörterbuch der Tigrē-Sprache* [Wiesbaden: Franz Steiner, 1958] p. 290; Wolf Leslau, *Lexique Soqotri [Sudarabique Moderne]* [Paris: Librairie C. Klincksieck, 1938] p. 86; *Corpus Inscriptionum Semiticarum* IV/2 [Paris: E. Republicae Typographeo, 1911] nos. 521 and 579 [pp. 234–35]; see also Isa 60:4).

[159] Jonah ibn Janaḥ, *Sepher Haschoraschim*, trans. J. ibn Tibbon, ed. W. Bacher [Berlin: H. Itzkowski, 1896; reprinted Jerusalem, 1966] p. 64; cf. *m. Menaḥot* 10:2, *m. Bikkurim* 3:1, and *t. Bikkurim* 2:8 as well as Lev 27:26, where *yĕbukkar* apparently means "designate" or "put ahead." For similar usages, see Edward Lane, *Arabic-English Lexicon*, p. 239 and 241, R. Payne-Smith, *Thesaurus Syriacus* (Oxford: Clarendon Press, 1879) p. 525, and E. S. Drower and R. Macuch, *A Mandaic Dictionary*, p. 64. W. von Soden ascribes this meaning to the Akkadian *bakīram* in *Archives Royales de Mari* vol. 1 (Correspondence de Šamši-addu, ed. Georges Dossin; Paris: Imprimerie Nationale, 1950) p. 70, line 5 (*Akkadisches Handwörterbuch*, p. 97).

ambiguity sometimes tolerable in matters of ownership. In many societies, including our own, entirely different principles are used for these two realms. An extreme example can be found among the Lurka Cole of southwestern Bengal, who are reported to have transmitted property according to the principle of ultimogeniture but leadership by primogeniture.[160]

To some extent, this distinction is illusory. Property is itself a form of status,[161] as is most clearly evident in cultures where estates are administered on behalf of an entire family by selected individuals, thereby obscuring the line between ownership and leadership. Even the frequently mentioned differences between these two realms are not always as clear-cut as one might expect. For example, offices need not be indivisible. The plot of *King Lear* is based on the reported incident of a ruler who intended to divide his domain among three daughters.[162] King Herod actually distributed his realm in this way so that each of his offspring would inherit a kingdom.[163] Other thrones have been shared, as in Sparta which Greek tradition reports as having been jointly ruled by the twins Procles and Eurysthenes.[164]

Even where the transmission of status and property are governed by different principles, the available choices are very much the same and the procedures used within any one culture usually similar.[165] In addition to the familiar lineal systems, leaders may be followed by an older brother, whether their own or their wife's.[166] In some cultures positions of

[160] William Dunbar, "Some Observations on the Manners, Customs, and Religious Opinions of the Lurka Coles," *Journal of the Royal Asiatic Society of Great Britain and Ireland* 18 (1861) 374; this is not entirely dissimilar from the juxtaposition of borough English and French in feudal Nottingham (see p. 38 above).

[161] E. Adamson Hoebel, *Anthropology: The Study of Man*, p. 356.

[162] For the historical background, see *The Historia Regum Britanniae of Geoffrey of Monmouth* 2.11 (ed. Acton Griscom; London: Longmans, Green and Co., 1929, pp. 262–65).

[163] Josephus, *Antiquities* 17.8.1 §188–89 (LCL vol. 8, pp. 458–59). ABL 870 describes an Assyrian king (generally considered to have been Esarhaddon) as having given one son (Ashurbanipal) the Assyrian throne and the other (Shamash-shum-ukin) the Babylonian; see Leroy Waterman, *Royal Correspondance of the Assyrian Empire* (Ann Arbor, MI: University of Michigan Press, 1930) pp. 102–4. Other examples can be found in Jack Goody, ed., *Succession to High Office* (Cambridge: Cambridge University Press, 1966) pp. 3–8.

[164] Herodotus 6.52 (LCL vol. 3, pp. 198–99). Early in the third century, the sons of the Roman emperor Severus looked forward to sharing their father's throne (Herodian 4.1.1–2 [LCL vol. 1, pp. 372–73]).

[165] A. R. Radcliffe-Brown, *Structure and Function in Primitive Societies*, p. 42. For a survey of systems, see Jack Goody's "Introduction" to *Succession to High Office*, which suggests that hereditary succession is characteristic of societies that place special importance on kinship ties (p. 4).

[166] The possibility of collateral succession was recognized already by Isaac Newton (*The Chronology of Ancient Kingdoms Amended* in *Opera quae Exstant Omnia*, ed. Samuel Horsley [London: Joannes Nichols, 1785; reprinted Stuttgart-Bad: Friedrich Frommann

authority are not hereditary at all. Leadership may be rotated among clans or tribes, in which case individuals cannot be succeeded by their kin, whether firstborn or otherwise.[167] Viewed historically, even the familiar British monarchy has been more variable than one might suppose. There was not a single case of father-son succession in Scotland until the introduction of primogeniture by David I in the twelfth century.[168] Some Celtic communities practiced collateral succession, and Irish heirs apparent ("tanist") were elected.[169]

Assuming Mesopotamian mythology to reflect familiar, if archaic, social practice, some have inferred that there was a system of "primitive democracy" in the ancient Near East, with rulers selected from among eligible citizens.[170] Hints of election have also been found alongside traces of dynastic succession at ancient Ebla.[171]

Few societies allow succession to be entirely automatic; instead, various methods are used to select one individual from a pool of eligible candidates. For example, Telepinus's sixteenth-century decree establishing dynastic succession among the Hittites stipulates only that the successor be one of the leading (*ḫantezzijaš*) princes.[172] However, limiting potential successors to members of the incumbent's family or, more narrowly, his offspring, does not guarantee how the ruler will be chosen from within

---

Verlag, 1964] vol. 5, p. 40). According to David Henige, filial succession is the most common and nearly always the ideal system (*The Chronology of Oral Tradition, Quest for a Chimera* [Oxford: Clarendon Press, 1974] p. 72), although he regards traditions describing long chains of father-son successions as inherently suspect (p. 90).

[167] E.g., S. F. Nadel, "Nupe State and Community" in *Comparative Political Systems, Studies in the Politics of Pre-Industrial Societies*, ed. Ronald Cohen and John Middleton (Garden City, NY: The Natural History Press, 1967) p. 303.

[168] J. H. Stevenson, "The Law of the Throne—Tanistry and the Introduction of the Law of Primogeniture: A Note on the Succession of the Kings of Scotland from Kenneth MacAlpin to Robert Bruce," *The Scottish Historical Review* 25 (1927) 1 and 9–10.

[169] James Hogan, "The Irish Law of Kingship with Special Reference to Ailechand Cenél Eoghain," *Proceedings of the Royal Irish Academy* 40 (1931–32) 188–89.

[170] Thorkild Jacobsen, "Primitive Democracy in Ancient Mesopotamia," *Journal of Near Eastern Studies* 2 (1943) 159–72; see, however, the methodological warnings of Robert A. Oden, "Method in the Study of Near Eastern Myths," *Religion* 9 (1973) 187–88.

[171] Giovanni Pettinato, "Gli Archivi Reali di Tell Mardikh-Ebla Riflessioni e Prospettive," *Rivista Biblica* 25 (1977) 235. David Noel Freedman's description of Dubuḫu-Ada as the oldest son (and heir apparent) of Ibbi-Sipiš ("A City Beneath the Sands" in *Science Year, The World Book Science Annual* [Chicago: Field Enterprises, 1978] p. 194; see Giovanni Pettinato, *The Archieves of Ebla, An Empire Inscribed in Clay* [Garden City, NY: Doubleday, 1981] p. 77) has no textual warrant.

[172] 2.36 in Inge Hoffmann, *Der Erlass Telipinus* (Heidelberg: Carl Winter Universitätsverlag, 1984) p. 32.

that group. In some cultures, eligible candidates had to fight among themselves to determine which would hold office. For three hundred years the Ottoman Empire was governed by a "Law of Fratricide," imposed in 1289 by Mehmed II in order to avoid fragmenting his domain.[173] Elsewhere, ultimate power has been vested in the incumbent, his family, or the community as a whole. Charisma often plays an important role, as do election and ratification, whether substantive or pro forma.[174] Such procedures minimize the risk of incompetence while ensuring that new leaders enter office with a modicum of popular support.

Mirroring a widespread approach to inheritance, incumbents are often allowed to choose a successor from among their own offspring. This practice appears to be reflected in the mythological description of El's request that Asherah designate which of her sons should be elevated to the throne.[175] The practice of rulers in some cultures, such as that of ancient Rome, of adopting their heirs apparent may have been intended to circumvent such systems. However, even in these cases, the individuals involved are typically made *sons*, not firstborns.[176]

In all of this, ancient Near Eastern practice conforms to patterns familiar from around the world. In some cases, the available sources suggest that leadership was not restricted to a specific family at all. Genesis, for example, lists a series of Edomite kings, not one of whom is related to his predecessor,[177] and only a handful of the many rulers mentioned in the Amarna texts from fourteenth-century Palestine are said to have been succeeded by their sons.[178]

---

[173] A. D. Alderson, *The Structure of the Ottoman Dynasty* (Oxford: Clarendon Press, 1956; reprinted Westport, CT: Greenwood Press, 1982) pp. 5–8; compare the Old Babylonian statement that "the brothers will compete for their father's throne" (*aḫū ana kussî abišunu iššanu*, YOS 10 31 i 52, quoted in the Chicago *Assyrian Dictionary*, vol. 1 [A]¹, p. 197) and the practice described by K. Oberg, "The Kingdom of Ankole in Uganda" in *African Political Systems*, ed. Meyer Fortes and E. E. Evans-Pritchard (London: Oxford University Press, 1940) pp. 158–60.

[174] See Jack Goody, *Succession to High Office*, pp. 13–14.

[175] *Corpus des tablettes en cunéiformes alphabétiques*, ed. Andrée Herdner, no. 6 i.43–46; this must be considered in the context of the methodological problems described by Robert Oden regarding the use of mythology to infer social practice (see note 170 above).

[176] The Roman examples are listed by Karl Loewenstein, *The Governance of Rome* (The Hague: Martinus Nijhoff, 1973) pp. 336–37; see also examples provided by Marc Bloch, *Feudal Society*, pp. 384–85. For broader discussion, see Fritz Kern, *Kingship and Law in the Middle Ages* (Oxford: Basil Blackwell, 1948) pp. 12–13.

[177] For arguments that the list in Genesis 36 is artificial, see J. R. Bartlett, "The Edomite King-List of Genesis XXXVI.31–39 and 1 Chron. I.43–50," *Journal of Theological Studies* n.s. 16 (1965) 302, and E. A. Knauf, "Alter und Herkunft der edomitischen Königsliste Gen 36, 31–39," *Zeitschrift für die Alttestamentliche Wissenschaft* 97 (1985) 245–53.

[178] See letters 253, lines 11–15, and 255, line 15 (about Labaya of Shechem) and 317, lines 14–16 (regarding Dagan Takala) in J. A. Knudtzon, *Die el-Amarna Tafeln* (Leipzig: J. C. Hinrichs'sche Buchhandlung, 1910) pp. 808–9, 814–15, and 922–23. Evidence of a

Even where power was concentrated within an individual family, leadership may have been transmitted in a variety of ways. Earlier in this century, Paul Koschaker discerned traces of what he called "fratriarchy," or collateral succession; additional cases have been added since.[179]

Most of the available evidence points away from the use of abstract or automatic principles for the selection of rulers. Numerous references assume that the incumbent could control royal succession. Besides the Ugaritic statement about Asherah's designating an heir, the North Syrian kings Kilamuwa and Panammuwa speak vaguely of a successor coming from among their sons, and Herodotus writes that "according to Persian Law, the king may not march with his army until he had named his successor."[180] Apologetic texts from the neo-Assyrian empire justify the successions of Esarhaddon and Ashurbanipal, both of whom appear to have been younger sons, by citing their superior qualities as the reason their fathers had selected them for the throne.[181] To be sure, the documents make it clear that the success of these figures was unexpected, but they also show that designation by the incumbent ruler was both a

---

Sidonian dynasty is found in the inscriptions of Eshmunazar and Tabnit of Sidon (*Kanaanäische und aramäische Inschriften*, ed. H. Donner and W. Röllig, nos. 13 and 14) almost a millennium later, and 2 Sam 10:1 alludes to one among the Ammonites. Abdi-ḥepa's statement that neither his mother nor father had given him (*nadnani, šaknani*) the throne (letters 286, lines 9–11, and 287, lines 25–27, in *Die el-Amarna Tafeln*, ed. J. A. Knudtzon, pp. 860–61 and 864–65) may cast some light on the succession in Jerusalem. However, none of this demonstrates how these offspring were selected nor their relative ages, although Rib-Addi of Byblos, Biridiya of Megiddo, and Yapahu of Gezer apparently had younger brothers (letters 137, line 16, 245, line 40, and 298, line 22; in *Die el-Amarna Tafeln*, ed. J. A. Knudtzon, pp. 572–73, 794–95, and 892–93); see, however, William L. Moran's comments in *The Amarna Letters* (Baltimore: The Johns Hopkins University Press, 1992) p. 300. G. Buccellati infers from the phrasing of other letters that more than one son of other rulers succeeded to the throne (*Cities and Nations of Ancient Syria* [Rome: Istituto di Studi di Vicino Oriente, 1967], p. 71). Regarding 2 Kings 3:27, see below.

[179] "Fratriarchat, Hausgemeinschaft und Mutterrecht in Keilschriftrechten," *Zeitschrift für Assyriologie* 41 (1933) 1–89; cf. Dietz O. Edzard, "Sumerer und Semiten in den frühen Geschichte Mesopotamiens" in *Aspects du Contact Suméro-Akkadien*, ed. Edmond Sollberger (IXe Rencontre assyriologique internationale; *Genava* n.s. 8; Geneva: Musée d'art et d'histoire 1960) p. 255. Cyrus Gordon has seen traces of this practice in ancient Israel ("Fratriarchy in the Old Testament," *Journal of Biblical Literature* 54 [1935] 223–31).

[180] *Kanaanäische und aramäische Inschriften*, ed. H. Donner and W. Röllig, nos. 24, lines 131–34, and 214, line 15; Herodotus 7.2 (LCL vol. 3, pp. 300–303). Compare his statement that Cyrus *intended* Combyses to be his successor (1.208, LCL vol. 1, pp. 262–63).

[181] The texts are presented in Riekele Borger, *Die Inschriften Asarhaddons Königs von Assyrien* (Graz: Archiv für Orientforschung, 1956) p. 40, and Maximilian Streck, *Assurbanipal und die letzten assyrischen Könige bis zum Untergange Niniveh's*, p. 396. For the details of Esarhaddon's succession, see Simo Parpola, "The Murderer of Sennacherib" in *Death in Mesopotamia* (XXVIe Rencontre assyriologique internationale), ed. Bendt Alster (Copenhagen: Akademisk Forlag, 1980) pp. 171–82.

legally sufficient and a theoretically justifiable basis for claiming legitimacy. A similar inference may be drawn from widespread claims that the accession of various rulers was the result of divine appointment.[182] Whatever the theological validity or the political realities such assertions are intended to obscure, it is readily apparent that in such cases succession was not always automatic or *expected* to be.

This conclusion is not contradicted by the Bible's comment that the *bĕkōr* son of Moab's king Mesha "would rule after him" (2 Kings 3:27).[183] Whether an accurate representation of Moabite practice or merely a reflection of Israelite expectations, the implications of this statement ought not to be exaggerated. The fact that Mesha's *bĕkōr* was heir apparent does not show how either status had been acquired, much less that they were causally related.

There is no evidence of primogeniture in the transmission of leadership during any period of Israelite history. Preserved lists of premonarchic tribal leaders give no indication that these positions were even hereditary, much less based on principles of seniority.[184] Later, Samuel is said to have appointed both his sons to be judges (1 Sam 8:1), and Abimelech to have let the people of Shechem decide, "Which is better for you, to be ruled by seventy men—by all Jerubbaal's sons—or to be ruled by one man?" (Judg 9:2), implying that all of Gideon's sons could have ruled over Shechem unless its citizens chose otherwise. Even after his brothers' death, the Shechemite populace had to act before Abimelech could be crowned (v. 6). An elective monarchy is also presumed by Jotham's fable, which describes how the trees *selected* a ruler (vv. 8–15).

Although the information about the monarchy provided by the Bible is far more extensive than that about other offices, its evidence is no more supportive of oldest children having been given preference. The theoretical principles governing transmission of the crown from one generation to the next are never explicitly elucidated; however, several relevant incidental

---

[182] For examples, see Henri Frankfort, *Kingship and the Gods, A Study of Ancient Near Eastern Religion as the Integration of Society and Nature* (Chicago: University of Chicago Press, 1948) pp. 238–40.

[183] Similar issues arise from Exod 12:29 (*bĕkōr parʿōh hayyōšēb ʿal-kisʾô*), if it is understood as referring to Pharaoh's *bĕkōr* as destined to sit on his [father's] throne (e.g., *Targum Onqelos ad loc*, cf. also *Mechilta Boʾ* 13, ed. H. S. Horovitz, p. 43); however, the phrase's syntactic parallelism with the subsequent reference to "the *bĕkōr* of the captive who is in the dungeon," which clearly refers to the captive as being in the dungeon, supports the more common understanding of Pharaoh as the one who sits on the throne.

[184] Numbers 1–2, 7, 10:14–28, 13, 26, 34, 1 Chronicles 27. Although inherited leadership is not at stake, Othniel is described as the son of Caleb's younger brother (Judg 1:13); for Israel's priesthood, see p. 22 above.

comments are scattered through the text. For example, the statement that Israel's King Ahaziah was succeeded by his brother Jehoram "because [Ahaziah] did not have a son" (2 Kings 1:17) supports the impression that both Israelite and Judean kingship normally followed lineal rather than collateral lines.[185] The most prominent exceptions (Jehoiakim and Zedekiah) took place late in the monarchy period, following the deportations of relatively young kings whose brief reigns may not have provided sufficient time for them to have children.

Less certain is the implication of 2 Kings' observation that Mesha would have been followed by his *bĕkōr* (3:27), whom he instead sacrificed in order to gain divine assistance for his confrontation with Israel. This could reflect Israelite assumptions based on its own culture rather than Moabite custom.[186] Equally ambiguous is 2 Chronicles' report that Judah's king Jehoshaphat "gave dominion (*mamlākâ*) to Jehoram because he [Jehoram] was the *bĕkōr*" (21:3), a statement without a corroborating parallel in the earlier book of Kings. Apart from the meaning of the Hebrew term *bĕkōr*, in neither this case nor that of Mesha is it clear whether these sons' elevation was the automatic result of their own seniority or because their fathers preferred to be succeeded by the *bĕkōr*. The phrasing—that Jehoshaphat "gave dominion" (*wĕʾet-hammamlākâ nātan*)—suggests that he acted for reasons of his own rather than because he was bound by legal or customary obligations.[187] From such cases, rabbinic tradition concluded that Israelite kings could entrust their throne to whomever they chose.[188]

The attested instances of Israelite succession are no more supportive of those who claim that birth order was a determining factor. To be sure, certainty in such matters is elusive, and the available information frustratingly vague. For the most part, we know relatively little about the

[185] For a different view, see Albrecht Alt, "The Monarchy in the Kingdom of Israel and Judah" in his *Essays on Old Testament History and Religion* (Garden City, NY: Doubleday, 1967) pp. 316–20, which must be evaluated in light of T. C. G. Thornton, "Charismatic Kingship in Israel and Judah," *Journal of Theological Studies* 14 (1963) 1–11. Tomoo Ishida cites David's description as Saul's son (1 Sam 24:11, 16, 26:17, 21, 25) as further evidence of the dynastic principle (*The Royal Dynasties in Ancient Israel* [BZAW 142; Berlin: Walter de Gruyter, 1977] pp. 61–62).

[186] See p. 74 above.

[187] Cf. *b. Ketuvot* 103b and the use of *ntn* described on pp. 50–51 below. A similar observation applies to Saul's apparent expectation that Jonathan should be his successor (1 Sam 20:30–31). Cf. Tomoo Ishida, "The 'People of the Land' and the Political Crises in Judah," *Annual of the Japanese Biblical Institute* 1 (1975) 25, and *Numbers Rabbah* 6:2. However Jehoram had come to the throne, his insecurity is evident from the report of his having purged his brothers (2 Chron 21:4). Regarding Exod 12:29, see note 183 above.

[188] *B. Keritot* 5b.

family status of the thirty kings who succeeded to the throne in Israel and Judah; the siblings of only seven are named, usually without reference to birth order. For example, the names of only two of King Ahab's seventy sons are given—because both became king[189]—but not the names or the relative ages of their sixty-eight brothers.

The Bible thus provides insufficient information to resolve the question posed here. Inferring birth order is especially difficult, since it is not clear that names are even listed according to seniority.[190] 1 Samuel gives Saul's sons as Jonathan, Ishvi, and Malchishua (14:49), to which 2 Samuel adds Ishbosheth (2:8).[191] However, the report of their death presents them as Jonathan, Abinadab, and Malchishua (1 Sam 3:12), while 1 Chronicles lists them as Jonathan, Malchishua, Abinadab, and Ishbosheth (8:33, 9:39).[192] Even if these lists were arranged chronologically, a manifest impossibility given the inconsistency of their sequence, they provide little support for either primogeniture or automatic succession. Ishbosheth's success was due to Abner (2 Sam 2:8–9), whose motivation is never stated. There is certainly no indication that Ishbosheth's age was a determining factor. Although Jonathan, Abinadab, and Malchishua had died by then, Ishvi's fate is never described.

The succession following David is not more helpful for those seeking evidence of Israelite primogeniture. In this case, some indication of his sons' relative ages can be gleaned from biblical statements as to whether they had been born at Hebron, where David ruled first, or at his later capital of Jerusalem; however, the two lists of Hebronite sons and the three lists of those born in Jerusalem are not identical.[193] It is particularly curious that the former group includes only one son by each of David's wives, suggesting that birth order was not its only concern.

Whatever the order in which these brothers are listed, there is no evidence that succession was based on age. Although Amnon is sometimes identified as David's *bĕkōr* (1 Chron 3:1),[194] that fact is given only to account for his having been the best loved of David's sons. Never is he in any way identified as David's heir apparent. Both Absalom and

---

[189] 2 Kings 10:1–7; cf. 1 Kings 22:40 and 2 Kings 3:1.

[190] See pp. 64–66 above.

[191] Two daughters, described as *habbĕkîrâ* and *haqqĕṭannâ* respectively, are also mentioned in 1 Sam 14:49.

[192] Ishbosheth is called Eshbaal in Chronicles, where the Peshitta lists Ishvi instead of Abinadab. For the problems with such lists, see pp. 64–66 above.

[193] 2 Sam 3:2–5, 5:13–16, 1 Chron 3:1–9, 14:3–7.

[194] See also the Septuagint and 4QSam^a at 2 Sam 13:21 (Eugene C. Ulrich, *The Qumran Text of Samuel and Josephus* [Missoula, MT: Scholars Press, 1978] p. 84) as well as Josephus, *Antiquities* 7.8.2 §173 (LCL vol. 5, pp. 452–53) and the Vulgate at 2 Sam 13:21.

Adonijah later claimed leadership, despite their being the sons of David's third and fourth Hebronite wives. To account for this, those arguing in favor of primogeniture must assume that David's second son Chileab had died by the time these events took place.[195]

Even if Amnon's death did contribute to Adonijah and Absalom's sense that they were entitled to the throne, their efforts to take power while David was still alive belie any assertion of automatic rights. Neither one is ever described as heir apparent, nor even as the oldest surviving son. Although Adonijah was surely older than Solomon (1 Kings 2:22), a similar claim could have been made by at least three other princes whom the Bible identifies as having been born in Hebron (Chileab, Shephatiah, and Itream).[196]

Both of these figures seem to have acted preemptively. Adonijah's public proclamation, "I shall rule" (*'ănî 'emlōk*, 1 Kings 1:5), itself shows that he did not assume the crown would automatically be his, in which case he could simply have awaited David's demise. Although possibly opportunistic and, as subsequent events would reveal, poorly realized, his efforts seem to have been made in good faith. The narrative's prior emphasis on his father's infirmity supports the verb's imperfect form in suggesting that rather than usurping the throne, Adonijah was most likely trying to position himself to take over after David's death.[197] At this early stage in Israel's national history, there was no dynastic tradition to define the rights of succession. Under the circumstances, it could hardly have been certain that David would be succeeded by a son at all, much less which son that would be. Nor does the Bible mention any public expression of his preference. It is the ambiguity of this situation, just what one would expect in a new dynasty and a culture with little monarchic experience and thus no accepted norms, that best accounts for Adonijah's actions.

---

[195] E.g., James A. Montgomery and Henry S. Gehman, *A Critical and Exegetical Commentary on the Book of Kings* (ICC; Edinburgh: T. & T. Clark, 1951) p. 72. The Peshitta gives the name as Caleb (at 2 Sam 3:3); 1 Chron 3:1 has Daniel.

[196] Some of David's Jerusalem-born offspring may also have been older than Solomon (see 2 Sam 5:13–16, 1 Chron 3:1–9 and 14:3–7, recognizing the uncertainty as to the significance of sequence in such texts; see pp. 64–66 above).

[197] So M. Garsiel, *Malkhut David: Meḥqarim be-Historiya ve-'Iyyunim be-Historiographia* (Tel Aviv: Don Publishing House, 1975) p. 170. This is not contradicted by the characterization of his actions as self-aggrandizement (*mitnaśśē'*). Note the Septuagint's effort to deflect some of the blame from him, though none of this is to imply biblical approval of his behavior; indeed, he is presented in a way that evokes memories of Absalom (1 Sam 1:6, 2 Sam 14:25); cf. Meir Sternberg, *The Poetics of Biblical Narrative, Ideological Literature and the Drama of Reading* (Bloomington, IN: Indiana University Press, 1985) p. 268.

The premise that the king could select his own heir pervades the Bible's depiction of the post-Davidic succession. Virtually every participant accepts that position. David clearly felt empowered to support Solomon against Adonijah's initiative, a right which was also assumed by Solomon's supporters when they sought his decree on the basis of a presumed prior assurance that Solomon would be the heir. Even Adonijah recognized his father's decision as irreversible when, after discovering that David had appointed Solomon, "he grasped the horns of the altar" (1 Kings 1:50) rather than challenge his brother's position. His later observation that "the kingdom was mine (*lî hāyĕtâ hammĕlûkâ*)... but [it] turned and became my brother's" (1 Kings 2:15) indicates how close his efforts had come to success. In none of this is there any evidence that any son expected the privilege to be automatic—only a struggle for succession, possibly exacerbated by the lack of accepted principles.

David's choice of Solomon could hardly have been based on age.[198] As one of his father's Jerusalemite sons, Solomon must have been younger than those born in Hebron. If the list in 1 Chronicles 3:5 is sequential, he may not even have been Bathsheba's oldest living child.[199] The importance of that passage should not be minimized. Although it is easy to understand why the court historian of 2 Samuel would have ignored the birth of intervening sons, making Solomon appear to have been born immediately after the stillborn fruit of David and Bathsheba's affair, it is hard to imagine what could have motivated the Chronicler to have moved his name to the end of such a list.[200]

However one chooses to resolve these well-known problems, the difficulties with theories of Israelite primogeniture do not stop with Solomon. Assertions such as one scholar's statement that "from the time of Solomon on the kings of Israel and Judah were regularly succeeded

---

[198] Abraham Malamat suggests that Solomon may have been chosen because of his foreign, aristocratic birth ("Comments on E. Leach, 'The Legitimacy of Solomon—Some Structural Aspects of Old Testament History," *European Journal of Sociology* 8 [1967] 166–67). Recall, however, those societies that grant priority to the first child born after his father's accession (see note 46 in this chapter).

[199] According to the Septuagint, Solomon was twelve at the time of his accession (1 Kings 2:12, cf. 3:7, 1 Chron 22:5 and 29:1), although he had apparently fathered Rehoboam a year before (1 Kings 11:42 and 14:21); cf. 2 Kings 16:2 and 18:2, which together suggest that Hezekiah was born when his father Ahaz was eleven.

[200] Despite the sequence of events described in 2 Sam 12:18–24, some have argued that it was Solomon who had been adulterously conceived and the tradition of that child's death subsequently invented to protect his legitimacy; e.g., Ernst Würthwein, *Die Erzählung von der Thronfolge Davids—theologische oder politische Geschichtesschreibung?* (Zurich: Theologischer Verlag, 1974) pp. 31–32, and Timo Veijola, "Salomo—der erstgeborene Bathsebas," Supplement to *Vetus Testamentum* 30 (1979) 230–41.

upon the throne by their firstborn sons"[201] are simply not supported by the evidence we have.

The persisting instability of the Northern Kingdom makes it difficult to ascertain the principles of succession that were followed there. Even where sons did succeed their fathers, the evidence is insufficient to determine the order of their birth. However, biblical accounts of Judean succession are no more supportive. Leaving aside the case of Ahaziah, who is said to have gained the throne only after his brothers had been taken captive (2 Chron 21:16–22:1), there are several other Southern kings who appear not to have been their fathers' oldest offspring. These include Abijah, who was the son of Rehoboam's second wife; his succession may, therefore, demonstrate the elevation of a favorite wife's offspring, but he is unlikely to have been the king's firstborn.[202] The same applies to Manasseh and Amon, both of whom are described as having been born when their fathers were over forty years old; such figures are surely unlikely to have been oldest sons.[203]

1 Chronicles lists Josiah's sons in the sequence Johanan, Jehoiakim, Zedekiah, and Shallum (3:15), the latter commonly identified with the son elsewhere called Jehoahaz. He ruled only three months immediately following the death of his father (2 Kings 23:30–31, cf. Jer 22:11). Twenty-three when he came to the throne, he was succeeded by his brother Jehoiakim, who was then twenty-five (2 Kings 23:36).[204] In other words, they did not reign in birth order.

Zedekiah, the last of Judah's kings, is usually regarded as another of Josiah's sons, so it is not surprising that he was older than his nephew Jehoiachin, who preceded him to the throne.[205] (He would also have been

[201] Julian Morgenstern, "Inheritance," *Universal Jewish Encyclopedia* (New York: Universal Jewish Encyclopedia Co., 1941) vol. 5, p. 566. Compare T. C. G. Thornton's comment, "There is no sign of any particular reason why the custom of primogeniture should not have prevailed" ("Solomonic Apologetic in Samuel and Kings," *Church Quarterly Review* 169 [1968] 161).

[202] See 2 Chron 11:20–22; Abijah's appointment as *rō's* recalls the reference to Shimri in 1 Chron 26:10 (see pp. 60–61 above). For other problems involved in this succession, see J. Maxwell Miller and John H. Hayes, *A History of Ancient Israel and Judah* (Philadelphia: Westminster Press, 1986) p. 240.

[203] According to Tomoo Ishida, the other Judean kings were all born when their fathers were between eleven and twenty-four (*The Royal Dynasties in Ancient Israel*, pp. 153–54).

[204] Whether Jehoiakim was elevated because Jehoahaz had no sons or, as Pinhas Ne'eman suggests, because of foreign intervention ("*Haqamat Melekh ve-Horashat ha-Melukhah be-Yisra'el*," *Beth Mikra* 15 [1970] 193) is not clear.

[205] 2 Kings 24:17, 1 Chron 3:15, and the Septuagint at 2 Chron 36:10. Jehoiachin was either eight (2 Chron 36:9) or eighteen (2 Kings 24:8) when he took the throne, while Zedekiah was twenty-one at his accession three months later (2 Kings 24:18, Jer 52:1, 2 Chron 36:11).

younger than Jehoahaz/Shallum, whose name follows his in the afore-mentioned list.) However, in one tradition he is identified as Jehoiachin's brother (MT 2 Chron 36:10), which would yield yet another instance of rulers not coming to power in the order of their birth.

In sum, David, Jehoram, and probably Rehoboam, Hezekiah, Manasseh, Josiah, and perhaps Jehoiakim were all succeeded by younger sons. Although foreign interference was a recurring fact of Israelite politics during this period, not one of these successions is ascribed to an outside power, despite the willingness of biblical authors to acknowledge it quite openly in other cases.[206] Jehoiachin's reign is simply noted, while Jehoahaz is said to have been made king by the people (*'am hā'āreṣ*, 2 Kings 23:30).

Granting the limits of the available evidence in terms of both quantity and historical reliability, it must nonetheless be emphasized that it offers no support for those who contend that succession to the throne, or any other Israelite office for that matter, was based on primogeniture.[207] Indeed, it appears questionable whether any prince could claim rights of automatic succession. The four-century chain of Davidic rulers demons-trates only Judean acceptance of that family as their dynasty, not how an heir was to be selected from within it.[208] David chose his successor; others were designated by military or even foreign supporters.[209] Numerous rulers are said to have been anointed by various functionaries or even the people themselves, while many kings and would-be kings seem to have needed popular support before they could rule. These include such figures as Absalom, Adonijah, Uzziah, Josiah, and Jehoahaz in the South and Sheba, Rehoboam, Jeroboam, Tibni, and Omri in the North.[210] The

---

[206] Cf. note 209 below.

[207] This holds true for both the priesthood (see p. 22 above) as well as later political rulers. Although the Hasmonean brothers are listed in the order John, Simon, Judah, Jonathan (1 Maccabees 2:2), Jonathan was chosen to succeed Judah (1 Maccabees 9:30) and was then followed by Simon (1 Maccabees 13:8). Josephus identifies Jannaeus as Hyrcanus' younger (third) son (*Antiquities* 13.2.1 §322–23 [LCL vol. 7, pp. 388–91]).

[208] Thus Psalm 132 speaks broadly in its assertion that "the Lord has sworn truthfully to David... 'If your sons (*bāneykā*) keep My covenant and My decrees that I teach them, then their sons (*bĕnêhem*) will sit on your throne to the end of time'" (vv. 11–12); cf. the vague reference to *ben melek* in Ps 72:1. See also Y. Liver, "*Melekh, Melukhah*," *Encyclopedia Miqra'it* (Jerusalem: Bialik Institute, 1950–88) vol. 4, pp. 1094–95.

[209] 2 Sam 2:8–9, 1 Kings 1:7, 2 Kings 10:5, 23:34, 24:17; cf. Isa 7:6. For the succession after David, see the first part of Chapter 5.

[210] 1 Sam 15:23, 26, 2 Sam 15:6, 16:18, 20:1–3, 1 Kings 2:15, 11:11–12, 12:1–17, 14:1–10, 16:1, 12, 21–22, 2 Kings 14:21, 21:24; note also the case of Abimelech (Judg 9:2, cf. vv. 7–15 as discussed on p. 74 above). Cf. C. Umhau Wolf, "Traces of Primitive Democracy in Ancient Israel," *Journal of Near Eastern Studies* 6 (1947) 98–108, and Hayim Tadmor, "'The People' and the Kingship in Ancient Israel: The Role of Political Institutions in the Biblical Period," *Journal of World History* 11 (1968) 62–66.

phrasing of Jehu's letter to northern officials may also reflect this practice in its invitation for them to "determine the best and most suitable of your master's sons to place on his father's throne" (*wĕšamtem ʿal-kissē' 'abîw*, 2 Kings 10:3). If this can be relied on as more than a provocative and rhetorical taunt, it demonstrates that any royal prince might be named to the throne, further weakening the likelihood that royal succession was in any way automatic. Admittedly, such procedures may have grown out of political reality or reflect ritual conservatism rather than legal theory, and the reliability of our evidence is not always assured. Nonetheless, the fact remains that there is simply no definitive support for the proposition that primogeniture was normative in determining Israelite succession.

Summary

In sum, despite von Rad's certainty that "the privilege of the first-born was absolutely uncontested (ein schlechthin unbestrittenes) in the ancient orient,"[211] Near Eastern practice in the areas of ritual, inheritance, and succession conforms remarkably well to what has been found elsewhere, with diverse approaches as its most notable characteristic. In some places property was shared or divided equally. Where a single individual did receive more than others, it is not at all clear how that person was selected. Testators (or other, less visible individuals) seem to have had substantial latitude in choosing who that would be. Leadership, too, was transmitted in a variety of ways, with the incumbent often playing a critical role in choosing his successor.

The evidence that primogeniture may not be as ancient or as universal a human practice as is commonly supposed raises the question of why it has been so widely assumed. If the roots of these beliefs do not lie in reality, their source must be within us, a product of our own particular history and culture. The widespread predisposition to equate seniority with ability no doubt accounts for much of this. Yet another factor may be the visibility of British royalty and its adherence to primogeniture as the last remnant of the far more pervasive English system of inheritance by which all of a family's real property passed to the oldest son.

Biblical accounts of Israelite inheritance and succession confirm the impression that holders of both property and hereditary office were free to grant preferential treatment to whichever offspring they wished. Israelite

---

[211] Gerhard von Rad, *Genesis, A Commentary* (OTL; Philadelphia: Westminster Press, 1973) p. 416; the original German is on p. 364 of *Das Erste Buch Mose, Genesis Kapital 25, 19–50, 26* (ATD, vol. 4; Göttingen: Vandenhoeck & Ruprecht, 1953) p. 364.

rulers were not inevitably the oldest children in their families, although many of them may have been firstborns, a fact that is not seen as calling for explanation in the way that the success of younger offspring does in the earlier, patriarchal narratives. Although the nature of our sources makes it more difficult to determine the details of Israelite inheritance practices, the key passage in Deuteronomy is significantly less useful than is usually assumed and, in any case, explicitly allows for both inheritance by several children in each family and also a father's right to determine which child would receive more than the others, so long as that decision was not based on the mother's favored status.

This system of fraternal sharing and paternal autonomy is confirmed by every incidental reference to inheritance in the Bible. Although the stories most commonly associated with inheritance are actually concerned with the transmission of a blessing rather than property, thus falling well outside of Israel's legal system, even they do not deviate from these principles. Nor have we found support for primogeniture in either Israelite ritual, where there is no evidence that firstborns actually played a special role, or philology, which has only raised questions as to the precise meaning of the term *bĕkōr* which looms so large in many of these texts.

In short, Israelite practice conforms to the patterns of inheritance and succession found in its own environment as well as throughout the world. In this, it is far different from what is often supposed. Rather than following an "iron law of primogeniture,"[212] property was typically divided among a decedent's heirs, most often his sons. Although one child may have been treated preferentially, that choice was left largely in the hands of the incumbent, whose decision need not have been based on age. Royal succession proceeded similarly, with no evidence of any rigidly automatic system. The dynastic principle presumes only that *a* son would succeed to the throne, not which son that would be—a determination apparently left open, as struggles for the throne and the involvement of third parties so clearly attest.

Recognizing that Israel's system of succession was not rigidly bound to birth order enables us to achieve an enriched understanding of the Bible's description of both Israel and her king as God's *bĕkōr*, for it suggests that this status was not necessarily automatic but could be earned. God's

---

[212] Robert Alter, *The Art of Biblical Narrative* (New York: Basic Books, 1981) p. 6; cf. E. Neufeld's statement that "the right of the firstborn...is the only right in Israel of which there is any real historical record" (*Ancient Hebrew Marriage Laws, With Special Reference to Special Semitic Laws and Customs* [London: Longmans, Green, and Co., 1944] p. 263).

right to choose whomever He preferred was that enjoyed by all Israelite fathers. For Israel to be the beneficiary of this designation, therefore, was the result of neither age nor merit, but a sign of God's favor for reasons which need not be divulged. That is precisely the point of Deuteronomy in its assertion that "it was not because you are more numerous than all the nations that the Lord loved you and chose you, for you are the smallest of all nations, but because of the Lord's love of you and His commitment to the oath which He swore to your ancestors..." (7:7–8).

Acutely aware of her own historicity, Israel could hardly have claimed a primordial relationship with God as did other cultures of the region. Drawing on the widespread view of God as father, she was able to adopt the legal metaphor of being *běkōr*, a paternally assigned status of superiority, as a way of expressing her theology of election without exaggerated claims of either merit or antiquity. This image was eventually adopted by Israel's ruling house in the psalmist's statement that David had been made God's *běkōr*, an assertion phrased in such a way as to accommodate theological sensitivities not felt by other cultures which had no hesitation at ascribing divinity to their rulers. Although the Bible obviously could not permit such assertions about David, describing the king as God's *adopted* son or *běkōr* granted him the metaphysical status other nations claimed for their rulers without compromising either history or theology.

Within this context, the repeated success of younger sons (and occasionally daughters) in the Bible cannot easily be interpreted as a protest against Israelite norms, any more than it can be understood as the natural result of accepted customs. The practice which this motif is said to reject simply did not exist. There is no evidence to prove that first-borns were regarded as having a natural right to either the throne or estate, any more than that they were prime candidates for sacrifice or even devotion in service to Israel's God, or any other ancient Near Eastern deity for that matter. This motif must, therefore, be studied on its own terms, in light of its internal dynamics and the various literary settings in which it occurs, before its significance and prevalence in the Bible can be understood.

3

The Last Shall Be First

The pervasiveness of younger siblings throughout so much of biblical literature demands an explanation. However, the lack of conclusive evidence demonstrating the practice of either primogeniture or ultimogeniture in ancient Israel precludes interpreting this as either a reflection or a rejection of actual norms governing inheritance and succession. Fortunately, the biblical accounts do not need to be treated as an isolated phenomenon. The success of younger children is a common feature of popular literature around the world. Particularly in folktales one finds youngest sons succeeding at tasks their older brothers are unable to achieve, defying the odds to kill dragons or marry princesses.[1]

This motif exists in ancient as well as modern sources. For example, the well-known Egyptian "Tale of Two Brothers" features a younger brother (*sn šri*) as its hero. In fact, once the title characters have been introduced, their names fade into obscurity as they come to be identified by their respective ages alone.[2] The god Horus, who plays a central role in Egyptian mythology and was considered the incarnation of the Pharaoh, is also presented as a younger brother.[3]

---

[1] Cf. motifs L 0–99 ("victorious youngest child") in Stith Thompson, *Motif-Index of Folk-Literature* (Bloomington, IN: Indiana University Press, 1925) vol. 5, pp. 6–8, and the analysis of over one hundred German fairly tales summarized by Brian Sutton-Smith and B. G. Rosenberg, *The Sibling* (New York: Holt, Rinehart and Winston, 1970) p. 3.

[2] See Alan H. Gardiner, *Late Egyptian Stories* (Brussels: La Fondation Égyptologique Reine Élisabeth, 1932) pp. 9–29.

[3] "The Contendings of Horus and Seth," especially 4.7 (in Alan H. Gardiner, *The Library of A. Chester Beatty* [London: Emery Walker Ltd., 1931] pp. 16 and 19; cf. J.

This motif is also well attested in Mesopotamian tradition. Prominent figures who are presented as youngest, or at least younger, siblings include the Assyrian emperor Esarhaddon, Alalakh's King Idrimi, and the Hittite ruler Hattusilis.[4] All three of these younger children were also kings, as was the Egyptian deity Horus. This is not simply coincidental. Although stories about royalty are inherently more likely to have been preserved than those dealing with less prestigious individuals, kingship is an integral and important element in the plot of many of these tales. In each case, the stories acknowledge that their protagonist had achieved power through an unusual chain of events. Moreover, many of their heroes are known to have been usurpers.[5] The stories thus serve a polemical function, justifying what was probably a questionable process of succession. The presence of folkloric features in several of these tales, many of which have parallels in various biblical accounts, strengthens the likelihood that they should not be treated as reliable, historical reports.

The book of Samuel's account of David, the greatest of Israel's kings, provides a biblical example of this genre. Like his Near Eastern counterparts, David's accession was irregular, following what the Bible presents as God's rejection of Saul. Although David is not presented as a usurper, given the biblical view that God was entitled to anoint or reject the king, his accession is acknowledged as having taken place against opposition from Saul's family and without his subjects' approval.

Gwyn Griffiths, *The Conflict of Horus and Seth, From Egyptian and Classical Sources* [Chicago: Argonaut, 1969] pp. 67–68). They are described as brothers in the Pyramid Texts §1742 (utterance 615 in R. D. Faulkner, *The Ancient Egyptian Pyramid Texts* [Oxford: Clarendon Press, 1969; reprinted Oak Park, IL: Bolchazy-Carducci Publishers, 1985] p. 256). H. Te Velde provides evidence of a connection between Seth and Bata, the younger brother of the "Tale of Two Brothers" (*Seth, God of Confusion, A Study of His Role in Egyptian Mythology and Religion* [Leiden: E. J. Brill] p. 41).

[4] Esarhaddon prism A I, line 8 (in Riekele Borger, *Die Inschriften Asarhaddons Königs von Assyrien* [AfO Beiheft 9; Graz: Archiv für Orientforschung, 1956] p. 40); Idrimi line 7 (in Gary H. Oller, "The Autobiography of Idrimi: A New Text Edition with Philological and Historical Commentary" [University of Pennsylvania, Ph.D. dissertation, 1977] p. 9); and the Apology of Hattusiliš, line 11 (in Heinrich Otten, *Die Apologie Hattusilis III, Das Bild der Überlieferung* [Wiesbaden: Otto Harrassowitz, 1981] pp. 4–5). For folkloristic features and biblical parallels, see Herbert M. Wolf, "The Apology of Ḫattušiliš Compared with Other Political Self-Justifications of the Ancient Near East" (Brandeis University, Ph.D. dissertation, 1967) pp. 36 and 112–28, and Mario Liverani, "Partire sul carro, per il deserto," *Annali dell'istituto Orientali di Napoli* 37 (1972) 414–15. Besides being younger brothers, several of these figures had been forced to flee their homeland, a motif found also in the stories of Jacob, Joseph, Jephtha, David, Jacob, and Sinuhe.

[5] Mario Liverani, "Partire sul carro, per deserto," p. 415; on methods of legitimation, see René Labat, *Le caractère religieux de la Royauté Assyro-Babylonienne* (Paris: Librairie d'amerique et D'orient, Adrien-Maisonneuve, 1939) pp. 74–79.

Although several passages mention David's older brothers, it is only in the story of his anointment by Samuel that family rank plays a noticeable role.[6] Because this is widely considered a relatively late addition to the Davidic saga, it is usually treated apart from the other stories relating to David's rise.[7]

According to the biblical account, Samuel was to anoint a new king from among Jesse's sons, but God did not tell him which son that should be: "I am sending you to Jesse, the Bethlehemite, for I have decided on (lit. "seen") a king from among his sons. . . . Invite Jesse to the sacrifice . . . then announce for Me the one I tell you" (1 Sam 16:1–3). It was only when Samuel was about to anoint Eliab, the first of Jesse's sons, that God warned him to ignore "his appearance and stature" (*mar'ēhû wĕ . . . gĕbōah qômātô*, v. 7).

Physical appearance plays a prominent role in this account, emphasized by its repeated use of the *Leitwort r'h* ("see"), which parallels the recurring distinction between chosenness (*bḥr*) and rejection (*m's*)[8]: Samuel had been sent to Bethlehem because God had seen (*rā'îtî*) a king among Jesse's sons (v. 1). Once there, he was impressed when he first saw (*wayyar'*) the eldest Eliab (v. 6), leading God to explain, "It is not that which a person sees (*yir'eh*), since a person sees (*yir'eh*) the outer appearance, but the Lord sees (*yir'eh*) the heart" (v. 7). There is more than a little irony in this last remark, since Samuel, to whom it refers, had been introduced as a *rō'eh* (lit. "seer," 1 Sam 9:19). But he did not see, at least not as God does.[9]

After the rejection of Eliab, Jesse brought forth each of his other sons in turn, but none was found acceptable. Besides prolonging the account and contributing to its suspense, this progression directs our attention to the youngest son, who is implicitly contrasted with his older

---

[6] 1 Sam 16:1–13; cf. 17:12–28 where David's youth, initially contrasted with his brothers (vv. 13, 14, 28), is critical for the contrast with Goliath (v. 42). This motif has been incorporated into Psalm 151 (cf. 11QPs[a] 28:3–4).

[7] Artur Weiser, "Die Legitimation des Königs David, Zur Eigenart und Entstehung der sogen. Geschichte von Davids Aufstieg," *Vetus Testamentum* 16 (1966) 326–27, but see Hans-Ulrich Nübel, *Davids Aufstieg in der frühe israelitischer Geschichtsschreibung* (Bonn: Rheinische Friedrich-Wilhelms-Universität, 1959) pp. 20 and 91–92.

[8] 1 Sam 15:23, 26, 16:1, 7–10; cf. Martin Kessler, "Narrative Technique in 1 Sm. 16, 1–13," *Catholic Biblical Quarterly* 32 (1970) 549–50; Ashley Rose notes the connection between *r'h* and selection, as in Gen 22:8, Deut 12:13, 2 Kings 10:3, Esther 2:9 ("The 'Principles' of Divine Election, Wisdom in 1 Sml 16," in *Rhetorical Criticism, Essays in Honor of James Muilenberg*, ed. Jared J. Jackson and Martin Kessler [Pittsburgh: Pickwick Press, 1974] pp. 49–50).

[9] Rashi at 1 Sam 16:6, citing 9:19; cf. Jer 11:20, 17:10, and 20:12.

siblings. The action is again delayed while David is summoned from tending sheep.[10]

In addition to demonstrating that God's choice need not correspond to our own expectations, focusing on David's youth and apparently small size may also be intended as a subtle repudiation of Saul, who was earlier described as a "goodly youth... taller than everybody else" (*bāḥûr wāṭōb...gābōah mikkōl hā'ām*, 9:2, cf. 10:23)—exactly as a king should be.[11] David's virtues are understood as internal, the kind that God most prizes. However, having made that point, the narrative then adds that he was "reddish with lovely eyes and good appearance" (*'admônî 'im-yĕpēh 'ênayim wĕṭôb rō'î*, 16:12; cf. 17:42). It seems odd that a description of David's physical excellence would follow a statement implying that he did not look like a king. Many interpreters have resolved this apparent contradiction by suggesting that the point is to show how God's choices conform to human criteria, even if the reasons for His selections differ from our own.[12] However, this explanation makes little sense. If David's presence really was worthy of a king, then the thrust of the whole account, with its contrast between inner reality and surface appearance, would be undermined, since this view would leave physical appearance as a reliable indicator of divine grace, even if it was not the reason for God's selection. Its effect would be to undo precisely what the author had worked so hard to convey—that David was not the sort of person one would expect a king to be, since God's concerns are different from our own.

A closer look at the way David is described suggests that the contradiction may be only apparent. Whereas male attractiveness is rarely mentioned in the Bible, and then usually in the most general of terms,[13] female beauty is often emphasized, and frequently with exactly the language applied here to David. Among those who are characterized in this way are Sarah, Rebecca, Rachel, Abigail, Bathsheba, Tamar, Vashti and the candidates to succeed her, as well as the prisoner of war who arouses her

[10] Like Joseph, this youngest son is physically separate from his brothers, although his caring for the sheep is the reverse of Gen 37:12 (however, David does stay home when his older brothers go to battle in 1 Sam 17:13–15); cf. Jakob H. Grønbaek, *Die Geschichte vom Aufstieg Davids (1 Sam. 15–2. Sam. 5), Tradition und Komposition* (Copenhagen: Prostant apud Munksgaard, 1971) pp. 96–97.

[11] E.g., George B. Caird in *The Interpreter's Bible* at 1 Sam 16:7 (ed. G. A. Buttrick; New York: Abingdon Press, 1952) vol. 2, p. 968.

[12] See, for example, David Qimhi at 1 Sam 16:12, C. F. Keil and F. Delitzsch, *Commentary on the Old Testament* (reprint Grand Rapids, MI: William B. Eerdmans, 1981) 2.169, and Hans W. Hertzberg, *I and II Samuel, A Commentary* (OTL, 2d ed.; Philadelphia: Westminster Press, 1964) pp. 138–39.

[13] Cf. 2 Sam 14:25, 1 Kings 1:6, Ezek 28:12, Ps 45:3.

captor's desire.[14] From even a cursory consideration of this list, it is obvious that what these terms describe is feminine sexual attractiveness. Nor is this contradicted by the case of Joseph, who is depicted in a similar way, since his "beauty" is mentioned in order to link him with his mother Rachel as well as to set up the lustful reaction of Potiphar's wife.[15] For David to be presented in such terms is in no way an evocation of his masculinity.

This conclusion is supported by his description as having been *'admōnî* (lit. "reddish"). That term, which is restated by Goliath as a sign of scorn (1 Sam 17:42), is the same one used to describe the newborn Esau (Gen 25:25).[16] This further weakens the likelihood that these characteristics convey aspects of adult masculinity. What they present is not a manly figure, but an unlikely hero. Seen in this broader context, there is no contradiction between David's physical appearance and the Bible's insistence that externals are of no interest to God. Rather than "ruddy and virile," he was pink and pretty, hardly an obvious candidate for the throne, as Goliath well saw.[17]

Biblical authors are unlikely to have intended this negative image as a criticism of David, particularly given the positive way he is understood in so much of the Hebrew Bible. Rather, its purpose is to show that his rise to power, like that of other Near Eastern rulers who are similarly portrayed, was not due to his physical appearance, but to destiny and inner worth. At one time this may have served to defend him from those who supported descendants of the more imposing Saul or from other critics of his dynasty, such as those in Northern Israel; in its present context, however, it functions as a literary and theological motif.

---

[14] Gen 12:11, 24:16, 26:7, 29:17, 1 Sam 25:3, 2 Sam 11:2, 14:27, Esther 1:11, 2:2, 3, 7; Deut 21:11.

[15] See p. 96 below.

[16] For usage of the root *'dm* to describe people's appearance, see Edward Ullendorff, "The Contribution of South Semitics to Hebrew Lexicography," *Vetus Testamentum* 6 (1956) 191–92.

[17] Cf. Robert Alter, *The Art of Biblical Narrative* (New York: Basic Books, 1981) p. 81, contra William McKane *I & II Samuel* (London: SCM Press Ltd., 1963) p. 112. Note also the depiction of Israelite children as *ṭôbê mar'eh* in Dan 1:4 (cf. v. 15). Cyrus Gordon compares the description to a heroic statue (*The Ancient Near East* [3d ed., New York: W. W. Norton, 1965] p. 125), but see Nahum M. Sarna, "The Anticipatory Use of Information as a Literary Feature of the Genesis Narratives" in *The Creation of Sacred Literature, Composition and Redaction of the Biblical Text*, ed. Richard E. Friedman (Berkeley, CA: University of California Press, 1981) p. 81. Meir Sternberg treats these texts quite differently in *The Poetics of Biblical Narrative, Ideological Literature and the Drama of Reading* (Bloomington, IN: Indiana University Press, 1985) pp. 354–63.

The unexpected nature of his success frees David, and other figures portrayed in this way, from the taint of having connived for the throne. In this regard, presenting them as younger sons takes advantage of the aura of innocence widely associated with youth.[18] As such, it is a particularly attractive device for figures whose accession may have been irregular. In the case of David, the implied contrast with his older brothers reinforces this same point.[19]

Vulnerability is another connotation frequently associated with younger figures. Often it is made manifest by presenting their encounters with disaster, several of which take place at the hands of older brothers. This feature, too, is common in folklore, where it is frequently associated with figures whose innocence and youth are prominently noted. For example, it was Bluebeard's youngest wife whose curiosity put her life at risk, while Servian legend tells of a youngest son whose wife was walled in because she had not been forewarned of the danger in bringing her husband food.[20]

Our sympathy is evoked by such characters' innocence and vulnerability. Unknowing and comparatively immature, their unexpected success implies both virtue and good fortune. The story of David exploits these connotations. By proceeding through his brothers sequentially while David is absent from the scene, the narrative emphasizes how unlikely a hero he is. This impression is strengthened when he subsequently appears with minimal qualifications for the position he is about to acquire. David's success cannot, therefore, be ascribed to his own merit, but demonstrates his good fortune and shows how much fate was on his side. Given the biblical setting, that is surely to be credited to God, as the text acknowledges with its observation that God looks at the heart (1 Sam 16:7), implicitly validating David's ultimate selection.

The popularity of this motif throughout world literature adds a paradoxical dimension to the way in which it functions. On the surface, it would appear to rest on the unlikelihood of these characters' success. This dimension is accentuated by a variety of devices. For example, many such heroes are identified as fools; one younger son is even named Dummling (lit. "simpleton"), as if to signal his limitations before the story

---

[18] In addition to the innocent brother in the Egyptian "Tale of Two Brothers," cited at the beginning of this chapter, see the Book of Mormon's description of Nephi as having been chosen over his sinful older brother (1 Nephi 2:12, 18–22).

[19] Cf. his brothers' attitude as presented in 1 Sam 17:17–28, to which Joseph's treatment by his brothers (Genesis 37) should be compared.

[20] Maria Tatar, *The Hard Facts of the Grimms' Fairy Tales* (Princeton, NJ: Princeton University Press, 1987) p. 157, and Edward B. Tylor, *The Origin of Culture* (New York: Harper & Brothers, 1958) p. 105.

has begun.[21] However, most of these protagonists turn out to be quite capable of the missions with which they have been charged. David, for example, does succeed in defeating Goliath. The unlikelihood of their success is thus a matter of appearance alone. Denying their ostensible qualifications for what is eventually achieved merely emphasizes the real virtues these heroes possess.

The frequent repetition of this motif compounds the paradox. Years of story hearing have accustomed us to younger offsprings' success in overcoming impossible odds and overthrowing the shackles of oppression.[22] Rather than catching us off guard, the appearance of a younger son attracts our attention, signaling his eventual success, even as we wonder how that will be achieved. With the outcome all but announced at the start, such accounts cannot accurately be described as unexpected. Only from the characters' point of view are the results truly unknown. Denied any doubt as to the conclusion, our attention is directed away from the denouement and towards the way in which it is achieved, particularly given the less than promising circumstances with which such stories begin.

This dynamic is well illustrated by Hans Christian Andersen's "Ugly Duckling," the hero of which is a youngest offspring who appears ill-suited for greatness.[23] Of course, the Ugly Duckling is really a swan and ultimately the best of the entire brood. The story's outcome is signaled from the start by the duckling's emergence from the largest egg, which alerts the reader to what the narrator already knows: there is a swan inside this duckling, and only time is needed for that which was present from the beginning to emerge.[24] Like so many of the Bible's youngest siblings, David is a swan, a point the narrative makes unmistakably clear. However unlikely his success and unpromising his appearance, the outcome is assured by his skill and by divine support. Nor is the reader expected to

---

[21] Maria Tatar adds such other characters as Blockhead and Numbskull (*The Hard Facts of the Grimms' Fairy Tales*, p. 96); as she comments, "To the question, 'Who is the stupidest of them all?' most fairy tale fathers would reply: my youngest son" (p. 87).

[22] Maria Tatar points out, "In fairy tales all over the world, the one least likely to succeed paradoxically becomes the one most likely to succeed (*The Hard Facts of the Grimms' Fairy Tales*, p. 87); cf. Meir Sternberg's reference to "foreshadowing by paradigm" (*The Poetics of Biblical Narrative*, pp. 268–69) and Robert Alter's description of type scenes (*The Art of Biblical Narrative*, pp. 47–58).

[23] Jean Hersholt, *The Complete Andersen: All of the 168 Stories by Hans Christian Andersen* (New York: The Limited Editions Club, 1942 and 1949) pp. 177–87.

[24] Similar signals are provided for Cinderella and, in its own way, the Tortoise and the Hare, both of which are ostensibly about unexpected results; see Bruno Bettelheim, *The Uses of Enchantment, The Meaning and Importance of Fairy Tales* (New York: Alfred A. Knopf, 1976) p. 241.

be fooled, given the number of devices used to ensure that our attention is focused on David. This notion is further strengthened by the way in which the book of Genesis has moved repeatedly to establish God's preference for younger siblings.

The theme emerges with the very first children mentioned in the Bible. Strangely, the text offers no explanation for why God accepted the offering of Abel while rejecting that of his older brother Cain. The possibility that God's response may have been utterly arbitrary has occasioned an endless stream of speculative interpretations.[25] Many have thought that this reflects the values of the society in which the story originated. Others have proposed that the account depicts the origins of Kenite ("Cainite") nomadism. Still others consider it a culture myth, reflecting the tension between farmers (Cain) and shepherds (Abel), with God's preference for the latter a reflex of Israel's own nomadic origins.[26]

Growing evidence of Israel's agrarian background makes this latter view an increasingly difficult position to sustain.[27] Cain's agricultural life-style is itself problematic; the same chapter credits him with having built the first city (Gen 4:17). More directly relevant is the fact that the brothers' differing lifestyles play no narrative role aside from accounting for the different kinds of offerings they brought, and that is nowhere said to have been the reason for God's preference.[28]

The text's statement that Abel had "brought some firstlings (*bĕkōrôt*) of his flock and their fat portions (*ḥelbēhem*)" may offer a slight hint,[29] particularly since Cain's offering is said to have consisted of "some produce of the ground" (*mippĕrî hā'ădāmâ*, Gen 4:3–4). Given the economy of biblical style, this contrast can hardly be accidental. Abel gave the best that he had, while his brother brought whatever was on

[25] See, for example, Judah Goldin, "The Youngest Son or Where Does Genesis 38 Belong," *Journal of Biblical Literature* 96 (1977) 32–33, note 36.

[26] See Walter Dietrich, "'Wo ist dein Bruder?' Zu Tradition und Intention von Gen 4" in *Beiträge zur alttestamentliche Theologie, Festschrift für Walther Zimmerli zum 70. Geburtstag*, ed. H. Donner, R. Hanhart, and R. Smend (Göttingen: Vandenhoeck & Ruprecht, 1977) pp. 94–103, and S. Mowinckel, *The Two Sources of the Predeuteronomic Primeval History (JE) in Gen. 1–11* (Oslo: I Kommisjon Hos Jacob Dybwad, 1937) pp. 27–28. Bruce Vawter compares the Syriac word *habla*, meaning "shepherd," to the Hebrew form of Abel (*hebel; On Genesis, A New Reading* [Garden City, NY: Doubleday, 1977] p. 91).

[27] See note 19 in chapter 1.

[28] Nahum M. Sarna, *Understanding Genesis, The Heritage of Biblical Israel* (New York: Schocken, 1970) p. 28; cf. Claus Westermann, *Genesis* (BKAT; Neukirchen Vluyn: Neukirchener Verlag, 1974), p. 387.

[29] For the significance of fat, see J. Heller, "Die Symbolik des Fettes im AT," *Vetus Testamentum* 20 (1970) 106–8.

hand.[30] God's reaction, therefore, turns out not to have been arbitrary at all. As with David, He sees more deeply than we can, recognizing what we readers only slowly discover—that Cain was a poor prospect for either the blessing or human ancestry.[31]

Although birth order is not the crux of this story, neither is it entirely absent. The reference to Abel's firstlings (*bĕkōrôt*) calls our attention to an issue the text does not make explicit. Although Abel's death leaves Cain as the only member of this second generation of human beings, the line does not proceed through him, but through Seth, yet another younger brother whose birth is interpreted as compensation for the loss of Abel; even his name, we are told, means "replacement" (Gen 4:25). It is as if the author of Genesis could not allow an oldest son to be the ancestor of humanity, even by default.

The fact that this tradition may have originally dealt with issues that are no longer obvious and that it has since gone through several stages that had their own concerns before achieving its present from makes its preference for younger siblings all the more impressive. Although fraternal conflict is a common literary and traditional motif, which is often presented in ways that are similar to various biblical accounts, rarely is it set so early in human history.[32]

The virtue of Abel, the very first of the Bible's younger children, is shared by many of his successors. Indeed, relative merit plays an important role in the development of this motif. Rather than the unfolding of unexpected results, the impact of which would become progressively weaker as these tales recur throughout the biblical corpus, what they highlight is the disparity between appearance and reality. It is this, rather than the

---

[30] Although Hermann Gunkel's assertion that both brothers naturally (*natürlich*) brought their best products (*Genesis* [5th ed., HKAT; Göttingen: Vandenhoeck & Ruprecht, 1922] p. 42) has no textual support, *Targum Pseudo-Jonathan* does preserve a tradition that Cain brought first fruits (*qrbn bykwry'*). Several ancient sources perceive differences of motivation in the biblical description (e.g., Philo, *Questions and Answers on Genesis* nos. 59–61 [LCL pp. 36–37]; cf. *On the Sacrifices of Abel and Cain* 1 §1 [LCL vol. 2, pp. 94–97], Josephus *Antiquities* 1.2.2 §53 [LCL vol. 4, pp. 24–25], Hebrews 11:4, and 1 John 3:12).

[31] Walther Zimmerli contends that Cain's wickedness was the result of God's preference (*1. Mose 1–11* [3d ed., Zurcher Bibelkommentar; Zurich: Zwingli Verlag, 1967, c. 1943] p. 210).

[32] This despite Cuno Lehrmann's assertion that "Die Geschichten aller antiken Völker beginnen mit einem Brudermord" ("Betrachtungen zum Thema: Kain, Wo ist dein Bruder?" in *Brudermord, Zum Mythos von Kain und Abel*, ed. Joachim Illies [Munich: Kösel-Verlag, 1975] p. 88); other examples are noted under motif S 73.1 "Fratricide" in Stith Thompson, *Motif-Index of Folk-Literature*, vol. 5, p. 302. The point is only strengthened if the tradition of Cain and Abel was originally separate from that of Adam and Eve, as some scholars believe (e.g., Walther Zimmerli, *1. Mose 1–11*, p. 224).

element of surprise, which accounts for much of their emotional appeal. Like folklore's handsome princes locked inside of hideous beasts, these stories teach that outward appearance is not always an accurate gauge of inner worth. That is a message which is appealing to all of us, for it holds out the hope that we will eventually be rewarded, no matter how much our virtues seem to pass unnoticed.[33]

This element of consolation makes it difficult to accept the theory that these stories were written by younger offspring.[34] One need not have an older brother to be a younger sibling, or at least to feel like one. We identify with the youngest, weakest, *seemingly* dumbest character—with underdogs of all kinds—because on the most basic level we are all younger siblings, assigned by fate to a position that is lower than we deserve. Having experienced rejection (undeserved, of course), we feel thwarted by a world that does not recognize our virtue or our merit. The consolation these stories offer is thus reassuring to us all. The innocence, vulnerability, and virtue which play so important a role in the portrayal of these figures reinforce the reassurance and the sympathy these tales arouse.

Several biblical accounts join this widespread convention of a younger son's success to other common literary themes. Among these, that of the barren woman is particularly prominent. The dynamics of this motif are best approached by beginning with those incidents where it stands alone; examples include the stories of Samson's birth and Elisha's encounter with a Shunamite woman.[35] In both of these, the motif's tone of sympathy for its protagonists, who find themselves unable to achieve the fulfillment represented by children in biblical literature despite their merit or proclaimed destiny, is readily apparent. For these women eventually to conceive marks the realization of their full potential. More important, by introducing them as barren, the narrative turns the biological event of their conception into a sign of divine intervention, signaling God's commitment to their offspring's survival and success.[36] (Although the Shunamite's son plays only a minor role, our sympathy is crucial for the report of his apparent death a few verses later, in 2 Kings 4:20.) That

---

[33] Cf. Maria Tatar, *The Hard Facts of the Grimms' Fairy Tales*, p. 171.

[34] Cf. Irving D. Harris, *The Promised Seed, A Comparative Study of Eminent First and Later Sons* (New York: Free Press of Glencoe, 1964) p. 174.

[35] Mary Callaway suggests that the motif's appearance in the Samuel story is based on its occurrence in the account of Samson (*Sing, O Barren One, A Study in Comparative Midrash* [Atlanta, GA: Scholars Press, 1986] p. 36). E. Lipinski has proposed that the name Peninnah is indicative of fertility ("Peninna, Iti'el et l'athlète," *Vetus Testamentum* 17 [1967] 70–71).

[36] Cf. Azila Reisenberger, "*Harbah 'Arbeh*," *Beth Mikra* 36 (1990/91) 82.

the sons constitute the real focus of these tales is confirmed by their mothers' frequent anonymity.

In this respect, the Bible's barren woman motif parallels that of the younger child. Both link their protagonists' virtue with God's role in overcoming an ostensibly problematic situation. Although the barren women are usually presented as deserving offspring, they do not or cannot conceive. Credit for their eventual motherhood therefore belongs to God, making their offsprings' destiny and special blessing manifest. Like the younger child motif, the frequency of the theme of barren women in the Bible makes it a virtual convention, with the outcome virtually assured from the start. Just as we can be confident that younger sons will emerge triumphant, it is also reasonable to anticipate the birth of a great hero every time we read of a barren women.

How much this is so, particularly in the patriarchal period in which every favored wife is characterized this way, can be seen in the case of Rebecca, whose barrenness is mentioned in a surprisingly offhanded fashion and has no evident narrative consequences.[37] Unlike the other women presented in this way, her pregnancy seems to have occurred rather easily. Nor does her barrenness serve to distinguish one son from another, as in the case of Isaac and Ishmael or Joseph and his brothers. Because Rebecca is her husband's only wife and therefore the mother of all his children, the conception of her twins, Jacob and Esau, must be ascribed to divine intervention.

The impact of this motif is often sharpened by the juxtaposition of the barren women with other, fertile wives. The contrast is made clearer still when these fertile women taunt their barren rivals (Gen 16:4, 1 Sam 1:6), which increases our sense of both the latters' righteousness as well as the injustice of their situation.[38] Frequently, additional devices help to confirm the barren women's higher status as well as that of their eventual offspring. For example, Sarah is presented as Abraham's full

[37] Cf. Mary Callaway *Sing, O Barren One*, p. 30.

[38] By way of contrast, Rachel's jealousy (Gen 30:1) is given no basis in Leah's behavior, which is itself said to have been motivated by feelings of inferiority (e.g., Gen 29:31–34). Other examples of juxtaposed females include Lot's two daughters, the Egyptian and Israelite women mentioned in Exod 2:19, Deborah and Yael, the two prostitutes arguing before Solomon for the same child, Vashti and Esther, and in the New Testament Elizabeth and Mary, to whom Athalya Brenner contrasts the presentation of Ruth and Naomi (*The Israelite Woman, Social Role and Literary Type in Biblical Narrative* [Sheffield, England: JSOT Press, 1985] pp. 92–102); cf. Axel Olrik's "das Gesetz des Gegensatzes," which is described in his "Epic Laws of Folk Narrative" in *The Study of Folklore*, ed. Alan Dundes (Englewood Cliffs, NJ: Prentice-Hall, 1965) p. 135, and the comments of Max Lüthi, *Das europäische Volksmärchen, Form und Wesen* (2d ed., Bern: Francke Verlag, 1960) pp. 34–35.

wife, whereas Hagar was only a concubine, and Rachel is said to have been more attractive than her sister Leah and to enjoy her husband's special love. The resulting contrast dramatizes these women's dilemma, simultaneously heightening both their worth and their lack of fulfillment. The result is a biblical version of the Cinderella syndrome in which better-positioned, though less worthy, rivals prevent the success of a deserving heroine.[39] It is this tension which the divine intervention resolves, by bringing these women's situation into harmony with their merit.

As a result of this pattern's prevalence in biblical literature, several of its heroes are left with older half-brothers. However, it is not their youth which is the central concern of these stories; that is but an incidental by-product of the fact that their mothers' initial barrenness has been emphasized by contrasting them with other, fertile wives.

This dynamic can be demonstrated by the stories of Samuel and Joseph, each of whom was born to the preferred of a pair of wives. Although Hannah is not explicitly said to have been better loved than Peninnah, her husband did give her a special gift, and she is presented in a consistently sympathetic way, whereas Peninnah comes across as a taunting shrew. Although Leah is not painted in these derogatory colors, she is contrasted with her sister at every opportunity. Jacob's preference for Rachel is clear from their first meeting.

Both stories ascribe their protagonists' eventual pregnancy to divine intervention (Gen 30:22, 1 Sam 1:19); that is also implied by earlier announcements crediting God with having closed their wombs (Gen 29:31, 1 Sam 1:6). God's role in the birth of Samuel is further emphasized by the explanation given for the newborn's name (*šĕmûʾēl*), which is said to have derived from the fact that Hannah had asked God (*šĕʾiltîw*) for the child (1 Sam 1:20).[40] God's part is their birth implies an interest in their future as well, thereby adding the implication of divine blessing to the special way in which they had been conceived.

Support for our observation that birth order is not central to these stories can be found in the Bible's acknowledgment that Hannah bore

---

[39] Cf. James G. Williams, "The Beautiful and the Barren: Conventions in Biblical Type-Scenes," *Journal for the Study of the Old Testament* 17 (1980) 107–19; these stories fit under Stith Thompson's rubric "Reversals of Fortune" (category "L" in *Motif-Index of Folk-Literature*, vol. 5, pp. 6–26) as do Jesus' birth to the virgin Mary and Luke's account of John the Baptist's birth to the barren and elderly Elizabeth.

[40] This explanation is widely considered originally to have referred to Saul, but see Yairah Amit, "'*Hûʾ šāʾûl l-YHWH*,' *Remizah Mehadeqqet, mi-Šiṭoteha shel ha-ʿArikhah ha-Sifrutit*," *Beth Mikra* 27 (1981/82) 238–43, and Mattitiahu Tsevat, "Die Namengebung Samuels und die Substitutionstheorie," *Zeitschrift für die Alttestamentliche Wissenschaft* 99 (1987) 250–54.

five children after Samuel (1 Sam 2:21). Joseph, too, was not his father's youngest child, nor even his mother's, a position reserved for Benjamin, who is repeatedly identified as the smallest (*haqqāṭān*) and whose birth is set long after that of his brothers.[41] Like Samuel, Joseph's age and birth order are barely mentioned in the text. This is particularly apparent in their absence from the dreams which play so central a role in this account, foreshadowing much of the story's development. Joseph described his first dream to his brothers by reporting, "We were binding sheaves in the field when suddenly my sheaf stood upright; then your sheaves gathered round and bowed down to my sheaf" (Gen 37:7). In his own telling, Joseph's sheaf seems to be just one among many, neither smaller nor larger than the rest. A similar view can be found in his second dream, in which "the sun, the moon, and eleven starts were bowing down to me" (v. 9). In this case, only his parents are distinct; their sons are represented equally, each with his own star, except for Joseph who has no symbol at all.

Although the impossibility of discerning the brothers' relative ages from this passage is remarkable, it may not be irrelevant, for despite their virtual anonymity and interchangeability, those brothers who have major roles are invariably the oldest or the youngest offspring of Jacob's full wives.[42] Still, what sets Joseph apart is not that he was the youngest son, but the fact that he was born in his father's old age (Gen 37:3) to Jacob's favorite wife, a connection made clear in the description of him as "attractive and good-looking" (*yph-tō'ar wyph mar'eh*), exactly the same phrase used earlier to describe his mother Rachel (Gen 29:17, 39:6).[43] It is this which makes Joseph distinct from his brothers, who have barely any distinguishing characteristics at all.

Although Joseph was not the youngest son, Benjamin, who does hold that position, functions as a kind of alter ego for him. They share both a common mother and the depiction as sons of Jacob's old age (Gen 44:20).[44] This parallel is extended in the account of the brothers' arrival

[41] Gen 42:13, 15, 20, 32, 34, 43:29, 44:2, 12, 20, 23, 26. His birth is presented in Gen 35:16–18; cf. Martin Noth, *A History of Pentateuchal Traditions* (Englewood Cliffs, NJ: Prentice-Hall, 1972) p. 210.

[42] The sole exception is Simeon, who, as his mother's second son, was a good equivalent for Benjamin (Meir Sternberg, *The Poetics of Biblical Narrative*, p. 291).

[43] Cf. *Genesis Rabbah* 86:6.

[44] For Joseph, this is problematic, since his birth is presented immediately after that of his brothers, all of which took place during Jacob's twenty-year Aramean sojourn (Gen 31:38), the first fourteen of which were devoted to earning his two wives. Joseph could not, therefore, have been substantially younger than the others, leading *Targum Onqelos* to render the Hebrew *ben zĕqunîm* as *bar ḥakkîm* (Gen 37:3); Nahmanides explains that all Jacob's sons had been born in their father's old age.

in Egypt, where they had come to purchase grain during a period of famine. By that time, Joseph had fulfilled his earlier dreams and achieved substantial power and importance in the Egyptian court.[45] But when his brothers failed to recognize him, Joseph seized the opportunity to determine whether their hostility had passed by using Benjamin to duplicate the conditions of his own earlier mistreatment: taking Simeon hostage and charging his brothers with espionage, Joseph demanded that they bring their "youngest brother," who had stayed behind with their father, just as Joseph used to do (Gen 37:12–13). After they had complied, he arranged the family in order of seniority, giving Benjamin an extravagant portion, five times that of the others (Gen 43:34), much as he had been favored by Jacob so long before. Then, he framed Benjamin for theft, announcing that "the one in whose possession the goblet is found shall be my slave; [the rest of] you go back to your father in peace" (Gen 44:17). In order to return home, therefore, the brothers had only to abandon this favored younger son of a different mother who had now become the cause of their problems; but they did not. Instead, Judah stepped forward in Benjamin's behalf, much as he had done earlier for Joseph. Convinced they had changed, Joseph then identified himself.

The impression of Benjamin's vulnerability is maximized by the emphasis on his youth, much as Joseph's fate had been the result of his brothers' collectively greater strength. God's interest in the offspring of a favored, once barren woman is thus emphasized again. Throughout this, however, the hero's being a youngest child is largely incidental, much as it was in the case of Cain and Abel, where God's preference was determined by other factors. For both Joseph and Samuel, being younger children is best understood as a by-product of other narrative motifs, whether their mothers' barrenness or the fact of their own youthfulness. Both of these themes share several connotations with that of youngest children, including blessedness, vulnerability, and innocence.

Another motif that frequently intersects with that of youngest children in the Bible is the sole survivor, which is also widely attested in world literature.[46] Its significance can be illustrated by two familiar examples drawn from popular American culture—Superman and the Lone Ranger,

---

[45] Thus Donald B. Redford's identification of the story's theme as "the boy who had a dream of future greatness" (*A Study of the Biblical Story of Joseph* [*Genesis 37–50*] [Supplement to *Vetus Testamentum* 20 (Leiden: E. J. Brill, 1970) p. 69]); cf. Antti Aarne and Stith Thompson's folktale type 725 ("The Dream") in *The Types of the Folktale, A Classification and Bibliography* (2d rev., FF Communications 184; Helsinki: Suomalainen Tiedakatemia, Academia Scientiarum Fennica, 1961) pp. 250–51.

[46] Stith Thompson, *Motif-Index of Folk-Literature*, Z 356 (vol. 5, p. 576); it is part of the much larger category "unique exception" (Z 300, p. 565).

the latter himself possibly a younger son.[47] (As the only inhabitant of the planet Krypton to have survived its massive explosion, Superman was an only child.[48]) For only a single individual to have survived such disasters emphasizes both the magnitude of the danger and the survivor's uniqueness and importance. Such stories marry the threat of overwhelming destruction with the hope implicit in anyone's having endured the unendurable. Like the offspring of barren women, those who escape such catastrophes are the sole hope for those they represent and are thereby marked for greatness. Innocence and vulnerability are inherent in the structure of such tales, along with the blessedness of their heroes, which follows from their having survived an otherwise all-encompassing act of devastation. This adds a further facet to their depiction—namely the mission with which their unique survival leaves them charged.

These narrative implications are enhanced when the sole survivor turns out to be a youngest child. The vulnerability and innocence inherent in youth are obviously increased by the circumstances they have endured as well as our sympathy, which is sometimes magnified by presenting the death of older siblings as having taken place one at a time. A familiar example is the Jewish legend of the woman whose seven sons were executed by a pagan king. These are typically presented in the order of their age, creating a sense of drama as the reader awaits the ruler's inevitable confrontation with the last child.[49] The impression of that son's innocence is enhanced by his offering a lengthy speech, which provides an opportunity to reiterate both his virtue and his right to survive.

Biblical literature includes a substantial number of sole survivors. Job learns of the various catastrophes to which he was subjected from such figures (Job 1:15–19). Lot and his daughters, who were the only ones to have escaped the destruction of Sodom and Gomorrah, belong

---

[47] Jim Harmon, *The Great Radio Heroes* (Garden City NY: Doubleday and Co., 1967) p. 196.

[48] As the Superman saga developed, other survivors emerged (see D. O'Neil, "The Man of Steel and Me" in *Superman at Fifty, The Persistence of a Legend*, ed. Dennis Dooley and Gary Engle (Cleveland, OH: Octavia Press, 1987) pp. 52–53. Biblical links are apparent in Superman's original name Kal-El; for parallels with Christ and medieval saints, see Edward Mehok, "St. Clark of Krypton," ibid., pp. 123–29.

[49] In some accounts, the children are simply numbered (e.g., *b. Giṭṭin* 57b), whereas the last son's being the youngest is emphasized in 4 Maccabees (e.g., 11:14 and 12:1; cf. *Lamentations Rabbah* 1:16 §50, where he is said to have been only two and one-half years old at the time). The mother herself is not always said to have been killed, although she does usually die. Other versions are in 2 Maccabees 7, *Seder Eliahu Rabbah* 30 (28; ed. M. Friedman, p. 151), and *Pesiqta Rabbati* 43 (ed. M. Friedman, p. 180b), which adds that their mother had previously been barren.

in this category, as do the inhabitants of Noah's ark. During the monarchic period, Joash was the only one of Ahaziah's sons to have survived the wrath of the queen mother Athaliah (2 Kings 11:2).[50]

This motif is frequently associated with the possibility of redemption. Outside the Bible, such figures' potential can be seen in the case of Zeus, king of the Greek gods, who was the youngest of Kronos's sons and the only one to have survived his father's murderous impulses.[51] Similar overtones can be found in Zechariah's description of those who endured God's punishing wrath as "a brand plucked from the fire" (*'ûd muṣṣāl mē'ēš*, 3:2).[52] Having barely avoided a great threat, the survivors of the exile offer a glimmer of hope.

Returning to the Bible's youngest children who are the focus of our attention, we find several who achieved positions of prominence as a result of their siblings' death or elimination from eligibility. An example from the early Israelite priesthood are Aaron's sons Eleazar and Ithamar, who received the responsibilities of their deceased brothers Nadab and Abihu (Leviticus 10). Although birth order is never stated outright in this account, Nadab and Abihu are consistently mentioned first in lists of Aaron's offspring and the former even identified once as his *bĕkōr*.[53] Although this story has been widely interpreted as legitimating certain elements of the Israelite priesthood, it cannot easily be explained as an expression of later generations' discomfort with the fact that these lines were not the oldest, given the absence of evidence that priestly status was based on seniority in ancient Israel.[54] For our purposes, it is sufficient to note that Eleazar and Ithamar's prominence was due to their siblings' transgression. As with the offspring of barren women, their being younger is apparently incidental to other narrative concerns. Their brothers' sin does, however, imply Eleazar and Ithamar's own innocence, while provid-

---

[50] Despite the inference of many interpreters from antiquity (e.g., Josephus, *Antiquities* 9.7.1 §142 [LCL vol. 6, pp. 76–77]) to the present day (e.g., Hugo Gressmann, *Die Anfänge Israels* [Göttingen: Vandenhoeck & Ruprecht, 1922] p. 215), the Bible never identifies Joash as a youngest child, although that may be inferred from the reference to his nurse (*mēniqtô*) in 2 Kings 11:2. For folkloric characteristics of this account, see M. Liverani, "L'Histoire de Joas," *Vetus Testamentum* 24 (1974) 438–53.

[51] Hesiod, *Theogony* 453–90 (LCL pp. 112–15).

[52] Cf. Amos 4:11.

[53] Num 3:2; cf. Exod 6:23, 28:1, Num 26:60, 1 Chron 5:29 (ET 6:3), and 24:1 (but see pp. 64–66 above).

[54] Contra John C. H. Laughlin, "The 'Strange Fire' of Nadab and Abihu," *Journal of Biblical Literature* 95 (1976) 562–63; see p. 22 above. A surprisingly persistent view links Nadab and Abihu with the sons of Jeroboam; e.g., Moses Aberbach and Leivy Smoler, "Aaron, Jeroboam, and the Golden Calves," *Journal of Biblical Literature* 86 (1967) 129–40.

ing circumstances that suggest they were able to survive when others could
not, nuances often associated with younger siblings.

The best example of a youngest sibling who was also a sole survivor
in the Bible is offered by the book of Chronicles' account of the accession
of Ahaziah, son of Jehoram, to the Judean throne. Whereas the book of
Kings mentions only that his reign followed his father's death (2 Kings
8:24), Chronicles presents Ahaziah as the youngest in his family, explaining his succession as the result of his brothers' having been taken captive
by the Arabs and the Philistines (2 Chron 21:16–22:1).[55]

Although Chronicles' reliability is no longer suspect in the way it
once was, there is reason to be skeptical about this particular episode.
For Ahaziah to have been forty-two at the time of his accession (2 Chron
22:2), he would have to have been older than his father, who died at the
age of forty (21:20). Following other traditions, which set his birth when
his father was between eighteen and twenty-four, raises questions about
2 Kings' reference to his having had forty-two older brothers (10:13–14).[56]
These difficulties are compounded by allusions to those brothers' having
been in Jerusalem well after Ahaziah's accession, this despite the tradition
of their captivity.[57]

In light of these problems and the "folkloric" portrayal of Ahaziah
as a sole survivor, it is reasonable to suspect that the Chronicler's account
of his accession may be more legendary than historical.[58] It marks this
king as both innocent, by virtue of being a youngest son, and blessed, as
demonstrated by his having escaped captivity. Not only did Ahaziah
benefit from God's protection, but the people of Judah were also lucky
that their royal line had been preserved by this thinnest of threads. What
a fortunate conjunction of circumstances that so blessed a figure was
available to protect Judah from the extinction of its divinely ordained

---

[55] The received text refers to him as Jehoahaz in 21:17, but the Septuagint, Peshitta,
Targum, and several Hebrew manuscripts preserve the reading Ahaziah.

[56] Cf. 2 Chron 21:17. On the basis of 2 Kings 2:24 and Revelation 13:5, John Gray
suggests that this number is typological (*I and II Kings, A Commentary* [OTL, 2d ed.;
Philadelphia: Westminster Press, 1970] p. 556). Evidence suggesting that Ahaziah was in
late adolescence or early adulthood at the time of his accession can be found in 2 Kings
8:26 and various ancient witnesses to 2 Chron 22:2.

[57] 2 Kings 10:13–14.

[58] So too Edward L. Curtis and Albert A. Madsen, *A Critical and Exegetical
Commentary on the Books of Chronicles* (ICC; New York: Charles Scribner's Sons, 1910)
p. 417, and Jacob M. Myers, *II Chronicles* (AB; Garden City, NY: Doubleday, 1965) p. 123.
Peter Ackroyd suggests that the theme contrasts Ahaziah with his father, who is identified
as *běkōr* (2 Chron 21:3, *I & II Chronicles, Ezra, Nehemiah* [London: SCM Press Ltd., 1973]
p. 232).

dynasty. As the sole link with Judah's royal past, Ahaziah thus functions as a sign of God's continuing concern.

Somewhat less dramatic is the case of Saul's daughters Merab and Michal. Like Leah and Rachel, these sisters shared a relationship with the same man, each having been promised to David, albeit at different times.[59] As in that better-known case, here too the younger daughter is clearly favored, even if Michal's youth is less prominent than Rachel's. It was her older sister Merab whom Saul had promised to David in return for defeating the Philistines, although by the time that task was completed she had been given to another man. However, Michal's love for David provides her father with another opportunity to send him into battle. Unfortunately, the revelation of her feelings leaves Michal emotionally vulnerable both to Saul and to David, whose actions seem to owe more to political considerations than to emotion. In this respect, too, Michal is distinguished from Merab, whose feelings, like those of Hagar and Leah, are largely ignored. Her frailty is also emphasized by the announcement of her barrenness, which varies from the common pattern in that it comes at the story's end (2 Sam 6:23), leaving no opportunity for rectification. Although the reason for her plight is not explained, it appears to have resulted from lack of conjugal attention, perhaps because of David's anger or his loss of interest after she had disapproved of his behavior when the ark was brought into Jerusalem (v. 20). In any event, Michal's inability to conceive contrasts with Merab's fertility.[60]

This story, then, provides a variation of the rival wife motif, but without the fulfillment that is usually expected. In it, youth is coupled with vulnerability and innocence, and these and Michal's expression of love for David evoke our sympathy. Ultimately she is dependent on others. The successful fulfillment of her initial goal—marrying David— owes less to her own merit than to her father's identity and the fact that her sister was no longer available. By the story's end, Michal is the lesser sister on all counts—a barren younger daughter chosen second by both her father and, apparently, her husband.

---

[59] The parallels between Rachel-Leah and Michal-Merab are enumerated by Adele Berlin, "Literary Exegesis of Biblical Narrative: Between Poetics and Hermeneutics" in *"Not in Heaven." Coherence and Complexity in Biblical Narrative*, ed. Jason P. Rosenblatt and Joseph Sitterson, Jr. (Bloomington, IN: Indiana University Press, 1991) pp. 120–21.

[60] Several Hebrew manuscripts, LXX[L], and the Targum support the scholarly consensus that the reference to Michal's children in 2 Sam 21:8 is a textual error for Merab; cf. also the Peshitta's *ndb*. For a different view, see J. J. Glück, "Merab or Michal," *Zeitschrift für die Alttestamentliche Wissenschaft* 77 (1965) 72–81.

The repetition of motifs in the Bible's description of David's relationships with these two sisters, each of whom was eventually given to another man, has been taken by some as evidence that the stories of Merab and Michal are variant versions of what was once a single episode.[61] If this is correct, the relationship between these women may owe more to editorial harmonization after the stories had been combined than to original authorship. Again, the fact that a biblical character is a younger sibling turns out to be a by-product of other circumstances, though this in no way reduces its importance in the way these stories are told.

Several of these elements converge in the story of Moses, one of the most familiar of the Bible's youngest sons. His birth is described immediately after the announcement of Pharaoh's edict that all newborn Israelite males be drowned, a juxtaposition that maximizes the connotations of innocence, vulnerability, and promise. This latter point is reinforced by several elements in the biblical narrative. For example, the inclusion of various phrases and motifs that will play a prominent role in the later account of Israel's escape from slavery foreshadow Moses' coming role,[62] much as his relationship to Egyptian authority is signaled by his mother's compliance with the letter of Pharaoh's decree to "throw every newborn son into the river" (Exod 1:22), which totally undermines its intent. From the start, there can be little doubt that this child represents Israel's hope in the coming annihilation.

Through it all, Moses' family rank is never made explicit. As a result and because of the narrative's phrasing, "A man from the house of Levi married a Levite woman who conceived and bore a son..." (Exod 2:1–2), some have thought that Moses was once regarded as firstborn.[63] The existing narrative makes such a contention implausible. Genealogical notices are not alone in presenting his siblings as older. There are also a number of indications, both implicit and expressed, which support Aaron's

---

[61] Cf. 1 Sam 18:17–19, 25–27, 25:44. The narrative concerning Michal is missing from several of the Greek texts; see Hans W. Hertzberg *I and II Samuel*, pp. 159–60, and P. Kyle McCarter, Jr., *I Samuel* (AB; Garden City, NY: Doubleday, 1980) pp. 305–7. Regarding 1 Sam 18:21b, see Shemaryahu Talmon, "The Textual Study of the Bible—A New Outlook" in *Qumran and the History of the Biblical Text*, ed. Shemaryahu Talmon and Frank M. Cross (Cambridge, MA: Harvard University Press, 1975) p. 363 and note 175 on p. 396.

[62] See James Ackerman, "The Literary Context of the Moses Birth Story (Exodus 1–2)" in *Literary Interpretations of Biblical Narratives*, ed. Kenneth R. R. Gros Louis et al. (Nashville, TN: Abingdon Press, 1974) pp. 94–103; so already *Midrash Sekhel Ṭov 'al Bereishit u-Shemot*, ed. Solomon Buber (Berlin: H. Itzkowski, 1900) p. 13.

[63] E.g., J. Coert Rylaarsdam in *The Interpreter's Bible* at Exod 1:2 (vol. 1, p. 858). Sensitive to the apparent implication of these verses, the rabbis inferred that Moses had been born only after a self-imposed separation by Amram and Zipporah (*b. Soṭa* 12a).

seniority[64] in addition to the reference to an unnamed sister who makes arrangements for her baby brother to be nursed by his natural mother, even as he is raised in the royal palace (Exod 2:4, 7). In light of these statements and the frequency with which the births of daughters and less important sons are ignored in biblical literature, the ambiguity of the opening sentence is hardly a strong enough basis on which to discredit the explicit presentation of Moses as a younger son, however prebiblical traditions may have understood his relationship to Aaron and Miriam.[65]

Presenting Moses as a younger child evokes all the nuances that we have found associated with this motif. Both innocence and vulnerability play an important role in the accounts that follow, as does the potential commonly associated with such figures. His ability to endure catastrophe marks him as blessed before the story has really begun, leaving the reader with little reason to worry whether Israel will emerge from Pharaoh's genocidal oppression. Both the people's salvation and the identity of their eventual savior have been signaled from the story's start.

By placing Moses' birth within the context of the Egyptian oppression, the nature of the looming disaster is blurred and a report of destruction set up to be evidence of God's beneficence. Israel's apparent doom constitutes the circumstance necessary for their salvation.

The powerlessness of Israel bound in Egyptian slavery is mirrored in Moses' later encounter with Pharaoh, whose decree of death he had only barely escaped. Moses' weaknesses, of which being a younger child is only one, make him an apt symbol for this suffering people, but his performance belies the vulnerability of his situation. Although lacking in self-confidence, Moses was firm and effective, a shift reasonably ascribed to his growing conviction and appreciation of God's power. In this, the narrative tacitly acknowledges the disparity between appearances and reality.

God's role is made explicit in His threat to the Egyptian *běkōrôt*, which we know to be justified on the basis that "Israel is My *běkōr* . . . . [so] let My son go that he may serve Me; if you refuse to let him go, then I will slay your *běkōr*" (Exod 4:22). In this, Moses does not, therefore, stand alone, nor will Pharaoh be the only one to suffer the consequences of his response. Each represents a larger constituency. Their meeting dramatizes the threat that powerful Egypt posed to vulnerable Israel.

---

[64] Exod 7:7, cf. 6:20. One Hebrew manuscript, the Septuagint, Peshitta, and Samaritan Pentateuch include Miriam in Exod 6:20. 15:20 notes her only as Aaron's sister.

[65] See Martin Noth, *Exodus, A Commentary* (OTL; Philadelphia: Westminster Press, 1962) pp. 122–23.

God's choice of a younger son with suspect capabilities (Exod 6:12, 30) to negotiate with this leader of a powerful empire illustrates the identity of Pharaoh's real adversary. The prominence of younger sons thus converges with the themes of barren mothers and sole survivors in its implication that the success of such figures rests not in their own strength, but in their being favored by God.

It is in this respect that the biblical account differs from occurrences of this motif in other bodies of literature, where the younger sons' success is a result of their own hidden skills. As the case of Moses demonstrates, biblical figures may be legitimately less capable than others. Moses uses that fact to justify his efforts to avoid the mission he has been given (Exodus 3-4). However, God's response—that it is He who provides the necessary skills (Exod 4:11)—is precisely the point. Human ability is irrelevant in the face of a God like that of Israel. The very frailty of her heroes emphasizes the locus of real power.

The familiarity of this theme comes to play a central role in the stories of Jotham and of Judah and Tamar. There these expectations provide a basis from which the narrative can then stray. The story of Judah and Tamar (Genesis 38) has already been discussed in the context of levirate marriage.[66] Tamar had been widowed when her husband, who was Judah's oldest son, died without children. She was then given to a younger son Onan in accordance with biblical law (Deut 25:5-10). When he in turn died, our attention is directed towards Shelah, Judah's sole remaining son, whom we expect will rise to the occasion and fulfill his biblically mandated duty. Shelah's status as a youngest son and the sole survivor of this threesome mark him as a figure of destiny; however, his brothers' fate heightens our awareness of Shelah's vulnerability and poses a threat to the whole of Judah's line.[67]

We have already seen that there is no evidence that levirate responsibilities were actually transmitted in the order of birth.[68] As in the biblical story of David and the later legend of the woman's seven sons, proceeding in order of the brothers' ages functions to heighten the readers' suspense while directing both our attention and our sympathies towards this threatened youngest child. The impact is strengthened by the account's conformity to the common "law of three" (*das Gesetz der Dreizahl*),[69] familiar from

[66] See pp. 52–54 above.

[67] Cf. Mordecai A. Friedman, "Tamar, A Symbol of Life: The 'Killer Wife' Superstition in the Bible and Jewish Tradition," *AJSreview* 15 (1990) 23–61.

[68] See pp. 52–53 above. Deuteronomy places the responsibility on "her brother-in-law" (*yĕbāmâ*), leaving the number of surviving sons who fall under this obligation indeterminate.

[69] Axel Olrik, "Epic Laws of Folk Narrative" in *The Study of Folklore*, p. 133.

such tales as The Three Little Pigs or the innumerable jokes involving a Protestant, a Catholic, and a Jew, in which repetition is used to build suspense until the climax arrives in the third instance.

While our expectations are thus focused on Shelah, the last remaining son, his brothers' fate suggests that his future, too, may be at risk. For Judah to withhold Shelah is what any parent might do, but he thereby violates God's will, forcing Tamar to contrive a plan in order to obtain the son to whom she was entitled. By protecting his youngest son, Judah ironically sealed his own fate.

Through all of this, Shelah himself plays no role. His passivity befits a youngest child and points to the incident's denouement. After producing only minor descendants, he disappears from the Bible, his heirs barely mentioned alongside his half-brothers Perez and Zerah in Chronicles' genealogy.[70] Instead, the promised line, leading eventually to King David, emerges directly from his father.

This account uses familiar themes in an unfamiliar way. Where the "law of three" and Shelah's status as a younger son and sole survivor mark him as destined for greatness, his passivity is a more accurate barometer of his ultimate fate. Prepared to see in him the story's climax, our attention has been misdirected. Rather than conforming to convention, its impact derives from the willingness to deviate from what it has led us to expect.[71]

A similar technique can be discerned in the story of Jotham. He is introduced as the only one of Gideon's seventy sons to have survived the bloodbath which his half-brother Abimelech perpetrated in an attempt to consolidate power over the city of Shechem (Judg 9:5). Neither this effort nor its results were unique. Several biblical rulers are said to have slaughtered their rivals,[72] and, as we have seen, it was not uncommon for only one person, particularly a youngest child, to survive such an onslaught. Like Shelah, Jotham's youth suggests innocence and vulnerability, while his survival demonstrates his blessed status. The stakes of their contest are raised by the powerful contrast with the vicious Abimelech, who also provides a foil.

As a sole surviving, youngest son, Jotham should be destined for greatness, with Abimelech (whose family rank is never stated) the obvious

---

[70] Intriguingly, one of Shelah's sons bears the same name (Er) as his father's older brother; see 1 Chron 4:21 as well as 2:3–6, 9:4–6, and Num 26:20–21.

[71] Cf. Robert Alter, *The Art of Biblical Narrative*, pp. 60–62.

[72] E.g., 2 Kings 10:1–7, 11:1, 2 Chron 21:4.

obstacle. Their antagonism was patently mutual. Jotham compared his half-brother, who had tried to kill *all* of Gideon's other sons, to a thorn-bush, threatening to send forth fire (Judg 9:15). The risk was magnified when Jotham proclaimed, "May fire come forth from Abimelech and devour the rulers of Shechem and Beth-Millo, and may fire come forth from the rulers of Shechem and from Beth-Millo and devour Abimelech" (v. 20).

Although his rival's days were numbered, Jotham's threat was not entirely realized. Abimelech fell, but not to the rulers of Shechem, nor was he replaced by the more appropriate, if younger brother. Defeat came instead at the hands of Gaal (lit. "dung beetle"), who seems even less worthy than he.[73] This son of a slave girl (v. 18, cf. 8:31) thus fell to the son of a slave (*ben 'ebed*, 9:26) before he was finally killed by a woman (9:53–54). Through all this, the city's leadership is left suspended. The story ends with Jotham, from whom great things were to be expected, in hiding as he was when it began (9:21, cf. v. 5). Our expectations are unful-filled. He was right after all: only the least likely come to rule.[74]

Although in its present context this conclusion may have a political point, the underlying message—that leaders are not always those most obviously suited for their positions—is a common theme in the Hebrew Bible. Gideon and Saul both questioned their appropriateness for divine assignments. Gideon asked, "How can I save Israel? My clan is the weakest in Manasseh, and I am the youngest in my father's household" (Judg 6:15). Later, Saul responded to Samuel's announced intention of making him king by pointing out that he was from the smallest family in Israel's smallest tribe (1 Sam 9:21), this despite the Bible's description of his impressive physique and indications that his father was a wealthy land-owner.[75] Gideon was also addressed as a *gibbôr ḥayil* (Judg 6:12) and his family as one of rank.[76] Whether these expressions of reluctance are formulaic elements in response to divine calls or rhetorical statements of humility by those who dared not admit their sense of worth,[77] they play a significant role as the biblical accounts unfold. A similar point can be

---

[73] A. D. Crown, "A Reinterpretation of Judges IX in the Light of Its Humor," *Abr-Nahrain* 3 (1961/62) 93.

[74] For the fable's background, see Eugene H. Maly, "The Jotham Fable—Anti-Monarchical?" *Catholic Biblical Quarterly* 22 (1960) 297–305.

[75] 1 Sam 9:1–3 and 15:17, to which Rashi compares Ps 68:28.

[76] If Gideon's response is taken seriously, the use of this title as a vocative may be rhetorical. J. Alberto Soggin cites especially Judg 8:18 (*Judges* [OTL; Philadelphia: West-minster Press, 1981] p. 119); see also Judg 6:25–27.

[77] N. Habel, "The Form and Significance of the Call Narratives," *Zeitschrift für die Alttestamentliche Wissenschaft* 77 (1965) 298–300; cf. Exod 3:11, 1 Sam 18:18, Isa 6:5, Jer 1:6, and Job 32:6.

sensed in the prophet's announcement that Israel's future ruler will come from "Bethlehem Ephrata, the smallest (ṣāʿîr) among the families of Judah" (Micah 5:1). By downplaying the stature of Israelite leaders, their achievements are maximized along with God's role in their success. As Samuel told Saul, "Was it not in your own eyes that you were small..." (1 Sam 15:17).[78] Or, in the psalmist's words: "The stone which the builder rejected has become the cornerstone" (118:22).[79]

The book of Judges makes this point explicit in its report of God's demand that Gideon reduce the number of his soldiers before going to battle against the Midianites: "The people with you are too many for Me to deliver Midian into their hands," God says, "lest Israel claim for themselves the glory due Me, thinking, 'It is my hand which has brought me victory'" (Judg 7:2).

God's preference for unlikely figures is a well-established theme of biblical literature, most vividly apparent in the remarkable succession of heroes who fill the book of Judges, including a woman, the son of a prostitute, and a left-handed guerilla.[80] Indeed, its most conventional hero, the mighty Samson, is the only one whose enemy remained unbeaten.[81] The nature of those who succeed in biblical lore demonstrates Israel's unique understanding of the importance of divine support as the source of true chosenness. A similar point can be seen in the prophetic concern for social justice and the Bible's widespread interest in orphans, strangers, and widows.[82] Deutero-Isaiah extends this into the eschatological realm with his assurance that "the small will become one thousand and the

---

[78] Arnold B. Ehrlich emends bĕ'êneykā ("in your eyes") to bĕ'amkā ("among your people," *Randglossen zur hebräischen Bibel, textkritisches, sprachliches und sachliches* [reprinted Hildesheim: Georg Olm Verlagsbuchhandlung, 1968] vol. 3, p. 218).

[79] Cf. Zech 4:6; in general, see Otto Bächli, "Die Erwählung des Geringen im Alten Testament," *Theologische Zeitschrift* 22 (1966) 385–95.

[80] Kenneth R. R. Gros Louis, "The Book of Judges" in *Literary Interpretations of Biblical Narratives*, ed. Kenneth R. R. Gros Louis et al. (Nashville, TN: Abingdon Press, 1974) p. 160.

[81] The Bible speaks of him as only "*beginning* to save Israel from the Philistines" (Judg 13:5, italics added); see Avraham Qariv, "Ḥidat Shimshon u-Fishrah," *Karmelit* 10 (1963) 36–37.

[82] E.g., 1 Sam 2:8, Isa 13:11, 40:29, 54:1, Pss 35:10, 68:6, 147:6, Job 5:11; cf. Matthew 5:3–11, 19:30, 20:16, Luke 1:52. This motif has widespread Near Eastern analogues; see, for example, lines 35–36 of the Egyptian inscription of Udjahorresne (Miriam Lichtheim, *Ancient Egyptian Literature, A Book of Readings* [Berkeley, CA: University of California Press, 1980] vol. 3, p. 39), Esarhaddon's inscriptions 8.18–31 (Riekele Borger, *Die Inschriften Asarhaddons Königs von Assyrien*, p. 25, cf. pp. 94 [line 35] and 110 [line 21]), and Shurpu 4.16–18 and 31–32 (Erica Reiner, *Šurpu, A Collection of Sumerian and Akkadian Incantations* [AfO Beiheft 11, Graz: 1958] pp. 25–26). Citations from several hymns are provided by Charles G. Cumming, *The Assyrian and Hebrew Hymns of Praise* (New York: Columbia University Press, 1934) pp. 140–42.

youngest a mighty nation" (*haqqāṭōn yiḥĕyeh lāʾelep wĕhaṣṣāʿîr lĕgôy ʿāṣûm*, 60:22). The prophet may have had Israel's return from exile in mind, but such activities were neither new nor out of character for this God, who "sets prisoners free... restores sight to the blind... straightens up those who are bent... loves the righteous... watches over the stranger, giving courage to the orphan and widow" (Ps 146:7–9). Committed to the least likely of partners, the power of Israel's God was dramatized in His commitment to society's weakest members.

Although this theme contrasts the world we know with that which God intends, it is not a call to revolt. Biblical authors have little confidence in the quality of our choices. Nor do they make much difference, since God's will can be done with the *least* likely of leaders. His power ensures that what is need not limit what will be, offering reassurance that the lowly status of so many of society's underclass is neither inevitable nor unending. Such unlikely figures demonstrate the divine basis for true accomplishment. Youngest children, sole survivors, and the offspring of barren women fit this collection well. Their precarious existence emphasizes God's responsibility for their success.

Setting the Bible's interest in youngest sons within this larger context of its preference for ostensibly unlikely heroes is illuminating for the way Israel is portrayed as a whole. Deuteronomy puts this most succinctly when it describes her as "the least among the nations" (7:7, cf. 9:5).[83] Although the words are unique to this setting, its point—that Israel was an ostensibly unlikely choice—is hardly idiosyncratic. Genesis begins Israel's history with God's assurance that a family of vagabonds would eventually fill their own land with descendants too numerous to count.[84] Elsewhere, the nation is said to have been fashioned from a "mixed multitude" of escaped slaves.[85]

That Israel saw herself this way helps to explain the number of her heroes who are presented as having been less than obvious choices for divine election. Moses in Pharaoh's court, David before the Philistines, and Elijah on Mount Carmel—all join the group of youngest siblings in reflecting Israel's perception of herself as outnumbered.

That view is not at all inaccurate. Despite Israel's claim to be God's favorite among the families of the nations, the evidence of history shows

---

[83] Herodotus provides a interesting parallel in his report that "the Scythians say that their nation is the youngest in all the world" (4.5, LCL vol. 2, pp. 202–3).

[84] E.g., Gen 15:5, 32:13; cf. Gen 16:10, 1 Chron 16:15–20, and, retrospectively, Deut 26:5. Contrast biblical enumerations of the number of Israelites, particularly in their early period (e.g., Gen 46:26).

[85] Exod 12:35, Num 11:4.

rejection to have been her lot. Not only was she a younger people but, most of the time, a weak nation as well. The Bible acknowledges that by presenting the ancestors of Israel's rivals as older and more powerful than her own.

Israel's image of herself as God's *bĕkōr* resolves this tension between Israelite theology and political reality. Drawing on a father's prerogative to choose whichever child he wishes, it reconciles Israel's doctrine of election with the reality of her political ineffectiveness.

The prominence achieved by younger sons throughout the Bible thus asserts Israelite merit while tacitly conceding the weakness of her case. These stories are fundamentally the self-reassuring triumphalism of a weak and unsuccessful tribe, what Max Weber called "a rational theology of misfortune."[86] It is no wonder that the powerlessness of exile has been proposed as the most natural environment for these tales,[87] although the evidence is insufficient to prove this hypothesis and other settings could have been equally propitious. This is, in the end, a literature of consolation, designed to reassure those whose oppression contradicted their belief in God's concern. Its message is that given to Samuel—that appearances are deceiving. We might choose Pharaoh, but God prefers Moses, Gideon, and David. As Jotham knew, human choices are often poorly made. Real power, the Bible tells us, lies elsewhere.

From this perspective, it is easy to understand the point of anthropologist Victor Turner, who observed that moral values are most strictly upheld in small nations or, to put matters in more Nietzschean terms, that humanitarianism is a "ruse" of the weak, its message a kind of consolation in a world not entirely just.[88] To use the German philosopher's own words, the Bible effects a "slave revolt in morals," which may in part explain its attraction for generations of dispossessed.[89] Narratives

---

[86] "The Social Psychology of the World Religions" in *From Max Weber, Essays in Sociology*, ed. H. H. Gerth and C. Wright Mills (New York: Oxford University Press, 1946) p. 274.

[87] Alan W. Miller, "Claude Lévi-Strauss and Genesis 37–Exodus 20" in *Shiv'im, Essays and Studies in Honor of Ira Eisenstein*, ed. Ronald A. Brauner (Philadelphia: Reconstructionist Rabbinical College; New York: Ktav Publishing House, 1977) pp. 32–35.

[88] Salo W. Baron, *A Social and Religious History of the Jews* (2d ed; New York: Columbia University Press, 1952–   ) vol. 1, p. 22; cf. Victor W. Turner, *The Ritual Process, Structure and Anti-Structure* (Chicago: Aldine Publishing Co., 1969) pp. 110–111.

[89] Friedrich Nietzsche, *Beyond Good and Evil, Prelude to a Philosophy of the Future* §195 (Harmondsworth, England: Penguin Books, 1973) p. 100. Lawrence Levine characterizes this motif as "wish fulfillment" ("'Some Go Up and Some Go Down': The Meaning of the Slave Trickster" in *The Hofstadter Aegis, A Memorial*, ed. Stanley Elkins and Eric McKitrick [New York: Alfred A. Knopf, 1974] p. 116).

such as these offer solace to those who suffer, with the assurance that their cause can eventually triumph.

In the end, Israel was as unlikely a choice as the heroes of her past. But like them, she believed herself both truly chosen and fundamentally deserving. Stories of their success thus demonstrate God's capacity both to recognize true virtue when appearances are deceiving and to work through unlikely figures. In this, the younger offspring motif joins its theme of consolation to a profoundly untriumphalistic recognition of Israel's origins and fate. Very much at the center of God's world, Israel looks forward to a time when her political power, like that of the Bible's younger brothers, will match her theological status.

4

Every Brother a Supplanter

The preeminence achieved by younger offspring in the Bible does not always come easily. As Abel found out only too late, there is often a heavy price to be paid for preferential treatment. Parental favoritism can easily spark fraternal jealousy and costly violence.[1]

Fratricide is particularly common as both a literary theme and a political reality. Abel's fate is that which awaited both Jotham and the brothers of several of Israel's actual or would-be rulers, who felt compelled to take protective action in the face of rivals.[2] Besides Abimelech, these include Absalom, Solomon, and Jehoram. Esau had also contemplated killing Jacob, much as Joseph's brothers discussed putting him to death, later even projecting their hostile intentions onto this newly powerful brother (Gen 50:15). Indeed, it is the very number of such cases which gives credibility to the wise woman of Tekoa's parable of her fighting sons (2 Sam 14:6).

Even when brothers and sisters do not respond violently, their subordination is often met with something less than equanimity. The amazement of Joseph's brothers—"will you really rule over us?" (Gen 37:8)—is hardly unique. Miriam and Aaron expressed the feelings of many siblings

---

[1] The reason for Cain's behavior is never actually stated in the Bible. Dan Jacobson comments on how God's choice ends disastrously for both brothers (*The Story of the Stories* [New York: Harper & Row, 1982] p. 53).

[2] This is hardly limited to Israel; cf. *Kanaanäische und aramäische Inschriften*, ed. H. Donner and W. Röllig (Wiesbaden: Otto Harrasowitz, 1966–69) no. 215, line 3, and *Corpus des tablettes en cunèiformes alphabétiques*, ed. Andrée Herdner (Paris: Imprimerie Nationale and Librarie Orientaliste Paul Geuthner, 1963) no. 12, ii.45–49.

when they complained, "Has the Lord spoken only through Moses? Did
He not also speak through us?" (Num 12:2).[3] Although Moses' youth is
never given as the reason for their statement, it must have played some
role in the evolution of their resentment.

The conflicts that emerge from these feelings seem ubiquitous in
biblical narrative, where brothers are killed, fathers deceived, mothers
expelled, and daughters switched so that one sibling can be given what
another expected. The impression that this motif is pervasive is shared
by the prophet Jeremiah, who speaks of *every* brother as a cheat (9:3).
However, the breadth of this theme should not be exaggerated. Its shadow
may loom large, but cases of fraternal tension are neither as widespread
nor as homogeneous as is commonly supposed.[4] Although many of the
prominent figures in biblical lore are younger offspring, stories involving
actual conflict with older brothers or sisters are largely confined to the
book of Genesis. Even there, not all sibling relationships are fractious.
For example, Noah's sons are typically listed as a group; the only sense
of individual identity we are given comes when Shem and Japheth carried
out what their brother Ham had implied needed to be done (Gen 9:22–23).
Nor is the prevalence of younger siblings universal, even in Genesis; most
notably, Abraham seems not to have been a younger brother at all.[5] In
fact, instances of actual friction are quite limited, centering both chronologically and genealogically around the figure of Jacob, who confronted
his brother Esau four separate times. His father, his beloved wife, and
his own favored son were also younger children whose success came at
the expense of older brothers or sisters. This theme extends to another
generation when Jacob overrules his own son's preference as to which of
two grandsons should receive the better blessing and when another pair
of grandsons vie to be born first.

The concentration of these stories around the figure of Jacob inevitably
suggests that they share a common purpose; however, this possibility must
be treated cautiously because these stories are not carbon copies of one

---

[3] Remarkably, this is the only instance of sibling conflict within Moses' family. A
conflict with members of his tribe is reported in Numbers 16. As with Michal, innocence,
both stated (Num 12:13) and confirmed by Moses' readiness to defend Miriam (v. 13), makes
this younger child vulnerable to mistreatment by others.

[4] Cf. Assyrian tradition, in which the undoubted conflict between Ashurbanipal and
Shamash-shum-ukin is most often presented as the rise of a younger son and only in one,
relatively late text as an actual conflict (Richard C. Steiner and Charles F. Nims, "Ashurbanipal
and Shamash-Shum-Ukin: A Tale of Two Brothers, from the Aramaic Text in Demotic
Script," *Revue Biblique* 92 [1985] 15).

[5] See note 16 in Chapter 1.

another. Even their ostensibly common theme is both less prominent and sometimes less relevant than their collective presence might seem to imply. Careful reading will reveal a surprising diversity of both structure and focus, with seniority not always a central feature and several protagonists not clearly understood as the youngest in their families. Of particular importance is the diversity of the advantage at stake in these tales, which extends from varying sorts of legal preference to simple narrative attention. In this regard, even the components of individual narrative cycles will be shown to be surprisingly heterogeneous. Rather than uniform and coherent compositions, many of the individual accounts are concerned with quite separate issues.

We have already encountered the ambiguous importance of birth order in the stories of Moses and David, not to mention that of Jacob's son Joseph who was both his mother's oldest son and his father's youngest. The relationship between Isaac and Ishmael provides a further example. On first reading, it appears obvious that Isaac was Ishmael's younger brother, born in his mother's old age after she had already given her maid-servant Hagar to Abraham in order to produce an heir.[6] Although these brothers had different biological mothers, the Bible seems quite clear in presuming that a concubine's offspring was legally the child of her mistress. This is most evident in the story of Leah and Rachel, each of whom wanted Jacob to sleep with her own maidservant in order to be credited with more children than her sister had produced (Gen 30:3–13). Ishmael's mother Hagar was also a slave, indeed, Sarah's own maidservant, whose pregnancy had been instigated by Sarah herself in order that Sarah might be "built up" (*'ibbāneh*, 16:2).[7]

At the same time, however, there are hints that the relationship between Ishmael and Isaac may once have been more complex than it initially appears. Although Isaac, like Joseph and Benjamin, is described

---

[6] George Heider observes that Isaac was, technically, a *peṭer reḥem* (*The Cult of Molek, A Reassessment* [Sheffield, England: JSOT Press, 1985] p. 276).

[7] As noted by Abraham ibn Ezra, this verb may be better rendered "be-sonned" (at Gen 16:2, so also AV; cf. Gen 30:3 and Deut 25:9). See L. Kopf, "Arabische Etymologien und Parallelen zum Bibelwörterbuch," *Vetus Testamentum* 8 (1958) 168, and Akkadian *bānû* ("beget"), A. Leo Oppenheim et al., *The Assyrian Dictionary of the Oriental Institute of the University of Chicago* (Chicago: Oriental Institute, 1964–) vol. 2 (B), pp. 94–95. For parallel customs, see Thomas Thompson, *The Historicity of the Patriarchal Narratives, The Quest for the Historical Abraham* (BZAW 133; Berlin: Walter de Gruyter, 1974) pp. 252–68. A quite different view can be found in *Genesis Rabbah* 71:7, which suggests that Hagar's conception might improve Sarah's fertility (see Samson Kardimon, "Adoption as a Remedy for Infertility in the Period of the Patriarchs," *Journal of Semitic Studies* 3 [1958] 123–26).

as having been born in his father's old age (21:2),[8] the narrative never says or seems concerned with the fact that he was younger than Ishmael.[9] Indeed, their legal relationship is relatively unimportant. The specific issues involved are surprisingly obscure. Although the story is frequently compared with provisions in several ancient Near Eastern law codes, none is entirely analogous.[10] Moreover, the biblical account itself never even hints that any law had been violated or that Ishmael had been deprived of something that was properly his. Instead, both versions of Hagar's departure present Sarah's actions and Abraham's discomfort (21:11) as having been personally motivated.

Given that, God's reference to Isaac as Abraham's *yāḥîd*, when commanding that he be sacrificed by his father (Gen 22:2, 12, 16), is striking. Although that term can have the broad meaning of "specialness," as it was understood by the Septuagint and has been occasionally since, it normally means an "only" child, a connotation particularly well suited to the story's interest in maximizing Abraham's faith in God.[11] It is possible, therefore, that the tradition of Isaac and Ishmael as brothers is not original, but that two separate figures have been connected as sons of Abraham to account for the relationship that was later perceived between their Israelite and Ishmaelite descendants.[12] If that is the case,

---

[8] Cf. note 44 in Chapter 3. *Targum Pseudo-Jonathan* Gen 22:1, which describes Isaac and Ishmael as having argued over their inheritance, is more explicit about their relative ages. According to one rabbinic tradition, Cain and Abel also quarreled over their inheritance (*Genesis Rabbah* 22:7); this fits one nineteenth-century derivation of the name Abel (Heb. *hebel*) from the Sumerian ibila ("heir"; Eberhard Schrader, *The Cuneiform Inscriptions and the Old Testament* [London: Williams and Norgate, 1885] vol. 1, pp. 44–45).

[9] Cf. the comment about Rebecca's being barren, which plays no narrative role and seems contradicted by her almost immediate pregnancy, leading to the suggestion that this had become a convention for patriarchal wives as noted on p. 94 above.

[10] Hammurabi's Code deals only with priestesses (§146, G. R. Driver and John Miles, *The Babylonian Laws*, vol. 2, pp. 56–57), although Thomas Thompson has suggested that it presupposes a more general practice (*The Historicity of the Patriarchal Narratives*, p. 262, but see p. 258). Expulsion of a concubine's children is prohibited by one Nuzi tablet (HSS 5:67, no. 2 in E. A. Speiser, "New Documents Relating to Family Laws," *Annual of the American Schools of Oriental Research* 10 [1928–29] p. 31); cf. lines 45–46 of ND 2307 in B. Parker, "The Nimrud Tablets, 1952—Business Documents," *Iraq* 16 (1954) 37–39.

[11] August Dillmann proposed that Isaac was the only child left after the expulsion of Ishmael (*Die Genesis* [3d ed., Leipzig: S. Hirzel, 1892] p. 291); for the juxtaposition of *yāḥîd* and *bĕkōr*, see pp. 62–63 above. The usage in Genesis 22 may be reflected in Christian allusions to Jesus as God's only son (*monogenēs*), e.g., John 1:14, 3:16, 18, 1 John 4:9, and Hebrews 11:17.

[12] See, for example, Henning Graf Reventlow, *Opfere deinen Sohn, Eine Auslegung von Genesis 22* (Neukirchen-Vluyn: Neukirchener Verlag des Erziehungsvereins, 1968) pp. 44–46. A similar development may account for the description of Enkidu as Gilgamesh's brother in some, relatively late versions of the Gilgamesh epic (Assyrian version 12.81, 87 in R.

then Isaac's status as a younger son is more an incidental by-product of the way in which these traditions evolved than a central feature of the account. Indeed, to the extent it can be discerned at all, the relationship between these figures is more a result of the tension between Sarah and her fertile maidservant Hagar than a function of Isaac's relationship with Ishmael.[13]

More surprising is the ambiguity found in the story of Perez and Zerah, the product of Tamar's efforts to bear the son to which she felt entitled from her deceased husband's family. These twins were the off-spring of Tamar's own father-in-law Judah, whom she had tricked into sleeping with her by disguising herself as a prostitute.

Birth order certainly seems to play a central role in this account when it describes how, at the time of delivery, one of the babies

> put out a hand. Then the midwife tied a scarlet thread on his hand, saying, "This one came out first." But when he pulled his hand back and his brother came out, she said, "What a breach (*pereṣ*) you have made for yourself!" So he was called Pereṣ. Afterwards his brother, who had the scarlet thread on his hand, came out, and he was called Zerah.

> (38:28–30)

But closer inspection reveals remarkable ambiguity. Although this incident is not treated as having any significance in Genesis, both Chronicles and Ruth connect it with David, whose line they trace through Perez.[14] Even if that issue can be discerned in the Genesis, account, there is little else there which is straightforward. The genealogy's significance remains particularly unclear, since Genesis is quite oblique as to which of the children it considers older. Although the scarlet thread is said to signify Zerah's having come out first (*zeh yaṣā' rī'šōnâ*, v. 28), it is David's ancestor Perez who was the first to emerge fully and whose name is, there-

---

Campbell Thompson, *The Epic of Gilgamesh, Text, Transliteration, and Notes* [Oxford: Clarendon Press, 1930] p. 69, see also 6.41 on p. 156 and lines 19 and 22 of the Hittite tablet published in Johannes Friedrich, "Die hethitischen Bruchstücke des Gilgameš-Epos," *Zeitschrift für Assyriologie* n.s. 5 = 39 [1930] pp. 18–19, and perhaps line 5 of the Hurrian tablet published by Arthur Ungnad, "Das hurritische Fragment des Gilgamesch-Epos," *Zeitschrift für Assyriologie* n.s. 1 = 35 [1923–24] p. 139).

[13] See pp. 94–95 above.

[14] Ruth 4:18–22, 1 Chron 2:3–15. Scarlet (*šānî*) is often associated with high class (cf. Jer 4:30 and Prov 31:21). A cord of that color was used to mark the home of the prostitute Rahab (Josh 2:18) who, like Tamar, came to be included in David's pedigree (Matthew 1:3–5). According to one rabbinic tradition, she received the cord from Perez and Zerah, who were Joshua's spies (*Midrash ha-Gadol*, ed. Mordecai Margulies [Jerusalem: Mosad Harav Kook, 1947] vol. 1 [Genesis] p. 371).

fore, explained as meaning "break out" (v. 29), a concept reminiscent of the Hebrew view that firstborns break their mother's womb (*peṭer reḥem*).[15] From the existing account, therefore, one can hardly tell whether Perez was considered a legitimate firstborn or a younger son who had displaced his older brother.[16] Nor does it make any real difference for Genesis, which has little interest in either of the twins, but proceeds instead through Joseph, barely mentioning Perez and Zerah even in genealogical passages. As it stands, the story plays virtually no part in the continuing biblical account.

Surprisingly, birth order is also vague in the story of Jacob and Esau, which lies so much at the center of this theme. Like that of Perez and Zerah, it too begins with a struggle. Although their wrestling seems to be connected with the order of their emergence, since it comes immediately before their birth is noted, the two incidents did not occur in immediate succession. The text acknowledges this by separating the incidents with the transitional phrase, "When [Rebecca's] days to bear were at hand" (25:24), indicating that a substantial interval of time had passed.

Although prenatal struggle is a common motif in traditional literature[17] and birth order frequently an issue, the two are not necessarily the same. For example, Greek tradition introduces the conflict between the brothers Acrisius and Proetus over their father's realm with a struggle *in utero*, but without indicating which was older.[18] There is some reason to

[15] See p. 66 above. A. Guillaume has compared instead the meaning "precede" associated with the Arabic root *frṭ* ("Paranomasia in the Old Testament," *Journal of Semitic Studies* 9 [1964] 285). The name Zerah is not explained in the text. Frank Zimmerman compares Aramaic *zĕḥôrît* ("scarlet," "The Births of Perez and Zerah," *Journal of Biblical Literature* 64 [1945] 377, cf. Rashi and R. Samuel ben Meir at Gen 38:30) and Otto H. Procksch connects it with Arabic *ḍrḥ*, meaning "bright red" (*Die Genesis* [5th ed., KAT; Göttingen: Vandenhoeck & Ruprecht, 1922] p. 204). August Dillmann suggests it is related to *'ezraḥ* (i.e., "indigenous," *Die Genesis*, p. 402).

[16] This ambiguity is recognized by J. A. Emerton, "Judah and Tamar," *Vetus Testamentum* 29 (1979) 408.

[17] Cf. Stith Thompson's motif T 575.1.3 "twins quarrel before birth in mother's womb" (*Motif-Index of Folk-Literature* [rev. ed., Bloomington, IN: Indiana University Press, 1955–57] vol. 5, p. 404); cf. motif A 511.1.2.1 (vol. 1, p. 116) and Nahmanides' comment on Gen 25:23. This may owe something to the widespread view of twins as having separate fathers (see E. Sidney Hartland, "Twins" in *Encyclopaedia of Religion and Ethics*, ed. James Hastings [New York: Charles Scribner's Sons, 1908–27] vol. 12, p. 496, and S. Thompson's motif T 587.1 [*Motif-Index*, vol. 5, p. 410], which lists tales in which the birth of twins is indicative of a wife's unfaithfulness; the Greek tale of Castor and Polydeuces, described in the Introduction, is an example of this view, which is also reflected in *Targum Pseudo-Jonathan's* understanding of the relation between Cain and Abel [at Gen 4:1–2]) and may contribute to the view of the birth of twins as a bad omen (Erle Leichty, *The Omen Series Šumma Izbu* [Locust Valley, NY: J. J. Augustin, 1970] pp. 39–43).

[18] Apollodorus, *The Library* 2.2.1 (LCL vol. 1, pp. 144–45); cf. Pausanius, *Description of Greece*, "Corinth" 2.16.2 (LCL vol. 1, pp. 326–27). J. Rendel Harris infers Proetus' priority

suspect that it made little difference. As a later Roman authority states, twins cannot be distinguished by age (*quoniam gemini essent nec aetatis verecundia discrimen facere posset*).[19] And so the birth of these figures is never even described; instead, our sources proceed directly to their later relationship, with each receiving part of his father's kingdom. Their wrestling foreshadows a state of tension, not one's priority over the other.

Like the conflict between Acrisius and Proetus, Jacob and Esau's prenatal struggle was concerned more with conflict than with sequence. The narrative never even distinguishes them, but simply states that "the children struggled within [their mother]" (*wayyitrōṣĕṣû bĕqirbāh*, 25:22). Indeed, the twins are not differentiated in any way. Neither is named as instigator; neither as victor. All we are told is that they struggled, a conflict which is presented as fully mutual with no winner even implied. This ambiguity persists at the moment of their birth, when Jacob came out of his mother's womb holding on to Esau's heel (25:26). Although this is commonly interpreted to mean that Jacob wanted to emerge before his brother did, that is not the only possibility, nor would it have been the best way to accomplish that goal.

Efforts by one twin to become the oldest are also well known in various traditions, where they typically involve the eager infant's finding some way out of the womb other than through the birth canal. For example, Ahriman, the Persian god of evil, left through his mother's navel, and Typhon broke out of his mother's side.[20] But Genesis says nothing of the sort, nor does it claim, or even imply, that Jacob was trying to displace Esau, even though the root *'qb* can mean "supplant" and was understood that way already in antiquity, as demonstrated by both Hosea

---

from his name (*Boanerges* [Cambridge:University Press, 1913] p. 279); however, Rudolf Hirzel contends that such names are more likely to reflect parental commitment than birth order (*Der Name, ein Beitrag zu seiner Geschichte im Altertum und Besonders bei den Griechen* [Leipzig: B. G. Teubner, 1918] p. 36).

[19] Livy 1.6.4 (LCL vol. 1, pp. 24–25); a remarkably similar perspective is apparent in the response of a Pepsi-Cola spokeswoman to learning that members of a space shutttle crew had drunk Coca-Cola about eight hours before they drank Pepsi: "It is about as relevant as who's first in the birth of twins" (Associated Press report, "Coke Gloats Over Space Race Victory," *Denver Post* August 10, 1985, p. 14A).

[20] Plutarch, *De Iside et Osiride* 12 (ed. J. G. Griffiths [Cambridge: University of Wales Press, 1970] pp. 136–37) and R. C. Zaehner, *Zurvan, A Zoroastrian Dilemma* (Oxford: Clarendon Press, 1955) pp. 60–66; the actual texts are on pp. 422–27. The imagery of Ohrmazd and Ahriman as twins is found in normative Zoroastrian tradition (Yasna 30:3–4, cited by Zaehner on p. 4). For other such stories, see Hermann Oldenberg, *Die Religion des Veda* (Darmstadt: Wissenschaftliche Buchgesellschaft, 1970) p. 134, Stith Thompson, *Tales of the North American Indians* (Cambridge, MA: Harvard University Press, 1929; reprinted Bloomington, IN: Indiana University Press, 1966) p. 15, and William W. Gill, *Myths and Songs from the South Pacific* (London: Harry S. King and Co., 1876) p. 10.

(12:4, ET v. 3) and Jeremiah (9:3)—but not by Genesis. There Jacob's name is understood as signifying that he had been born holding on to Esau's heel (*'āqēb*), which could have been the entirely innocent result of their physical proximity and virtually simultaneous birth or, perhaps, the outcome of Jacob's independent effort to escape from the womb.[21] From the narrative's perspective, all that matters is that it was Esau's heel (*'āqēb*, Gen 25:25–26) onto which he was holding.

As ambiguous as the importance of birth order can be, the benefit at stake in these contests is also quite different from what is often supposed. We have already seen how difficult it is to connect these stories with actual inheritance or leadership, particularly given the question as to how much authority their beneficiaries actually exercised.[22] Isaac never ruled over Ishmael, nor Jacob over Esau. To the contrary, after obtaining the blessing, Jacob had to flee, leaving Esau to exercise whatever dominance there was to be, at least for the ensuing twenty years. The dubious impact of Perez and Zerah's struggle has also been noted. Surprisingly, much the same can be said for the prenatal struggle which opens the Jacob-Esau cycle.

Although the oracle that Rebecca received prior to her delivery ends with the phrase "*rab ya'ăbōd ṣā'îr*" (25:23), which is conventionally translated "the older shall serve the younger,"[23] this has nothing to do with the twins at all, and certainly not with which one would be born first or achieve prominence later for that matter. Instead, it deals with a much larger context, as its opening sentence makes clear: "Two countries (*gôyîm*) are in your womb," God tells Rebecca, "two nations (*lĕ'ummîm*) shall separate from your belly, and one nation (*lĕ'ôm*) shall be stronger than the other" (25:23).

This national dimension is not unique to the oracle section of the Jacob-Esau cycle. Esau is later called Edom and said to have lived in Seir (Gen 36:1, 8), a connection implied also by the description of him as having been born "ruddy (*'admônî*) like a hairy (*śē'ār*) cloak" (25:25). Some have suggested that these terms are traces of an earlier tradition in which the lifestyle of the pastoralist Jacob was contrasted with that of

---

[21] Cf. Leroy Waterman, "Jacob the Forgotten Supplanter," *American Journal of Semitic Languages* 5 (1938) 28.

[22] See pp. 54–56 above.

[23] The connection of those terms, which need not be rendered so specifically, with inheritance has been noted by E. A. Speiser, *Genesis* (AB; Garden City, NY: Doubleday, 1964) p. 195; see also pp. 42–47 above. Arnold B. Ehrlich takes *rab* adverbially ("for a long time," *Randglossen zur hebräischen Bibel, textkritisches, sprachliches und sachliches* [reprinted Hildesheim: Georg Olms Verlagsbuchhandlung, 1968] vol. 1, p. 119).

the hunter Esau.[24] It is certainly conceivable that such a story of competing lifestyles has been adapted to reflect on the ancestor of all Israel and thus the people as a whole.[25] Whatever its early history, however, the allusion to Edom is hard to miss in the present context, especially when it recurs in the description of the pottage Esau bought from Jacob as red (*'ādôm*, 25:30).

This national orientation emerges once again in the blessings given Jacob and Esau by their father Isaac. "May peoples (*'ammîm*) serve you and nations (*lĕ'ummîm*) bow down before you" (27:29), he told Jacob, who, despite all that the story has led us to expect, is never placed above Esau at all, but only given a vague and generic kind of superiority: "Be master over your brothers (*'aḥeykā*); may your mother's sons (*bĕnê 'immekā*) bow down to you" (27:29)—a rather odd blessing for a boy with only one sibling. As in the prenatal oracle, Jacob (whom Isaac would have thought to be Esau) is not even mentioned. It is only in the blessing given Esau after his return from the field that the brothers' relationship is spelled out, with initial subordination ("you shall serve your brother"— *wĕ'et 'āḥîkā ta'ăbōd*, 25:40) offset by the assurance of eventual independence ("but when you rebel you shall break his yoke from over your neck"—*wĕhāyâ ka'ăšer tārîd ûpāraqtā 'ullô mē'al ṣawwā'rekā*, 25:40).

Significantly, neither this nor anything else foretold by the story was actually fulfilled during Jacob and Esau's lifetimes. In fact, Jacob's flight made it impossible for him to achieve the kind of domination suggested here. But even when he returned, Esau was not put under his brother's control, and he certainly never rebelled. Given the repeated links between Esau and Edom as well as Jacob's subsequent identification as Israel (32:29), there can be little doubt then that these stories have their eye on a larger canvas than one family.

---

[24] Hermann Gunkel, *Die Schriften der alte Testaments* (2d ed.; Göttingen: Vandenhoeck & Ruprecht 1921) vol. 1, p. 197, who notes also the priority Jacob gave to family ties in contrast to Esau's concern with immediate gratification. See also Ronald S. Hendel, *The Epic of the Patriarch, The Jacob Cycle and the Narrative Traditions of Canaan and Israel* (Atlanta, GA: Scholars Press, 1987) p. 128, who compares Enkidu's hairy body (*šu''uram pagaršu*, cf. Jeffrey Tigay, *The Evolution of the Gilgamesh Epic* [Philadelphia: University of Pennsylvania Press, 1982] p. 277) to that of Esau in order to justify placing these figures under the headings "nature and culture" (p. 117). Norman O. Brown observes that tricksters are often culture heroes (*Hermes the Thief, The Evolution of a Myth* (New York: Vintage, 1969) p. 24. For similar concerns in the story of Cain and Abel, see p. 91 above.

[25] Victor Maag, "Jakob-Esau-Edom," *Theologische Zeitschrift* 13 (1957) 418–29 and J. R. Bartlett, "The Brotherhood of Edom," *Journal for the Study of the Old Testament* 4 (1977) 2–27.

The incongruity between the blessings actually given and what readers have been led to expect is enhanced by another of its provisions. The assurance that Jacob will be blessed with "dew from the sky and fat of the earth (*miṭṭal haššāmayim ûmišmannê hāʾāreṣ*), much grain and wine" (25:28) is duplicated almost verbatim in the blessing given Esau, who is also promised "the fat of the earth and the dew of the sky" (*mišmannê hāʾāreṣ ... ûmiṭṭal haššāmayim*, 25:39).[26] In short, even what concrete benefit is offered Jacob turns out to be of doubtful advantage in comparison to that given Esau.

A similar observation can be made regarding the blessings Jacob gave his grandsons Ephraim and Manasseh. Although Joseph was at pains to make sure that Manasseh stood at his grandfather's right side and Jacob was equally insistent that Ephraim be blessed with his right hand, the two of them received only one, common blessing, with each jointly assured of having numerous descendants and being known by his ancestors' names (48:15–16). Moreover, they continued to be treated together when Jacob subsequently told Joseph that both would be great peoples (*gam-hûʾ yiheyeh-lĕʿām wĕgam hûʾ yigdāl*), even though the younger will be greater (*ʾāḥîw haqqāṭōn yigdal*, 48:19).[27]

As with the blessings given Jacob and Esau, this statement has nothing at all to do with Ephraim and Manasseh, whose moment on the stage of biblical narrative has passed by the time the account is over. As the text itself acknowledges, the purpose of this report is merely to explain why Ephraim is mentioned first in a traditional Hebrew blessing (48:20). In a broader context, it alludes to that tribe's much later prominence, as it effectively eclipsed Manasseh in Israel's Northern Kingdom.

In sum, the recurring preeminence of younger siblings in the book of Genesis is not as self-evident as it initially appears. Relative age is a minimal and sometimes ambiguous element in several of these accounts, and surprisingly few of the victors win anything at all, much less something of personal benefit. Even the special blessing (*bĕrākâ*) for which Jacob worked so hard is not as conspicuous in other accounts as it is there. When Joseph's son Ephraim was blessed with his grandfather's right hand, the

---

[26] Although translating these occurrences the same way is "the most obvious interpretation" (T. Nöldeke, "Edom" in *Encyclopedia Biblia*, ed. T. K. Cheyne and J. Sutherland Black [New York: Macmillan, 1901] vol. 2, p. 1184; cf. the Septuagint, Vulgate, *Targum Onqelos, Targum Pseudo-Jonathan*, AV and NJV), the implied contrast has sometimes led the latter occurrence to be rendered "away from the fat of the earth and dew of the sky" (e.g., RSV and NAB).

[27] This is echoed in Deut 33:17, see W. J. Phythian-Adams, "The Boundary of Ephraim and Manasseh," *Palestine Exploration Quarterly* 61 (1929) 229.

only advantage given him was the expectation of future success. The *bĕkōrâ* was certainly never transferred, nor is it even mentioned in his grandfather's promise that "the younger brother will be greater" (*haqqāṭōn yigdal*, 48:19), an advantage achieved by his tribal descendants rather than by himself, as is clear from the way in which Manasseh continues to be regarded as *bĕkōr*—by the narrator (48:14), by his father Joseph (48:18), and apparently by Jacob as well (48:19).

In fact, the "brighright" (*bĕkōrâ*), which seems so prominent in the story of Jacob and Esau, appears nowhere else in Genesis, providing one more indication of these tales' lack of commonality.[28] It is true that the book of Chronicles does observe that Reuben had been *bĕkōr*, "but when he defiled his father's bed, his *bĕkōrâ* was given to Joseph's sons" (1 Chron 5:1).[29] However, Genesis shows no awareness of this, despite its reference to the elevated status of Joseph's sons, which it presents as a result of their having been adopted by Jacob: "They are mine," by says, "like Reuben and Simeon" (48:5).[30] In other words, Genesis understands Ephraim and Manasseh to have been made sons of Jacob ("like Reuben and Simeon"), whereas Chronicles regards them as having split the special inheritance portion given their father Joseph after he was made *bĕkōr*.[31]

These two, separate traditions share a common purpose—to explain how the tribes of Ephraim and Manasseh, which did not claim to be

---

[28] Contrast various claims that it was precisely the *bĕkōrâ* which was at stake in Isaac's elevation over Ishmael (e.g., *Genesis Rabbah* 61:6, Rashi at Gen 21:10, and Thomas E. McComiskey, "The Status of the Secondary Wife: Its Development in Ancient Near Eastern Law, A Study and Comprehensive Index" [Brandeis University, Ph.D. dissertation, 1965], p. 69) and the struggle between Perez and Zerah (S. E. Loewenstamm, "Zerah," *Encyclopedia Miqra'it* [Jerusalem: Bialik Institute, 1950–88] vol. 2, p. 941, and Arnold B. Ehrlich, *Miqra' ki-Feshuṭo*, at Gen 38:28 [New York: Ktav, 1969] vol. 1, p. 105).

[29] The Septuagint reflects *bĕrākâ* instead of *bĕkōrâ*.

[30] Taking *kir'ûbēn wĕšim'ôn* as "like" rather than "instead of Reuben and Simeon"; contra Hans-Jürgen Zobel, *Stammespruch und Geschichte, Die Angebe der Stammessprüche von Gen 49, Dtn 33 und Jdc 5 über die politischen und kultischen Zustände im damaligen "Israel"* (BZAW 95; Alfred Töpelmann, 1965) p. 124. Cf. Sara Japhet, *'Emunot ve-De'ot be-Sefer Divrei ha-Yamim u-Meqomo ba-'Olam ha-Maḥshavah ha-Miqra'it* (Jerusalem: Mosad Bialik, 1977) p. 274, n. 198. Even if Reuben were rejected because of his earlier sin, there is no reason for Simeon to have been displaced. See also Isaac Mendelsohn, "A Ugaritic Parallel to the Adoption of Ephraim and Manasseh," *Israel Exploration Journal* 9 (1959) 180–83 and Herbert Donner, "Adoption oder Legitimation?" *Oriens Antiquus* 8 (1969) 107–109.

[31] Hugh G. M. Williamson, *Israel in the Book of Chronicles* (Cambridge: Cambridge University Press, 1977) p. 91. This is supported by the omission of *bĕnê* from some versions of 1 Chron 5:1 and by Joseph's adoption of Ephraim's sons (Gen 50:23), which Otto Kaiser suggests was done to replace Ephraim and Manasseh as his legal sons ("Stammgeschichtliche Hintergründe der Josephsgeschichte, Erwägungen zur Vor- und Frühgeschichte Israels," *Vetus Testamentum* 10 [1960] 9).

descended directly from Jacob's sons, had come to hold equal status with other tribes in the Israelite confederation—but they do so in quite different ways. According to Genesis, that was the result of their ancestors' having been adopted as Jacob's sons, whereas Chronicles ascribes it to their having inherited the double portion of the *bĕkōrâ* given their father Joseph after it had been taken away from Reuben.

Other biblical passages confirm that this issue was widely discussed in ancient Israel. For example, the book of Joshua, which preserves a Josephite complaint about having been given only one portion (17:14), also lists Ephraim and Manasseh as two separate units (*kî-hāyû bĕnê-yôsēp šĕnê maṭṭôt*, 14:14), which is there explained as compensation for the fact that Levi had no portion at all.[32] This is the same anomaly with which the book of Genesis is concerned when it offers the observation that the ancestors of those tribes had been adopted by Jacob, just as Chronicles ascribes that to Joseph's having been given a double share (the *bĕkōrâ*)— two very different ways of explaining the same thing.

The Chronicler did not invent his reference to Reuben's sin, but found it briefly mentioned in the book of Genesis: "When Israel was dwelling in that land, Reuben went and lay with Bilhah, his father's concubine, and Israel heard" (35:22). Within its original context, however, that statement is remarkably laconic. No motivation is provided for Reuben's behavior, nor does it have any narrative consequences. The incident is not even condemned, although similar actions elsewhere in the Bible are typically performed by sons who are attempting to displace their fathers.[33] But Genesis neither claims nor implies that Reuben had that goal in mind. Instead, the incident appears to have been primarily lustful, the kind of behavior condemned by subsequent biblical legislation.[34]

---

[32] So too Ezek 48:4–5; cf. Num 34:23–24 and Ezek 47:13. Although *ḥăbālîm* is formally plural, it has long been understood as dual (e.g., the Vulgate, Targum, Rashi, and David Qimhi). This tradition supports those who understand the Genesis adoption tradition as an attempt to maintain the twelvefold character of Israel's confederation (cf. Martin Noth, *Das System der zwölf Stämme Israels* [Stuttgart: W. Kohlhammer, 1930] p. 13) although that reason is not stated in Genesis itself.

[33] Cf. 2 Sam 16:21–22. Hermann Gunkel cites Schiller's "Bride from Messina" and an incident from the Iliad (11.448–56 [LCL pp. 414–15]) as parallels (*Genesis* [5th ed., HKAT; Göttingen: Vandenhoeck & Ruprecht, 1922] pp. 384 and 479); however, the latter incident was instigated by the woman.

[34] Lev 18:8 and Deut 23:1. Nahum M. Sarna proposes that the Genesis statement was included to "save [Gen 49:3] from unintelligibility" ("The Anticipatory Use of Information as a Literary Feature of the Genesis Narratives" in *The Creation of Sacred Literature, Composition and Redaction of the Bible*, ed. Richard E. Friedman [Berkeley, CA: University of California Press, 1981] p. 82).

This incident was recalled when Jacob lay on his deathbed and gathered his sons to be blessed. There, Reuben's fate ("you shall excel no more" [ʾal-tôtar]) is ascribed to his having "ascended your father's bed, bringing defilement [by] ascending my couch" (ʾāz ḥillaltā yĕṣûʿî ʿālâ, Gen 49:3–4). Although Reuben's status as bĕkōr, which was not noted in the earlier passage,[35] is mentioned here alongside of other descriptions of him as Jacob's "strength" (kōḥî), "the best of my vigor" (rēʾšît ʾônî), "very exalted" (yeter śĕʾēt), and "very strong" (yeter ʿāz, 49:3), there is no evidence of its having been revoked, despite the explicit repudiation of Reuben's behavior.

The fact that it is only in Chronicles that the bĕkōrâ is said to have been taken away from Reuben suggests that this assertion was the Chronicler's own interpretation of these traditions. In other words, he was aware of the basic facts found in Genesis, but did not accept Genesis' ascription of Ephraim and Manasseh's tribal status to their ancestors' having been adopted as Jacob's sons. Instead, he explained it by drawing on Deuteronomy's statement about a double portion being given to the bĕkōr. Juxtaposing that with the account of Reuben's transgression, he inferred that Ephraim and Manasseh's position was the result of their father Joseph's having been given that status when it was taken away from Reuben.[36]

The sole obstacle to this conclusion is Chronicles' surprising persistence in identifying Reuben as Jacob's bĕkōr (1 Chron 5:3), even after claiming that he had lost the bĕkōrâ. However, that is a very minor difficulty, easily resolved by a careful look at the structure of that passage. For although the chapter opens by announcing a list of Reuben's descendants ("The sons of Reuben, Israel's bĕkōr..."), the actual enumeration is not provided until after the presentation of Reuben's sin, when the opening phrase is repeated. This syntactic awkwardness suggests that the account of Reuben's losing the bĕkōrâ has been inserted into a list of his descendants which identified him as Israel's bĕkōr. Because this insertion separated the genealogy from its introduction, the now anomalous identification of Reuben as Jacob's bĕkōr was repeated (*Wiederaufnahme*).[37]

---

[35] It is mentioned only in Gen 35:23, immediately after the account of Reuben's sin.

[36] Contrast *Targum Onqelos*'s understanding that Reuben deserved three portions (at Gen 49:3).

[37] J. Wilhelm Rothstein and Johannes Hänel, *Kommentar zum ersten Buch der Chronik* (KAT; Leipzig: A. Deicherstsche Verbuchhandlung D. Weiner Scholl, 1927) p. 91; note, however, Rashi's view that the title bĕkōr is retained even after an individual has lost the bĕkōrâ (at Gen 25:23).

Collectively, these observations leave the story of Jacob's purchase of the *bĕkōrâ* as the only true instance where that status changes hands in the book of Genesis. As such, it demonstrates the diversity of issues with which these various stories are concerned and supports the importance of caution before they are read as restatements of a common theme. Moreover, as we will now see, even the centerpiece of this motif—Jacob's purchase of the *bĕkōrâ*—does not entirely conform to the pattern which these accounts are usually claimed to represent.

That account is straightforward in describing how Esau returned famished from a hunt, only to be told that he would have to give up his *bĕkōrâ* before he could eat from Jacob's pot, a price he reluctantly paid. One senses an element of ambivalence in his comment, "I am about to die, so what good is the *bĕkōrâ* to me?" (25:32), which is followed by the sale and the statement that "Esau despised the *bĕkōrâ*" (25:34).[38]

There is certainly ample evidence that this status was conceived as transferable.[39] Nor does the narrative cast any doubt on the transaction's legality, despite the questionable way in which Jacob had acquired his prize. But that leaves serious questions about a strange detail in the narrative which follows.

When Esau, who had already sold the *bĕkōrâ*, returned from the hunt to receive his dying father's blessing, he presented himself as "your son, your *bĕkōr*" (27:32).[40] Nor would Jacob have disagreed with that identification, since when he earlier approached Isaac, disguised as his older brother, he identified himself by saying, "I am Esau, your *bĕkōr*" (27:19). It will not suffice to explain this as having been necessary because Isaac was ignorant of the earlier transaction. In that case, there would have been no need for the entire deception; Jacob could simply have informed his father of the sale and explained that the *bĕkōrâ* was now his. It is, therefore, reasonable to suspect that the stories of Jacob's buying the *bĕkōrâ* and then stealing the *bĕrākâ* were originally separate. In fact,

---

[38] The transaction may actually have taken place in two stages, with sale of the *bĕkōrâ*—for an unstated price—a precondition for Esau's obtaining food (see Nahmanides at Gen 25:31). Only after acknowledging that it had been sold (25:33) does the text allow that Jacob "gave him bread and lentil soup" (v. 34).

[39] See pp. 58–59 above. Cassuto concludes that Jacob only stole what was already his ("*Ya'aqov*," *Encyclopedia Miqra'it*, vol. 3, p. 719). The evidence of Nuzi contracts is discussed by Thomas L. Thompson, *The Historicity of the Patriarchal Narratives, The Quest for the Historical Abraham* (BZAW 133; Berlin: Walter de Gruyter, 1974) pp. 281–83.

[40] Contra J. P. Fokkelman, *Narrative Art in Genesis, Specimens of Stylistic and Structural Analysis* (Assen/Amsterdam: Van Gorcum, 1975) pp. 107, and H. Y. Hamiel, "'*Em Ya'aqov ve-'Esav* (Gen 28:5)," *Beth Mikra* 32 (1986/87) 334.

several similarities between them suggest that they may be variants of a common, earlier tradition about how Jacob had come to take Esau's place[41]: Food plays a central role in both, as does Esau's hunting in the fields. Death is also a presence, with Isaac's imminent fate (*hinnēh-nā' zāqantî lō' yāda'tî yôm môtî*, 27:2) rhetorically balanced by Esau's observation, "I am about to die..." (25:32). (In fact, Isaac does not die until eight chapters later, just as Esau's life was probably not in serious danger.) Rather than progressing from Esau's sale of the birthright under duress to Jacob's exploitation of that status to gain his brother's blessing as well, the narrative seems to have joined two quite separate stories without harmonizing them entirely.

On close examination, then, the stories of triumphant younger brothers which fill so much of biblical literature turn out to be a far more diverse group than is usually thought. Moreover, the centrality of youngest offspring, which initially seemed so important an element in these tales, is often less significant and sometimes more ambiguous than its recurrence had led us to suppose. Even allowing for that ambiguity, the stories themselves have little in common, but cover a wide variety of issues, ranging from God's acceptance of one brother's offering over that of another to a grandfather's decision regarding which of his two grandchildren should be blessed with his right hand. Surprisingly few of them are concerned with the *bĕkōrâ*, which one would have expected to lie at their center. It appears only in the stories of Jacob and of Reuben, and even there is limited to but one of Jacob's many encounters with Esau and to Chronicles' complex reinterpretation of the Reuben incident, with its interweaving of several originally distinct traditions.

Where sibling conflict can be found, it is often remarkably indeterminate. Jacob and Esau wrestled in Rebecca's womb with no evident concern from the narrator as to who had started the fight or who won. Likewise, in the case of Tamar's twins Perez and Zerah, it is all but impossible to ascertain which was considered to have been born first.

Where victory does seem obvious, its consequences are frequently inconsequential. This is particularly evident from the number of accounts devoted to blessings rather than actual inheritance or succession, many of which are further mitigated when both contenders emerge with equivalent prizes. Where one sibling does succeed in displacing another, the loser is seldom totally rejected. Ishmael and Esau simply proceed offstage, as did Manasseh and (from the point of view of Genesis) Leah's offspring.

---

[41] J. Chaine, *Le Livre de la Genèse* (Lection Divina 3; Paris: Le Editions du Cerf, 1948) pp. 307–11.

A remarkable diversity thus permeates the Bible's presentation of what is widely considered a prevailing theme.

In large part, this lack of uniformity can be ascribed to the diverse origins and varied interests of the traditions in which this motif appears. As has been noted throughout, such tales grow out of everything from culture myths to tribal polemics. In one scholar's words, "Behind the Genesis stories . . . lurk many remote historical migrations, institutions and conceptions of right, social norms, feuds and victories, tribal units and larger compounds of peoples, and perhaps individuals too."[42] Originally separate accounts with quite different interests have thus been woven together, sometimes around a single pair of siblings, despite their often originally distinct agendas and separate narrative dynamics. The combined blessing *and* adoption of Jacob's grandchildren Ephraim and Manasseh are but one example of this phenomenon.

It would, however, be a serious mistake to leave matters at that. The number of younger figures with central roles in the Bible remains as testimony to a remarkable consistency in the way biblical heroes are portrayed. This is made all the more striking by their concentration within the patriarchal period as presented in the book of Genesis. Just as the wife-sister motif's threefold recurrence within two generations of a single family requires some explanation,[43] so the repeated emergence of younger offspring within the patriarchal traditions cannot be accidental.

The narrative itself has several ways of acknowledging the connection among these tales. Most explicit is Esau's complaint to Isaac, after discovering Jacob's deception, that he had been cheated *twice* (Gen 27:36), thereby presupposing the prior sale of his *běkōrâ*.[44] Also binding the stories together is the progression to Jacob's distinct, if assonant goal of acquiring the blessing (*běrākâ*) and the cycle's underlying theme of chosenness (*běḥîrâ*).[45]

Of particular importance in holding the various Jacob-Esau episodes together is the oracle given Rebecca prior to their birth. Whatever the ambiguities of that tale and its allusions to the national rivalry between Israel and Edom, within the present context it serves to announce the continuing struggle between these brothers as well as to foreshadow their

---

[42] Judah Goldin, "The Youngest Son or Where Does Genesis 38 Belong?" *Journal of Biblical Literature* 96 (1977) 36.

[43] See, for example, Robert Polzin, " 'The Ancestress of Israel in Danger' in Danger," *Semeia* 3 (1975) 81–98.

[44] The comment also tacitly excludes both the wrestling in the womb and their subsequent birth.

[45] Avraham Qariv, *Shiv'at 'Amudei ha-Tanakh, 'Ishim ve-'Ide'ot be-Sefer ha-Sefarim* (Tel Aviv: Am Oved, 1968) pp. 10–16.

outcome, with Jacob repeatedly victorious over Esau. Introducing, as it does, a series of encounters between these two figures and employing terms such as *rab* and *ṣā'îr*, with their well-known basis in the realm of inheritance and succession, this brief report provides the context in which the following narratives are read. It is, therefore, no accident that however ambiguous the text, generations of readers have understood Jacob's emergence from the womb holding on to Esau's heel as yet another instance of his ongoing effort to supplant his brother.

Just as the oracle introduces these themes, so do they reach their denouement in the description of Jacob's return to his homeland more than twenty years after his earlier flight (Gen 31:38, 41). On encountering Esau, Jacob bowed before his brother, who responded that he had enough (*rāb*) and did not need Jacob's beneficence (33:9). Jacob, in turn, offered Esau *birkātî* (lit. "my blessing"), symbolically returning what he had earlier taken (33:11)[46] in order to bring the conflict to a close. Their reconciliation thus joins the prenatal oracle in bracketing the confrontation between these brothers, so that the conflict which is announced before their birth is finally resolved in adulthood.

As a result, for all the complexity of its literary history, the Jacob saga turns out to have a well-integrated, symmetrically arranged structure.[47] Nor is its thematic coherence limited to those narratives involving Jacob and Esau.

These themes reappear in the description of Jacob's encounter with his uncle. Belying the purity implied by his name,[48] Laban (lit. "white") disguised his older daughter Leah so that Jacob would not realize that his bride was not the younger Rachel, whom he loved and expected to marry after seven years of service. Laban explained that "it is not the practice in *our* region to marry off the younger before the older" (*lō' yē'āśeh kēn bimqômēnû lātēt haṣṣě'îrâ lipnê habběkîrâ*, Gen 29:26), language which cannot help but recall the earlier instances of age reversal. This literary connection is strengthened by the absence of substantive support for Laban's contention that allowing Rachel to marry first would have violated local custom.[49]

---

[46] For this connotation of *běrākâ*, see Josh 15:19 (= Judg 1:15), 1 Sam 25:27, 30:26, 2 Kings 5:15, 18:31 (= Isa 36:16); cf. Sirah 44:23. Among the other puns in this story are Edom and *ādôm*, *bārûk*, *bēkōr*, *mkr*, and by implication *bḥr*, Seir and *ṣā'îr*, and *tām* and *tě'ômîm*.

[47] See Michael Fishbane, *Text and Texture, Close Readings of Selected Biblical Texts* (New York: Schocken Books, 1979) p. 42.

[48] Cf. *Genesis Rabbah* 60:7.

[49] Other biblical instances are not ascribed to law or custom; cf. 1 Sam 18:17 and Judg 15:1–2 where the younger daughter is described as more attractive. Jubilees 28:6–7

Laban's actions have long been recognized as just retribution for Jacob's earlier deceit.[50] The Bible reinforces the connection by characterizing this incident with the same Hebrew root (*rmh*) as was used to describe Jacob's treatment of Isaac (29:25, cf. 27:35). Laban's use of nighttime darkness to substitute his older daughter for the younger Rachel—only the next morning did Jacob discover that "Behold, it was Leah" (29:25)— recalls Jacob's earlier exploitation of Isaac's weakened vision. A further allusion may be discerned in the reference to Leah's dim (*rakkôt*) eyes (29:17), although it is not entirely clear whether they are to be understood as an asset or a flaw.[51] Switching brides is a common element in folk literature, where the substitute is typically less attractive than the intended wife and often downright ugly.[52] In any event, the incident causes no lasting damage. Rachel married Jacob, just as Esau received his father's blessing. But whatever the facticity of Laban's statement that this is not done in *our* place (*bimqômēnû*), it does serve to remind both Jacob and the reader that birth order has been reversed somewhere else. Nor will this be the last time in Jacob's life that it occurs.

---

does ascribe the regulation to "heavenly tablets"; however, the practice is also apparent in some folklore (Stith Thompson's motif T 131.2 and C 169.2 [*Motif-Index of Folk-Literature*, vol. 1, p. 503, and vol. 5, p. 356], although the latter is limited to Jewish attestations). Other examples are provided by Theodor H. Gaster, *Myth, Legend and Custom in the Old Testament* (New York: Harper & Row, 1969) pp. 199–202. Sinuhe was given the oldest (*wrt*) daughter of a Canaanite ruler (line B78, Alan H. Gardiner, *Notes on the Story of Sinuhe* [Paris: Librairie Honoré Champion, 1916] p. 140) and Gilgamesh married an older daughter while making her younger sister his concubine (Aaron Shaffer, "Gilgamesh, The Cedar Forest and Mesopotamian History," *Journal of the American Oriental Society* 103 [1983] 309–10, lines 168 and 172). The frequently cited instance mentioned in Edward W. Lane's *An Account of the Manners and Customs of the Modern Egyptians* (3d ed., London: Rock & Bowden, 1842, p. 144) demonstrates parental preference rather than custom. Henry Callaway describes an African story in which a younger, more desirable son must await his older brother's marriage (*Nursery Tales, Traditions, and Histories of the Zulus in Their Own Words* [Springvale, Natal: J. A. Blair; London: Trübner and Co., 1868] vol. 1, p. 323).

[50] Cf. *b. Bava Batra* 123a, *Midrash Tanḥuma* (Buber) *Vayeṣe'* §11 (p. 152), *Genesis Rabbah* 70:19, and Richard E. Friedman, "Deception for Deception," *Bible Review* 2 (Spring 1986) 22–31 and 68. Biblical awareness of this principle is apparent in 2 Sam 12:10. Retributive symmetry is common for tricksters (cf. Mac L. Ricketts, "The North American Indian Trickster," *History of Religions* 51 [1965/66] 343).

[51] This is understood as a virtue by *Targum Onqelos*, Rabbi Samuel ben Meir (at Gen 29:17), and E. A. Speiser (*Genesis* [AB; Garden City, NY: Doubleday, 1964] p. 255), whereas the Septuagint, Aquila, Symmachus, David Qimhi, and S. R. Driver (*The Book of Genesis* [9th ed.; London: Methuen and Co., 1913] p. 270) regard it as a flaw; cf. Gen 27:1.

[52] Stith Thompson, *Motif-Index of Folk-Literature*, motif K 1911 (vol. 4, pp. 450–51); for a sample of its forms, see Stith Thompson, *The Folktale* (New York: Dryden Press, 1946) pp. 117–20, and P. Arfert, *Das Motiv von der Unterschobenen Braut in der internationalen Erzählungslitteratur* (Schwerin: Bärensprungschen Hofbuchdruckerei, 1897).

The earlier struggles of Jacob and Esau are recalled when Jacob's son Judah became the father of twins through the deceit of his own daughter-in-law Tamar. The announcement, "And behold, there were twins in her womb (*wĕhinnēh tĕ'ômîm bĕbiṭnāh*)!" (Gen 38:27), uses precisely the same words as the story of Jacob and Esau's birth (25:24).[53]

Echoes of the confrontation with Esau are also evident in the way Jacob blessed his grandsons Ephraim and Manasseh, with the verb *r'h* ("see") repeated frequently. Here Jacob, who now had lost the ability to see (48:10) and expected never to see Joseph again (v. 11), is said to have seen his grandsons (v. 8), just as Joseph saw (v. 17) that his father's hands were reversed.[54] Within the immediate context, these statements emphasize the intentionality of Jacob's actions. However weak his vision, his intellect had not failed; Jacob knew precisely what he was doing. However, within the larger context, they recall his earlier exploitation of his own blind father, who had been unable to ascertain which of his sons was standing before him. This is, therefore, a familiar Jacob, rearranging relationships and favoring younger siblings to the end.

Collectively, there is more to these tales than simply the recurring preference for younger children. They form a thematic whole, centering around the figure of Jacob, whose conflict with Esau is announced before their birth, confirmed by his brother's frustrated cry, avenged in his uncle's substitution of an unloved older sister, and resolved in his reconciliation with Esau as an adult. Further, their uterine struggle is reenacted by his grandsons Perez and Zerah, his displacement of Esau repeated in the favoritism he granted Joseph's younger son Ephraim, and his deception of Isaac amply repaid in the anguish visited on him during his old age by his own children. Indeed, so central is this theme that Jacob's deceitfulness became legend, his name the basis for the pun: "Never trust a brother, for every brother cheats" (*'āqôb ya'qōb*, Jer 9:3).[55]

Through all of this, it is the oracle introducing the birth of Jacob and Esau that provides the context in which these events are to be understood.

---

[53] Another connection is provided by the genealogical link between Zerah and Esau/Edom (Gen 36:13, 17, 33, 1 Chron 1:37).

[54] See also v. 3 and *r'h* in v. 15 as well as Gen 44:28, 45:27–28, 46:4, 30; for connections with other stories (especially 1 Sam 16:1–13, discussed on pp. 85–88 above), see Robert Davidson, *Genesis 12–50* (Cambridge: Cambridge University Press, 1979) pp. 293–95.

[55] Meir Sternberg discerns similar parallels with the story of Isaac, *The Poetics of Biblical Narrative, Ideological Literature and the Drama of Reading* (Bloomington, IN: Indiana University Press, 1985) p. 352. For parallels with the Joseph story, see Peter D. Miscall, "The Jacob and Joseph Stories as Analogies," *Journal for the Study of the Old Testament* 6 (1978) 28–40. Claus Westermann adds parallels from the story of Cain and Abel (*Genesis* [BKAT; Neukirchen Vluyn: Neukirchener Verlag, 1974–82] pp. 398–99).

Like the prophecy that the sword would not depart from David's house (2 Sam 12:10), it unifies the stories that follow and provides them with a coherent meaning. But in this case, it serves another function as well, casting the hero of these tales in a very different light than would otherwise be the case.

Although there is no reason to doubt that Jacob is the focus of this cycle, as shown by his transformation into Israel (Gen 32:29), he is not a very positive figure. Indeed, unlike David or Moses, there is not even much evidence of hidden virtue with which his selection might be vindicated. Although, he is described as an *'îš tām* (25:27), which would normally be translated "an innocent person,"[56] that interpretation is already compromised by the way he pulled himself from the womb at his brother's expense, only to be further weakened when he exploited Esau's immediate needs for his own personal gain, however one judges the nature of Esau's behavior.[57] It is, therefore, appropriately Esau who evokes our sympathy as the victim of repeated unfair treatment. Even his patently inferior intellect redounds to his narrative advantage by his well-intentioned if clumsy efforts to please Isaac by marrying an Ishmaelite, rather than a Canaanite woman (28:8–9).[58] As a victim, Esau may be mocked, but he is never condemned.[59] Jacob's behavior, however, is wholly lacking in moral justification, contradicting both the innocence typically associated with youth and our expectations for one called "Israel."

Jacob's descendants may have found his antics amusing, but there is no reason to think that they were proud. That point becomes clear in his

[56] Robert Alter, *The Art of Biblical Narrative* (New York: Basic Books, 1981) p. 43; Arnold B. Ehrlich comments that here it means he was not a fighter ("eine Menschen, der keine Waffe führt," *Randglossen zur hebräischen Bibel* vol. 1, p. 120), and Susan Niditch understands it as "acculturated" (*Underdogs and Tricksters, A Prelude to Biblical Folklore* [San Francisco: Harper & Row, 1987] p. 165 note 31; cf. S. R. Driver, *The Book of Genesis* [9th ed.; London: Methuen & Co., 1913] p. 247). Norman J. Cohen notes the pun on *tômîm* in 25:24 ("Two That Are One—Sibling Rivalry in Genesis," *Judaism* 32 [1983] 335). Cf. several youngest sons' characterization as "simpletons."

[57] Robert Alter notes the animalistic overtones of Esau's desire to "gulp" (*l'ṭ*) Jacob's porridge (Gen 25:30; *The Art of Biblical Narrative*, pp. 44–45; cf. *m. Shabbat* 24:3); so also *Midrash Tanḥuma* (Buber) *Toledot* §4 (p. 63b) and *Genesis Rabbah* 63:12. It is worth remembering that whatever the reason for Esau's acceptance of a "mess of porridge" in payment for his *bĕkōrâ*, it was Jacob who offered that price.

[58] There is some irony in the fact that his Edomite descendants are often regarded as paradigms of wisdom (Jer 49:7, Obadiah 8); cf. K. Luke, "Isaac's Blessing: Genesis 27," *Scripture* 20 (1968) 36.

[59] In this respect, the biblical treatment is more complex than later interpretations in which Jacob and Esau symbolize good and evil (e.g., *Genesis Rabbah* 63:10 and St. Ambrose, "De Cain et Abel" 1.2 [*PL* vol. 14, p. 318]).

subsequent experiences. Forced to flee the brother whom he had supposedly displaced, never again would this blessed son see his mother, whose favor had played so critical a role in his success. Instead, it was her brother Laban whom he confronted. Later still, his daughter was raped and his favorite son sold into slavery.[60]

Jacob's behavior may owe something to his own circumstances. The Bible presents him as having been a mamma's boy (Gen 25:28), but in literary terms he is a "trickster," one who overcomes physical and social limitations by relying on decit.[61]

Jacob is not the only figure from Israel's past who is lacking in heroic stature. Isaac was, after all, largely passive and Joseph self-important. The only advantage they can claim over their respective brothers has to do with the identity of their mothers, and Ephraim and Perez cannot claim even that.

These are appropriate "founders" for the nation their descendants would become. Israel portrayed herself as a deeply flawed culture, with repeated biblical references to sinfulness, despite her election. From the endless murmurings of the wilderness "honeymoon" to the unrelenting infidelity of life in the Promised Land, from Abraham's deception to the syncretism of the monarchy period, the Bible presents Israel as falling far short of God's expectations. The stories of how her blessing had been acquired through the deceit of a blind, old man and her interests served when a pregnant slavegirl was driven into the wilderness are a fitting introduction to the Bible's doubts about Israel's own merit. Just as the protrayal of her ancestors reflects Israel's sense of worth, her fate cannot be divorced from their experience, and particularly those of her namesake Jacob. Oppressed, ravaged, defeated, and exiled, her history was not what one would expect for God's chosen people.

The Bible's heroes are thus appropriate to its understanding of the nation's own worth. Convinced that God had chosen her, Israel was no less cognizant of her being an unlikely and maybe even undeserving choice.[62] It is this which makes Israel's system of inheritance such a powerful backdrop against which to tell these tales. Rather than deviating from a legally foreordained conclusion, these stories exploit the arbitrariness of a social

---

[60] Umberto Cassuto, "*Ya'aqov*," *Encyclopedia Miqra'it*, vol. 3, p. 719.

[61] See Kathleen A. Farmer, "The Trickster Genre in the Old Testament" (Southern Methodist University, Ph.D. dissertation, 1978) pp. 87–106. E. E. Evans-Pritchard regards such figures as "never really malicious... [but they have] an endearing innocence" (*The Zande Trickster* [Oxford: Clarendon Press, 1967] p. 28).

[62] Cf. *Deuteronomy Rabbah, Shofetim* 7.

system in which preeminence was a function of paternal designation. The rivalry underlying so many of them is the struggle for a father's love and all which that meant, or could mean, in ancient Israel.

Given the national overtones to be found in so many of these stories— most explicitly regarding Jacob, who is Israel—as well as Israel's description of herself as God's *běkōr*, these accounts reflect Israel's understanding of her relation with her heavenly Father, a blessing conceived as an acquired rather than an automatic privilege.[63] Israel's chosenness was not, therefore, something taken for granted. Indeed, she realized that it had been paid for by someone else, that her theology of election left others dispossessed.[64]

Such apprehension would not have been without cause. Jacob had extorted the birthright, and Isaac's success been achieved at Ishmael's expense, God's role notwithstanding. Whether these figures' accomplishments were deserved or not, their hands had been stained in the process. As national heroes, their adventures must have made ancient Israelites uncomfortable, recalling how rarely people portray themselves or their forebears as having acquired their position through cheating or the cost others pay so they can gain power. Working through the psychological implications of this may have been the purpose of these accounts. After all, Manasseh would surely have read the story of Jacob's crossed hands differently than did Ephraim.[65] That is why Jacob had fled to Aram and Cain had killed Abel, a fate to which Joseph came perilously close. One wonders whether Isaac lived in fear of Ishmael's possible return.

This may be the reason that biblical authors portrayed Esau so sympathetically, along with many of the other rejected siblings in these tales. For example, despite the fact that Leah's earlier marriage and more numerous offspring suggest a privileged position over that of Rachel, her longing for Jacob's love is reiterated at almost every turn. Thus, Rachel's complaint about being barren comes close to whining (Gen 30:1), whereas Leah's fate is presented poignantly through the explanations she offers for the names given to her sons—"Surely now my husband will love me" (v. 32), "the Lord has heard that I am hated" (v. 33), "this time my husband will be joined to me" (v. 34).

---

[63] See p. 83 above.

[64] A similar awareness is implicit in the biblical acknowledgment that Israel was not indigenous to her land (cf. *Genesis Rabbah* 1:2).

[65] Cf. Anne Roiphe's comment, "If history is always seen as the struggle between the valiant and good David against the brutish and huge Goliath, then one forgets that Goliath has a story too and his people mourn him also" (*Generation Without Memory, A Jewish Journey in Christian America* [New York: Linden Press, 1981] pp. 26–27).

Although the Bible's portrayal of Isaac is not particularly negative, the behavior of his mother Sarah directs whatever sympathy we might feel towards his brother Ishmael. Abandoned by his father and two mothers (both legal and natural), this older brother was cast under a desert bush, ultimately to be blessed with the same promise of eventual nationhood given all the patriarchal heroes (21:18, cf. 16:10)—a share in Abraham's becoming a father of nations (17:6).[66]

In focusing on these rejected siblings, biblical authors tacitly acknowledge the price others had paid for Israel's theological success. Indeed, it is striking how much more attention many of the ostensibly rejected children receive than do their chosen siblings. A particularly dramatic example is the case of Adam and Eve's younger sons, who are shadowy figures with little narrative role and not much personality. Abel's very name (*hebel*) means "wind," a word which often bears the connotation "nothingness," and appropriately so since, aside from his sacrifice, Abel does not act through most of the story nor speak any lines, despite the prevalence of dialogue in Genesis 4.[67] Unlike Cain, whose name is said to mean "acquired from God" (Gen 4:1) and whose fate the narrative follows and laments, the text has no interest in the meaning of Abel's name, much less any sympathy for its bearer. Even the chosen line bypasses him, continuing instead through his brother Seth.

Not only does the Bible treat the displaced older siblings more sympathetically, but it also emphasizes the positive, if not effusive, blessings bestowed upon many of these "rejected" children. Both Leah and Rachel married Jacob, just as both Isaac and Ishmael founded nations; both Jacob and Esau were given dominion and fertility, and both Ephraim and Manasseh promised future greatness.

Israel's deeply felt superiority, her certainty of having been chosen, is thus tempered by acceptance of at least partial responsibility for the deceptive and manipulative way that had been achieved. The underlying triumphalism is therefore scarcely chauvinistic. The ambiguity of these accounts yields a kind of inchoate universalism, in which God's blessings are bestowed on both Israel and her rivals. Moreover, her sense of superiority is leavened with a substantial, and frequently overlooked, element

---

[66] For other ambiguous blessings, see pp. 119–20 above.

[67] Walther Zimmerli, *1 Mose 1–11*, (3d ed., Zürcher Bibelkommentar; Zurich: Zwingli Verlag, 1967, c. 1943) p. 207; see already Josephus, *Antiquities* 1.2.1 §52 (LCL vol. 4, pp. 24–25). *Hebel* is, as Ecclesiastes repeatedly observes, something one strives to apprehend without fully grasping (Qoh 1:14, 2:11, 17, 26, 4:4, 6:9; cf. Ps 144:4 and Job 7:16). For other interpretations of the name, see note 26 in chapter 3 and note 8 in this chapter.

of humility and self-derogation, laying the groundwork to counter any arrogant inclinations Israel, or her eventual daughter traditions, might otherwise have felt.[68] Israel's ancestors, these stories suggest, were every bit as manipulative as younger children are said to be, but without the engaging style their parents usually perceive.[69]

The displacement theme is thus a two-edged sword, cutting off Israel's neighbors, albeit with substantial blessings of their own, but hardly leaving Israel unscathed. Neither the technical legality of the process nor her own merit could obscure how Israel believed that status to have been gained. God may work through the shortcomings of such figures, but their characters are flawed nonetheless, chosen by God almost in spite of themselves.[70]

The image of a trickster, which pervades so much of the way Jacob and his family are portrayed in the Bible, is often associated with groups that are politically weak. Like trickster tales worldwide, these stories preach resilience to a people whose fulfillment lies ever in the future.[71] The centrality of Jacob thus reflects Israel's own struggles, and his tactics those on which powerless cultures have always needed to rely. Put in impossible situations, B'rer Rabbit's cleverness is necessary for survival in a world filled with those whose inherent strength puts him at an inevitable disadvantage, but it also creates the risk that he will become entangled in his own traps.

In Genesis, it is neither Jacob's self-interest nor the "tit for tat" retribution to which he was subjected that mitigates his behavior, however much these may enhance the story's appeal. What ultimately enables him

---

[68] Hans R. Schiltknecht perceives the self-critical element in these traditions ("Konflikt und Versöhnung in der biblischen Erzählung von Jakob und Esau," *Reformatio* 22 [1973] 525).

[69] Kevin Leman, *The Birth Order Book, Why You Are the Way You Are* (Old Tappan, NJ: Fleming H. Revell, Co., 1984) p. 11; cf. *Midrash Psalms* 9:1 (ed. Buber, p. 40a). Paul Radin reports an Indian tale in which the hero's out-of-control penis is carried in a box and addressed as "younger brother" (*The Trickster, A Study in American Indian Mythology* [London: Routledge and Kegan Paul, 1956] pp. 18–19). A similar typology is apparent in a Hurrian myth that identifies an older twin as Evil and the younger as Good (Hans G. Güterbock, *Kumarbi, Mythen von churritischen Kronos aus den hethitischen Fragmenten zusammengestellt, übersetzt und erklärt* [Zurich: Europaverlag, 1946] pp. 120–22). It may be not entirely irrelevant that the prodigal son of Jesus' parable is also a younger child (Luke 15:11–32). Alfred Adler ascribes younger children's "desire to overcome all others" to their need to prove themselves (*Understanding Human Nature* [Garden City, NY: Garden City Publishing Co., 1927] p. 150).

[70] Cf. Terence E. Fretheim, "The Jacob Traditions, Theology and Hermeneutic," *Interpretation* 26 (1972) 423.

[71] Kathleen A. Farmer "The Trickster Genre in the Old Testament," pp. 22–28 and 67. Susan Niditch draws particular attention to Jacob's (the biblical trickster par excellence) wrestling with God (*Underdogs and Tricksters*, p. 117).

to emerge a hero from these accounts in their introduction by God's assurance of his eventual success. Once that promise had been made, Esau could no longer claim preeminence by right. Instead, his hunger and Jacob's aggressiveness are transformed into the means whereby God's will is achieved. It is this which removes the blame from both Jacob and Rebecca, their all-too-human motivations notwithstanding.

The introductory oracle thus creates the context in which everything that follows must be understood, integrating these tales into a coherent whole even as it justifies Jacob's behavior and eventual primacy. The success of Israel's ancestor and namesake thus emerges as the salutary outcome of a long series of complicated events whereby God's plan, announced before the characters were named or even born, came to fulfillment as leadership devolved to the chosen figure. That does not turn Jacob into a righteous man. Instead, these stories tend to invert the conventional image of youngest children as morally innocent. It is true, as Samuel had been told, that God can recognize virtue that we do not see, but His choices do not need to conform to our moral standards, any more than they must meet our physical expectations. The fulfillment of God's will is not dependent on the merits of those assigned to carry it out. As is made most vivid in the book of Judges, God's power is actually maximized when it is manifest through unlikely figures.[72] In developing this theme, biblical authors created a cadre of heroes whose skills and virtue are questionable, to say the least. This is illustrated most conspicuously through the success of Jacob, who may be the Bible's consummate trickster, but he is still Israel.

The prevalence of this motif within the book of Genesis tends to obscure the fact that it is not the only way rivalries can be portrayed. Conflict is hardly restricted to family settings, nor to those involving members of a single generation, and there is certainly no reason why such tensions have to revolve around sibling pairs, much less those of a single sex. The message of these tales could surely have been expressed in terms of generation or of gender.[73]

The Bible itself had other ways in which to present contests, even when the rivals were unequal. The most obvious example is the story of

---

[72] See p. 107 above.

[73] Contrast the Freudian tendency to locate tension in generational relations (e.g., Sigmund Freud, *The Interpretation of Dreams*, trans. James Strachey [New York: Basic Books, 1958] pp. 260–64); in the Bible, cf. David and Absalom and less conspicuously Laban and Rachel and Saul and Jonathan and Michal. The two are connected by Melville and Frances Herskovits ("Sibling Rivalry, The Oedipus Complex, and Myth," *Journal of American Folklore* 71 [1958] 1).

David's battle with Goliath, which makes no recourse to models of family tension. There are also sibling configurations that do not involve a single pair. Besides Moses, who had both a sister and a brother, there is Joseph with his eleven brothers and a sister and David, who was one of seven or eight.[74] Gideon and Saul are described only as "the smallest" in their respective families. But except for Joseph, these figures encountered little conflict, especially from older family members who are not presented as having posed any significant obstacle to their success.

Yet time and again in the Bible, sibling pairs do turn into the locus of competition, and almost always they involve members of the same sex. The centrality of this perspective may even be discerned in the way biblical authors projected fraternal conflict back into the time of Eden, normally a symbol of tranquility and eschatological reconciliation.[75] From Israel's vantage point, the struggle between siblings was as old as humanity itself.

Whatever this owes to the nature of biblical narrative, which tends to focus on two figures at a time,[76] it is not merely a requirement of the Bible's narrative style. The fact that it is sibling relations in which the Bible repeatedly locates family conflict, particularly as it emerges out of parental favoritism, points to a deeper reality. As countless cliches (and not a few biblical quotes) affirm, no one deserves better treatment than a brother. And Israel clearly did not preceive herself, or her ancestors, as inherently superior to other peoples. That, indeed, is the utility of both the sibling metaphor and the occasional references to Israel as God's *bĕkōr*, the one chosen—for reasons of His own. Yet displace them she had, engendering an element of guilt into her own relationship with God.

This point can be clarified by observing the correlation between this motif and the other kind of rivalry which is remarkably prevalent in the Bible, that involving wives with a common husband. As we have already seen, these barren and fertile women (e.g., Sarah and Hagar, Rachel and Leah, and Hannah and Penninah) are regularly juxtaposed in such a way as to maximize the differences between them while emphasizing the heroines' virtue and, more important, the blessed status of her eventual

---

[74] According to 1 Chron 2:13–15 he was the seventh son, whereas 1 Sam 16:10–11, 17:12, and the Peshitta at 1 Chron 2:15 present him as the eighth. From this ambiguity, Cyrus Gordon has inferred an earlier poetic version of the story (review of *Ancient Near Eastern Texts Relating to the Old Testament* ed. James Pritchard in *Journal of Biblical Literature* 70 [1951] 161).

[75] Cf. Isaiah 11:6–9 and 51:3.

[76] Cf. Axel Olrik's observation of folklore's tendency to focus on two characters at a time (*das Gesetz der scenischen Zweiheit*), "Epic Laws of Folk Narrative" in *The Study of Folklore*, ed. Alan Dundes (Englewood Cliffs, NJ: Prentice-Hall, 1965) p. 135.

offspring.[77] Sibling pairs function similarly in many respects. The clearest example is that of Esau and Jacob, whose differing complexions (Gen 27:11) correlate with their different ways of life and the support that each derives from a different parent (25:28). A similar point could be made with regard to Cain and Abel, Isaac and Ishmael, or Leah and Rachel.

As with rival wives, the Bible's sibling pairs provide the narrator with an opportunity to emphasize certain features of those whom God had chosen by setting them alongside others. Common parentage and gender makes their differences all the more salient. By portraying these heroes as younger offspring, the narrative is then able to suggest the kind of innocence and fraility often associated with this motif. Older brothers (or, on rare occasions, sisters) thus dramatize both their younger siblings' strengths and vulnerability, thereby maximizing the importance of their success.

At the same time, the Bible's predilection for same-sex siblings suggests that the narrative has an investment in something more. After all, brother-sister rivalries are not unknown and could even have enhanced the possibilities for character contrast. Yet the Bible never takes advantage of the opportunities such a configuration would have offered, despite its presence in both literature and real life.[78] Biblical brothers may have harbored protective (e.g., Genesis 34) or aggressive (e.g., 2 Samuel 13) impulses towards their sisters, but aside from one instance of friction between Moses and Miriam (Numbers 12), it offers no examples of brother-sister conflict. Instances of biblical twins—Jacob and Esau and Perez and Zerah—further support the importance attached to the similarity of these figures.

World literature is filled with tales of cooperative siblings, despite their relative absence from the Bible.[79] Among the best-known exemplars of this theme is the story of Romulus and Remus, twin founders of Rome. Although most often cited to demonstrate fraternal conflict, in light of Remus' death at his brother's hands,[80] their relationship was fundamentally

---

[77] See note 38 in chapter 3 regarding *das Gesetz des Gegensatzes*. For the correlation with the more numerous fraternal rivalries, see Northrop Frye, *The Great Code, The Bible and Literature* (New York: Harcourt, Brace, Jovanovich, 1982) p. 183.

[78] For the possibilities in other cultures, see Donald Ward, *The Divine Twins, An Indo-European Myth in Germanic Tradition* (Berkeley, CA: University of California Press, 1968) p. 3.

[79] See pp. 3–4 above.

[80] Other versions, such as that of Ovid, credit that to an aide, albeit in accordance with Romulus' unwitting guidelines (*Fasti* 4.843 [LCL, pp. 250–51], cf. Plutarch's *Lives*, "Romulus" 9.10.1 [LCL vol. 1, pp. 116–17], and Livy 1.7.2 [LCL vol. 1, pp. 24–25]).

harmonious, filled with common adventures undertaken for common purposes. In this regard, their story belongs to the vast literature of fraternal harmony, in which siblings travel together, help each other overcome obstacles, and rescue one another from potential disaster.[81] Many such siblings are almost indistinguishable, their collective existence exemplified by anonymity as much as by joint action. In the case of Romulus and Remus, this may owe something to their having been differentiated from what was once a single figure.[82]

Even among biblical brothers, whose relations seem so lacking in harmony, complementarity need not entail complete separateness. After all, whether hunter and shepherd males or beautiful and fertile females, these sibling rivals regularly embody different facets of the *same* reality. Indeed, by portraying such twosomes as brothers, the Bible suggests how much the "other" may, in fact, have been an inextricable part of Israel's own consciousness.[83] This may explain why so many of its rejected sons are described as having left "civilization" for the desert (Cain, Ishmael, and Esau).[84] Although surely related to the fact that Israel's was an agrarian culture for which the desert was irretrievably alien,[85] it was also part of Israel's own past, a past she could no more deny than Isaac could remove Ishmael from his life story. Traits that coexist, whether as complementary social functions or competing individual ideals—yin and yang

---

[81] The literature on this theme is itself vast; for a broad overview, see Heino Gehrts, *Das Märchen und das Opfer, Untersuchungen zum europäischen Brüdermarchen* (Bonn: H. Bouvier, 1967), Raymond Kuntzmann, *Le symbolisme das jumeaux au Proche-Orient ancien, Naissance, fonction et évolution d'un symbole* (Paris: Beauchesne, 1983) pp. 13–21, and the several works of J. Rendel Harris, especially *The Cult of the Heavenly Twins* (Cambridge: University Press, 1906). According to Paul Ehrenreich, fraternal conflict is especially common at the end of such cycles (*Die Mythen und Legenden der südamerikanischen urvölker und ihre Beziehungen zu denen Nordamerikas und der alten Welt* [Supplement to *Zeitschrift für Ethnologie*; Berlin: A. Ascher, 1905] p. 51). For a contemporary version of this theme, cf. Sigmund Freud's fraternal horde as described in *Moses and Monotheism* (New York: Vintage Books, 1939) pp. 102–4.

[82] C. Joachim Classen, "Zur Herkunft der Sage von Romulus und Remus," *Historia* 12 (1963) 446–57; see also Th. Mommsen, "Die Remuslegende," *Hermes* 16 (1881) 9.

[83] Cf. Ralph Tymms, *Doubles in Literary Psychology* (Cambridge: Bowes & Bowes, 1949) pp. 14, 24, and 29, and, for a broader, psychoanalytic view, Otto Rank, *The Double, A Psychoanalytic Study*, trans. Harry Tucker, Jr. (Charlotte, NC: University of North Carolina Press, 1971) and Bruno Bettelheim, *The Uses of Enchantment, The Meaning and Importance of Fairy Tales* (New York: Alfred A. Knopf, 1976) pp. 90–92.

[84] Those who remain, such as Leah and Adonijah, become complicating elements in the ongoing plot.

[85] Cf. Shemaryahu Talmon, "The 'Desert Motif' in the Bible and Qumran Literature" in *Biblical Motifs, Origins and Transformations*, ed. Alexander Altman (Cambridge, MA: Harvard University Press, 1966) pp. 42–43.

as one author has felicitously, if somewhat incongruously, put it[86]—are thus separated in order to reflect the tension which is within us all.

That tension accounts for the number of these stories that end in reconciliation. Joseph provides a good example, as the brothers' final reunion resolves the conflicts with which the narrative began.[87] Even Jacob and Esau reunite, unlike siblings in many other cultures where the pattern of Cain and Abel seems more likely to prevail.[88] The biblical denouement thereby demonstrates the extent to which these siblings' real conflict had been with themselves—Jacob with his deceptive past and Esau with his undeserving present—rather than with each other.[89]

This may also account for the surprising fact that, despite the prevalence of this theme in the Bible, it does not embrace Israel's greatest enemies, who are not presented as siblings at all. The Philistines, Egyptians, and Assyrians posed a far greater threat than the Edomites or Ishmaelites, but do not figure in these tales. In part, this may be a function of historical reality. The Egyptians and Assyrians were patently outsiders, for whose losses Israel could hardly have felt much guilt, particularly since they rarely lost. However, the Philistines had arrived in Canaan at approximately the same time as Israel and would, therefore, have been suitable candidates for stories of fraternal strife. But they are seen as outsiders in the Bible, dangerous strangers with whom no real relationship is possible. On the other hand, those presented as brothers had, at various times, come under Israelite control, as several of the stories reviewed here quite freely

[86] Norman J. Cohen, "Two That Are One," *Judaism* 32 (1983) 332. cf especially Claude Lévi-Strauss's view of myth as a means to resolve opposites (*Structural Anthropology*, trans. Claire Jacobson and Brock Grundfest Schoepf [Garden City, NY: Doubleday, 1967] p. 221). Paul Radin notes that, as halves of a unified personality, such figures must be integrated before constructive action is possible ("The Basic Myth of the North American Indians," *Eranos-Jahrbuch* 17 [1949] 387–88).

[87] James Ackerman, "Joseph, Judah, and Jacob" in *Literary Interpretations of Biblical Narratives II*, ed. Kenneth R. R. Gros Louis, et al. (Nashville, TN: Abingdon Press, 1982) pp. 95–98; cf. Arthur Waskow's comment about Ephraim and Manasseh that "Genesis is unable to come to an end until there is a peaceful pair of brothers" (*Godwrestling* [New York: Schocken Books, 1978] p. 15).

[88] Cf. Maria Tatar, *The Hard Facts of the Grimms' Fairy Tales* (Princeton, NJ: Princeton University Press, 1987) p. 182. Fraternal reconciliation is also found in the Dahomean story of Sagbata and Sogbo, which begins with a quarrel involving their rule over the world (Melville J. Herskovits and Frances S. Herskovits, *Dahomean Narrative, A Cross-Cultural Analysis* [Evanston, IL: Northwestern University Press, 1958] pp. 129–31). Later versions of the biblical tales do not always end so peacefully, as when they report Jacob's killing Esau (e.g., Jubilees 38:2 and Testament of Judah 9:3), albeit at the latter's instigation.

[89] Drawing on the work of René Girard, Devora Steinmetz comments on the correlation between similarity and violence (*From Father to Son: Kinship, Conflict, and Continuity in Genesis* [Louisville, KY: Westminster/John Knox Press, 1991] p. 21).

acknowledge. This seeming paradox, in which the fraternal rivals of Genesis represent people who were only minimally problematic for ancient Israel from a political or military perspective, mirrors our common tendency to focus less on those forces which really govern our lives than on those which are the nearest and least threatening. Like Joseph, Israel struggled more with her equals than with those who actually controlled her fate. The fact that the other tribes are portrayed as brothers itself suggests the ambivalence of this relationship, which incorporates both closeness and conflict. Unable to get along with the siblings over whom she claimed superiority, Israel behaved like Joseph, exploiting paternal favoritism at the expense of fraternal harmony.

In the end, the Bible's ambivalence towards Jacob ("Israel") and his family is that which Israel felt about herself. Her deepest struggle seems to have had less to do with foreign states and outside forces than with suppressed aspects of her own being—or even those she most proudly proclaimed. Deeply aware of her own shortcomings, both historical and existential, Israel's doctrine of election was itself at odds with the reality of her daily existence. Only eschatologically did she look forward to some kind of reconciliation between her historical experience and theological reality, her status and her worth.

5

The Son God Has Chosen

The stories of younger childrens which so fill the pages of Genesis have been woven together into a common work with values similar to those found in several other biblical accounts, including those devoted to rival wives and the various hero narratives which comprise the book of Judges. Nontheless, it is reasonable to expect the younger sibling stories to have their own unique focus. The nature of that can be inferred from the prominent role accorded national concerns in so many of these accounts, such as the Jacob-Esau cycle, with its dominant characters standing for Israel and Edom. This orientation sometimes becomes explicit, as in the oracle given Rebecca when Jacob and Esau are described as two countries (*šĕnê gôyim*, Gen 25:23) or Isaac's assurance that peoples (*'ammîm*) would serve Jacob (27:29). The relationship of rivalry (*yitrōṣĕṣû*, 25:22), in which Edom (Esau) *appeared* to have the upper hand (*rab*, v. 23) but found itself subordinate (*ya'ăbōd* *šā'îr*, v. 23) to the scrappy (*'āqēb*, vv. 25–26) Israel from whom they would eventually be free (*ûpāraqtā 'ullô*, v. 40), is generally traced to the period of Israel's United Monarchy, when upstart Israel gained control over the older Edom.[1]

A similar focus can be detected in the account of Ephraim and Manasseh's adoption, which culminates when Jacob blesses each of his grandsons with the promise of becoming a great people (*gam-hû' yihĕyeh-llĕ'ām*), although the smaller one will be dominant (*wĕ'ûlām 'āḥîw haqqāṭōn*

---

[1] Hermann Gunkel, "Jacob" in his *What Is Left of the Old Testament and Other Essays* (New York: Macmillan, 1928), p. 178, and J. R. Bartlett, "The Brotherhood of Edom," *Journal for the Study of the Old Testament* 4 (1977) 18–20.

yigdal mimmennû, Gen 48:19, cf. Deut 33:17). The book of Chronicles gives this a distinctly Southern slant by connecting it with Reuben's loss of the *běkōrâ* and the rise of Judah, who is said to have "prevailed over his brothers and become their leader (*nāgîd*), even though the *běkōrâ* was Joseph's" (1 Chron 5:2). This, too, came to fulfillment in the time of David, a focus some have detected in the Genesis version of this incident where the story has no explicit purpose unless it can be placed in some such larger context.[2]

The Davidic kingdom is also, of course, the focus of the birth of Perez and Zerah, as presented in both Chronicles and Ruth, a link some have perceived in Genesis' telling of that event as well.[3] Evidence of Southern adaptations have also been found in the narratives of Joseph and of Jacob, even though these are usually thought to stem from Northern groups.[4] To this evidence of a Southern focus should be added the fact that so many of these stories are found within the J level of tradition, widely acknowledged as having links with Israel's Southern Kingdom.[5] Broader still are the connections between the United Monarchy and Genesis as a whole.[6] Indeed, any number of scholars have found parallels and connections between the patriarchal traditions and the Davidic kingdom, most conspicuously in the repeated concern with blessings which came to be fulfilled in the time of David and Solomon.

This thesis—that there is a Davidic/Solomonic *tendenz* behind the fascination with younger sons' eclipsing their older brothers—is supported,

[2] See B. J. van der Merwe, "Joseph as Successor of Jacob" in *Studia Biblica et Semitica Theodoro Christiano Vriezen* (Wageningen: H. Veenman Zonen, 1966) pp. 223–24.

[3] Moshe Weinfeld, "Book of Ruth" in the *Encyclopedia Judaica* (Jerusalem: Keter Publishing House, 1972) vol. 14, p. 518, and Gary A. Rendsburg, "David and His Circle in Genesis XXXVIII," *Vetus Testamentum* 36 (1986) 441.

[4] See Donald B. Redford, *A Study of the Biblical Story of Joseph (Genesis 37–50)* (Supplement to *Vetus Testamentum* 20; Leiden: E. J. Brill, 1970) pp. 141, 178–79, and 252–53, and J. R. Bartlett, "The Land of Seir and the Brotherhood of Edom," *Journal of Theological Studies* 20 (1969) 3–5; see also B. J. van der Merwe, "Joseph as Successor of Jacob," pp. 225–28, and J. Robin King, "The Joseph Story and Divine Politics: A Comparative Study of a Biographic Formula from the Ancient Near East," *Journal of Biblical Literature* 106 (1987) 577–87. Robert B. Lawton describes the parallels between Jacob's relation with Rachel and Leah on the one hand and David's with Merab and Michal on the other ("1 Samuel 18: David, Merob, and Michal," *Catholic Biblical Quarterly* 51 [1989] 423–25).

[5] Eduard Meyer, *Die Israeliten und ihre Nachbarstämme* (Halle: Max Niemeyer, 1906) pp. 127–28. For the connection between J and the United Kingdom period, see Hans W. Wolff, "The Kerygma of the Yahwist," *Interpretation* 20 (1966) 131–58.

[6] R. E. Clements, *Abraham and David, Genesis XV and Its Meaning for Israelite Tradition* (Naperville, IL: Alec R. Allenson, Inc., 1967) pp. 16–47; and, in a quite different way, Benjamin Mazar, "The Historical Background of the Book of Genesis," *Journal of Near Eastern Studies* 28 (1969) 73–83.

though hardly proven, by ancient analogues, which range from the ancient Near Eastern stories of Idrimi, Ashurbanipal, Esarhaddon, and Hattusilis to the classical accounts of Romulus and Remus or Acrisius and Proetus, and beyond, as in Egyptian myths about Horus and Seth or those of the Persian deities Ahriman and Ohrmazd. Without trying to homogenize these obviously diverse traditions, which range from prenatal struggles to personal combat, it is possible to identify a common thread. Ultimately, they are all interested in rulership. For in the end, what is at stake time and again in these stories is the question of succession to the throne. That is to say, the point in each and every tale is to explain or justify the one who became king.[7]

For reasons both intrinsic to the Bible as well as drawn from a broader, comparative context, then, it is perfectly reasonable to look to Israel's monarchy as a possible focus for these accounts. More particularly, given the observations above, it should be the period when the two kingdoms were joined under the house of David that raises the specific issue with which these stories are concerned, one which, in the nature of things, must have something to do with a younger son whose preeminence was achieved through the displacement of his older brother.

Although the book of Samuel presents David as a younger son, there is no evidence that his rise to power took place within a family setting of the sort that is so central to these accounts. To be sure, his accession was perceived as involving the displacement of a prior king, whose imposing physical presence may affect the way David's older brothers are described[8]; however, it is not really sibling rivalry which lies at the center of that story, which in any event is widely considered a late accretion to the biblical traditions about David.[9] However, the accession of his son Solomon does incorporate the central elements of this theme in a variety of significant ways. We have already observed that Solomon's accession to the throne could not have been automatic, since, at the time, Israelite culture had no experience with a hereditary monarchy.[10] As the founder

---

[7] See pp. 85 and 117 above; additional cases of childhood fraternal conflict where subsequent rulership is the underlying issue include the stories of Eteocles and Polyneices (Apollodorus, *The Library* 3.5.8–6.1 [LCL vol. 1, pp. 348–49]), Neleus and Pelias (ibid., 1.9.8–16 [LCL vol. 1, pp. 82–95]), Atreus and Thyestes (Apollodorus, Epitome of *The Library* 2.11 [LCL vol. 2, pp. 163–64]), Tyndareus and Hippocoon (Pausanias, *Description of Greece*, "Laconia" 3.14 [LCL vol. 2, pp. 4–5]), and Procles and Eurysthenes (Herodotus 6.52 [LCL vol. 3, pp. 196–99]).

[8] See pp. 86–87 above.

[9] See note 7 in chapter 3.

[10] See p. 77 above.

of a dynasty in a country that had scarcely a generation of kings, David's successor could hardly have been certain. The Bible itself gives no indication that Solomon was expected to be David's heir. Not only is there no evidence that he was the oldest of David's sons, but he may not even have been one of the royal family's older princes and possibly not even Bathsheba's oldest child.[11]

The Bible leaves no doubt that Solomon's accession was the result of having been appointed by his father (1 Kings 1). Whether this promise, first mentioned by Nathan near the time of David's death, had actually been offered earlier is not clear. Be that as it may, the practice of designation by an incumbent is both typical of Israelite culture and central to this motif. However, the complexity of the events described suggests that the process whereby Solomon achieved the throne may well have been suspect.

Evidence that Solomon's legitimacy was a matter of some dispute can be inferred from the polemics supporting it, even outside the book of Samuel. Most notable is the way in which the later Chronicler "remedies" 1 Samuel's vagueness as to whom God intended to be David's successor, taking great pains to show not only that David had been promised a dynasty, but that it was through Solomon that this promise would be fulfilled.[12] Whether the impetus for this justification grew out of embarrassment with the biblical account or from awareness of more ancient traditions, there can be little doubt that the way in which Solomon had come to the throne was a matter of some discomfort. The collective thrust of the Genesis stories—that a younger son can be chosen over older, more obvious candidates so long as he has been designated by his father—thus defends the emergence of Solomon, a younger brother whose accession, like that of the younger sons who so fill the pages of Genesis, seems to have entailed considerable difficulties with family members.

The key to understanding the treatment of this issue in the book of Kings lies in its reference to David's promise to Bathsheba that her son would replace him (1 Kings 1:13, 17).[13] Such a commitment would

---

[11] See p. 78 above.

[12] 1 Chron 28:5; see Yehezkel Kaufmann, *Toledot Ha-ʾEmunah ha-Yisraʾelit* (Jerusalem: Bialik Institute; Tel Aviv: Dvir, 1937–56) vol. 8, pp. 462–64, and Roddy L. Braun, "Solomonic Apologetic in Chronicles," *Journal of Biblical Literature* 92 (1973) 506–7. The closest analogue in 1 Kings is David's expression of gratitude for having lived to see his successor (1:48), who is not even named there. Joachim Conrad notes 2 Samuel's statement that God loved Solomon, (12:24, *Die junge Generation im alten Testament, Möglichkeiten und Grundzüge einer Beurteilung* [Berlin: Evangelische Verlagsanstalt, 1970] p. 59), which is a patent aetiology for the name Jedidiah.

[13] Even this does not specify Solomon, since according to 1 Chron 3:5 Bathsheba had other sons.

certainly have been realistic. David's attraction to Bathsheba is evident from both the story of their early affair and his response to her later in life. It would certainly have been reasonable for David to have wanted the succession to proceed through her, as rulers in many cultures have done by choosing heirs on the basis of affection for a particular wife.[14] Israelite tradition itself records God's assurance that Abraham's line would be reckoned through Sarah rather than Hagar, and Jacob's preference for Joseph seems largely the result of his love for Rachel. In a later generation, there are even hints that Abijah was chosen to succeed Rehoboam on account of his mother (2 Chron 11:21–22).

Granting the reasonableness of this choice does not, however, prove that such a promise had actually been made. Of particular significance is the Bible's failure to mention it at the time of David's affair with Bathsheba. It is hard to imagine any reason why this should have been omitted. Biblical authors are seldom reluctant to repeat information when the occasion demands it, sometimes providing lengthy and even verbatim repetitions.[15] With everything that is at stake in the biblical depiction of David's relationship with Bathsheba, mentioning such a promise would have been an effective way both to demonstrate the king's commitment to his new wife and to support Solomon's eventual claim to the throne. Indeed, the absence of such a promise only raises doubts as to whether it had actually been made. Even God, who has much to say about the future of David's line, never indicates who the successor would be or how he would be chosen, but only that the king would be followed by his son(s). In fact, Chronicles is at great pains to remedy this omission in the book of Samuel.

This kind of discrepancy between the way an event is initially presented and how it is later reported is not without precedent in the Bible, where such changes often play an important role in characterization and subsequent narrative development. There are numerous examples that illustrate how this dynamic can work.[16] Joseph's brothers say that their father Jacob, who by then was dead, had asked him to forgive their earlier mistreatment (Gen 50:17). Not only is there no support for this in the earlier narrative, but it is reasonable to suspect that it was not true. The brothers' misrepresentation shows how their father's death had left them feeling painfully vulnerable to Joseph's anticipated vengeance, itself possibly a

---

[14] See note 45 in chapter 2.

[15] The most extensive example is the description of the tabernacle incorporated in God's commandment to Moses (Exodus 25–31) and then repeated in the account of its execution (Exodus 35–40).

[16] See George W. Savran, *Telling and Retelling in Biblical Narrative* (Bloomington, IN: Indiana University Press, 1988) chapter 3, especially pp. 64–65 and 81–82.

projection of their own guilty consciences, while depriving Joseph of any way to verify the accuracy of their claim.

Similarly, Jonah reacts to the Ninevites' repentance by chiding God for not having accepted his earlier explanation that he fled in order to avoid this inevitable turn to events (4:2). In fact, the book records no such earlier statement, which would, in any case, be rendered suspect by Jonah's general behavior and more typical cowardice. His claim is, therefore, most likely a demonstration of after-the-fact self-righteousness, rather than an accurate report.

This phenomenon is also evident in the Israelites' assertion at the Red Sea that they had earlier asked Moses to leave them in Egypt, since "It is better for us to serve the Egyptians than to die in the wilderness" (Exod 14:12). Although this too is not impossible, it is an all-too-convenient recollection with no support in previous chapters. Rather than the report of an incident which was actually believed to have occurred, it, therefore, seems best understood as illustrating the mentality of this people, who blamed Moses in order to avoid responsibility for their now undesired plight.

A final example can be found in the Garden of Eden story. Although Eve told the snake that God had prohibited her and Adam from both eating and touching the tree in the middle of the garden (Gen 3:3), only eating is mentioned in the original report of God's prohibition (2:16–17). Eve's statement thus reveals a significant gap between her impression and what God actually said, providing an opportunity the snake exploits. Eve's statement had not been volunteered, but was offered in response to the snake's carefully phrased question: "Did God really say, 'You may not eat from any tree in the garden'?" (3:1). Of course, God had said nothing of the sort, as the snake surely knew. Although a query cannot, by its very nature, be inaccurate, this one was plainly intended as a conversational gambit, giving Eve an opportunity to create her own trap.[17]

The exchange between Eve and the snake is uniquely relevant to the biblical account of Solomon's accession. Nathan used the snake's technique in approaching Bathsheba. According to the biblical account, David's son Adonijah had gathered a band of supporters, before whom he proclaimed, "I shall rule" (*'ănî 'emlōk*, 1 Kings 1:5). Rather than simply

---

[17] The midrash recognizes this in its description of the snake as having pushed Eve into the tree, pointing out that just as she had not died from touching it, so would she not die after eating it (*Genesis Rabbah* 19:3). Interestingly, the commandment was originally given to Adam before the account of Eve's creation. For an alternative interpretation of "touching" as mere rhetoric, see Umberto Cassuto, *A Commentary on the Book of Genesis* (Jerusalem: Magnes Press, 1961) vol. 1, p. 145.

informing Bathsheba of this event, Nathan "innocently" inquired as to the extent of her information: "Have you not heard that Adonijah, the son of Haggith, has become king and our[!] lord David does not know?" (1:11). This is far different from what we have been told had actually taken place. Whereas Adonijah's proclamation used the imperfect form of the verb (*'emlōk*), implying only his intention to succeed, Nathan's report uses the perfect (*mālak*), suggesting that this had already taken place. This is scarcely an oversight or a matter of mere style. Nathan's phrasing was not intended to be objective. His reference to Adonijah's mother Haggith demonstrates an effort to capture the queen's attention. In case the message was still unclear, he urged Bathsheba to "save your own life and the life of your son Solomon" (1:12), appealing to her self-interest, much as the snake had done with Eve.

The emotional nature of Bathsheba's response makes it clear that Nathan succeeded in arousing both her maternal and her wifely instincts. "When my lord, the king, lies down with his fathers," she told David, "my son Solomon and I will be regarded as traitors" (1:21). Cast in the position of Sarah, Bathsheba recognized the implications for her own future should her husband's heir be some other woman's offspring.

Knowledge (*yd'*) plays a central role throughout this account. Having been told by Nathan that "our master David does not know" (1:11), Bathsheba reported Adonijah's actions to the king with the comment, "but you did not know" (1:18). Later, Nathan himself asked the king, "Did this come from my lord, the king, without your letting your servant know?" (1:27). Nor is that the only kind of knowledge that David was lacking. The text earlier uses common biblical terminology to tell us that he had not known (*lō' yĕdā'āh*) Abishag, the beautiful young woman who had been brought to keep him warm (1:1–4), a remarkable admission for a king of David's earlier sexual enthusiasm.

Knowledge, in all its dimensions, is, of course, also a central theme in the Garden of Eden story, where another woman was manipulated by a different instigator seeking to reach her husband.[18] Although there is no reason to think that the story of Solomon has been modeled on that Genesis account, comparisons of this sort can draw attention to important features which illuminate our understanding of biblical narratives.[19] In

---

[18] Meir Sternberg points out that knowledge is a common theme throughout the Bible (*The Poetics of Biblical Narrative, Ideological Literature and the Drama of Reading* [Bloomington, IN: Indiana University Press, 1985] pp. 176–79).

[19] See Yair Zakovitch, "*Sippur Bavu'ah—Meimad Nosaf le-Ha'arakhat Demuyot ba-Sippur ha-Miqra'i,*" *Tarbiz* 54 (1984/85) 165–76, which should be considered in the light

this case, the analogy between these two incidents supports the appropriateness of setting Nathan alongside the snake and thus the likelihood that this cunning figure had invented, or at least manipulated, the facts rather than reported them accurately. The probability that David had never made such a promise thus casts its shadow over the characters and events that follow.[20]

Although Nathan encouraged Bathsheba to follow his lead and approach David with a question—"Did you not, my lord king, swear to your maidservant, saying, 'Solomon, your son, shall reign after me, and he shall sit on my throne'?" (1:13)[21]—her own approach was more straightforward, if still of questionable accuracy: "My lord, you yourself swore to your maidservant by the Lord, your God, 'Solomon, your son, will rule after me, and he will sit on my throne'" (1:17), before encouraging him to action with the observation, "The eyes of all Israel are upon you, my lord king, to tell them who shall succeed my lord king on the throne" (1:20). It was at that precise moment that Nathan entered in accordance with his earlier plan,[22] referring twice to the one who "sits on the throne" (*yšb 'l ksʾ*) while asking the king, "Did you really say, 'Adonijah will rule after me'? for ... he has assembled all the royal princes and army officers as well as Abiathar the priest ... and they have said 'Long live King Adonijah'" (1:24–27). This again goes well beyond what was earlier reported. By carefully orchestrating the presentation of this "information," Nathan was able to emphasize the situation's gravity and create the impression of two independent witnesses to the events he described.

We can only speculate as to the motivation for Nathan's behavior. The Bible's comment that he had been excluded from Adonijah's party

---

of Adele Berlin, "Literary Exegesis of Biblical Narrative: Between Poetics and Hermeneutics" in *"Not in Heaven": Coherence and Complexity in Biblical Narrative*, ed. Jason P. Rosenblatt and Joseph Sitterson, Jr. (Bloomington, IN: Indiana University Press, 1991) pp. 120–28.

[20] For a detailed exposition of this issue, see Pinhas Neʾeman, "*Shevuʿat David u-Ṣevaʾato (Heʿarot le-Sippur ha-Miqraʾi ʿal ʿAliyato shel Shelomoh la-Melukhah*," *Beth Mikra* 10 (1965) 70–76, to which should be contrasted Shaul Zalevsky, "*Ha-Maʾavaq ʿal ha-Melukhah bein ʾAdoniyahu li-Shelomoh*," *Beth Mikra* 20 (1975) 490–94. Yehezkel Kaufmann helps focus the issue by contending that whatever the historical reality, the author believed there to have been such an oath ("*Ha-Sippurim ʿal David u-Shelomoh*," *Molad* 15 [1957] 99).

[21] This interchange is discussed by Robert Alter, "Biblical Narrative," *Commentary* 61:5 (May 1976) 63–64; for the entire passage, see also Harry Hagan, "Deception as Motif and Theme in 2 Sm 9–20; 1 Kgs 1–2," *Biblica* 60 (1979) 320–31.

[22] Nathan's instructions to Bathsheba (1 Kings 1:13) are followed by his stated intention to come back before the king after she has spoken in order to confirm what she had said (*ûmillēʾtî ʾet-dĕbārāyik*).

(1 Kings 1:8) suggest that self-interest may have played a role, with Nathan attempting to protect his position or maybe even his life. In the absence of any evidence that Solomon was an obvious, much less the best choice for the crown, it may have been Bathsheba's closeness to the king that led Nathan to focus on him as an alternative candidate for the throne. In any event, Nathan's actions left the dottering king with a simple choice: to acknowledge an oath he did not, for good reason, remember having made or to admit having lost control over both his household and his land. Under the circumstances, it is not surprising that David announced having made such a promise—it would, after all, have been a reasonable thing for him to have done—nor that he did so in the most forceful royal form: "Just as I swore to you by the Lord, God of Israel, saying, 'Solomon, your son, will succeed me to sit on my throne after me,' so will I do this [very] day" (1:30). Rather than proving such a commitment to have been made, the announcement shows only that David believed that he had made such a promise.

Although its abundant detail and apparent familiarity with court procedure are often cited to support the Succession Narrative's historicity, its intricate literary construction and underlying apologetic make this a doubtful proposition.[23] Rather than reporting facts, it seeks to explain and to justify Solomon's position as David's heir, a turn of events which was neither required by Israelite practice nor understood as inevitable by the biblical account.[24]

Neither father nor son is presented here in wholly positive terms, but the succession is portrayed in such a way as to spare both of them blame for the unlikely turn of events. The implication that David had lost control over both his memory and his kingdom leaves his integrity intact. His endorsement of Solomon is ultimately ascribed to Nathan's manipulation, but in a way that avoids undercutting the proclamation's legitimacy, just as the validity of Isaac's blessing of Jacob is not undermined by the deception through which it had been attained.[25] Nor did Solomon behave

---

[23] Cf. David M. Gunn, "Narrative Patterns and Oral Tradition in Judges and Samuel," *Vetus Testamentum* 24 (1974) 286–317, to which should be contrasted Gerhard von Rad, "The Beginnings of Historical Writing in Israel" in *The Problem of the Hexateuch and Other Essays* (New York: McGraw Hill, 1966) p. 195, and P. Kyle McCarter, Jr., "The Apology of David," *Journal of Biblical Literature* 99 (1980) 489–504, which summarizes recent discussion of this issue.

[24] Cf. T. C. G. Thornton, "Solomonic Apologetic in Samuel and Kings," *Church Quarterly Review* 169 (1968) 160–62, and Joachim Conrad, "Zum geschichtlichen Hintergrund der Darstellung von Davids Aufstieg," *Theologische Literaturzeitung* 97 (1972) 329.

[25] Tomoo Ishida notes the similarity of the parental roles to those in Genesis 27 ("Solomon's Succession to the Throne of David—A Political Analysis" in *Studies in the*

illegitimately, even if his selection, like that of Isaac and Joseph, owed more to his mother's identity than his own accomplishments.[26] Indeed, what sets him apart from the successful younger brothers who are so prominent throughout the Bible is Solomon's total absence both before and during these events. Spoken of, he never speaks, nor even appears on the biblical stage until after being proclaimed king. He never receives a divine promise, nor is he the subject of an oracle in the manner of Isaac and Jacob. Neither a braggart nor a cheat, he is not even mentioned until the actual struggle for the throne, and even then remains strangely silent. Following the death of two older brothers, the eldest of whom had raped a half-sister and the next attempted to usurp his father's crown, it is Adonijah who is presented as having taken the initiative—and paid the price. Never cheated like Esau, displaced like Manasseh, or expelled like Ishmael, Adonijah appears to be the displacer, leaving Solomon with the crown almost by default, the unexpected beneficiary of his brothers' transgressions and his supporters' success.

Given the obviously convoluted circumstances of his succession, this passivity effectively shields Solomon from suspicion of having connived for the throne. However complex that process may actually have been, later generations could at least find some solace in its not having been Solomon's fault nor, for that matter, David's. The biblical account is, therefore, neither anti-David nor anti-Solomon, but portrays both as having been pawns in the plot of Nathan and Bathsheba.[27]

While acknowledging that Solomon's road to the throne had been rock-strewn, the book of Kings does allow him one element no other candidate could claim—designation by the incumbent, albeit at the very close of David's life and under circumstances that rendered its legitimacy inherently suspect.[28] Yet it is precisely in this that the book of Kings' account of Solomon's rise conforms to the pattern that pervades so much of Genesis. It accepts the authority of paternal designation, quite apart from the circumstances under which it was obtained or the merit of its

---

Period of David and Solomon and Other Essays, ed. T. Ishida [Winona Lake, IN: Eisenbrauns, 1982] p. 180).

[26] The biblical reference to David's supposed promise conforms to this pattern by emphasizing that it had been made to Bathsheba (1 Kings 1:13-17).

[27] Contrast Ernst Würthwein, *Die Erzählung von der Thronfolge Davids—theologische oder politische Geschichtsschreibung?* (Zurich: Theologischer Verlag, 1974) pp. 11-15, and F. Langlamet, "Pour ou contre Salomon? La Rédaction prosalomonienne de I Rois, I–II," *Revue Biblique* 83 (1976) 321-79, 481-528.

[28] Shaul Zalevsky, *'Aliyat Shelomoh li-Melukhah—Pirqei 'Iyyun be-Sefer Melakhim uve-Sefer Divrei ha-Yamim* (Jerusalem: J. Marcus, 1981) p. 15.

beneficiaries, whether younger offspring whose success followed the disqualification of older siblings (Abel, Isaac, Joseph, Rachel, Ephraim), or on tempermental (Cain, Esau) or moral grounds. Lest that point be missed, one case even involves premature access to a father's woman (Reuben), much as Absalom had demonstrated publicly with his father's concubines (2 Sam 16:21–22) and as Adonijah sought to achieve with Abishag, even after having been denied the crown (1 Kings 2:17). Fratricide (Abel and almost Jacob and Joseph) and deceptive exploitation of an older father's frailties (Jacob, Ephraim) are also common elements in these tales, along with the centrality of conjugal favoritism (Isaac, Joseph) and an emphasis on supporters' ambition (Isaac, Jacob).[29] The presentation of Solomon's accession in 1 Kings thus incorporates a variety of elements that are conspicuous in the Genesis description of younger sons' ascendance, revolving around the central point that neither age nor status nor even merit is crucial for the chosen line, so long as the blessing has been bestowed by their father, a concept rooted in actual patterns of Israelite inheritance and succession. The eyes of Genesis are thus on Solomon, even as Cain and Jacob are on its lips, providing a theological and political *Sitz im Leben* for the displacement theme.[30]

That is not to say that these tales were necessarily composed or collected during Solomon's own lifetime. The Pentateuch's J tradition, with its widely recognized interest in the United Kingdom, is no longer assumed to have been written during that period which it considers the fulfillment of God's promises.[31] A closer look at the stories which collectively constitute this theme will provide ample evidence that they, too, could have been written later.

The United Monarchy period to which the Jacob-Esau traditions are so widely ascribed would certainly have been an appropriate time for an apparently Northern hero of Transjordanian origins to have been absorbed into this cycle with its Southern focus, but it was not the only time during which there was tension between Israel and Edom. The Bible mentions an Edomite rebellion as having taken place during Joram's ninth-century

---

[29] Other patriarchal motifs that recur in the accounts of David and Solomon include flight from an enemy (Jacob, David, and Absalom), performance of an assigned task (Jacob and David), and rape of a sister (Dinah and Tamar).

[30] See already Peter F. Ellis, *The Yahwist, The Bible's First Theologian* (Notre Dame, IN: Fides Publishers, 1968) p. 134; other connections between Genesis and the time of David are noted by Benno Jacob, *Das Erste Buch der Tora, Genesis* (Berlin: Verlag Schocken, 1934) pp. 1048–49.

[31] Cf. John van Seters, *Abraham in History and Tradition* (New Haven, CT: Yale University Press, 1975) pp. 149–53 and note 23 in this chapter.

reign (2 Kings 8:21) and her defeat by Amaziah early in the eighth (2 Kings 14:7). Fifty years later, Edom appears to have enjoyed a resurgence (2 King 16:6, emended). All these hint at Judean hegemony and Edomite restlessness, precisely the conditions implied by the Jacob-Esau tales. Similar circumstances may be reflected in the report of an Edomite king who accompanied an unnamed ruler of Israel (presumably Jehoram) against Moab's King Mesha (2 Kings 3:9). The theme of ongoing tension between Israel and Edom, with the former unexpectedly successful, thus fits several chronological contexts within the monarchy period.[32]

A similar ambiguity attends the reference to Reuben's displacement of Ephraim and Manasseh. It is certainly reasonable to date these traditions after the tribe of Reuben had fallen from a presumably prominent position within Israelite affairs.[33] However, that scarcely limits their possible origin to the regins of David or Solomon. To the extent that Chronicles draws on the deuteronomic formulation of Israel's law of inheritance, the account may be no earlier than the seventh century.

The adoption of Ephraim and Manasseh to positions of equality with the other tribes, represented by Reuben and Simeon, as described in Genesis 48, may also have to be dated after the tenth century, when the tribe of Reuben appears to have weakened and Simeon was absorbed into Judah[34]; however, it is difficult to identify the Ephraimite superiority over Manasseh which that chapter's description of Jacob's blessing seeks to justify so early in Israelite history. Manasseh is not even mentioned in the Song of Deborah, which does name several other northern groups. Nor do the references to Ephraimite separateness in the book of Judges provide an appropriate setting, since those efforts rarely met with success. Only in the story of Gideon does Ephraim begin to emerge as an independent force, and even there narrative centrality need not include political preeminence. It is not until the time of Hosea, when its name blossomed into full equivalence with "Israel," that one can find firm evidence of Ephraimite priority. The eighth century is thus as credible a setting for this tradition as any other.[35]

---

[32] For a survey of Edomite history, see J. R. Bartlett, "The Rise and Fall of the Kingdom of Edom," *Palestine Exploration Quarterly* 104 (1972) 26–37.

[33] Cf. Roland de Vaux, *The Early History of Israel* (Philadelphia: Westminster Press, 1978) pp. 577–81; this theme is echoed in Deut 33:6.

[34] See Roland de Vaux, *The Early History of Israel*, pp. 528–29 and 578.

[35] Cf. Roland de Vaux, *The Early History of Israel*, pp. 650–52, and Otto Kaiser, "Stammesgeschichtliche Hintergründe der Josephsgeschichte, Erwägungen zur Vor- und Frühgeschichte Israels," *Vetus Testamentum* 10 (1960) 8–10. W. J. Phythian-Adams and Edwin C. Kingsbury both see this as an early tradition, the former as a reflex of Ephraim's

The possibility that a Solomonic apology could have been written significantly later than the events it seeks to justify is not weakened by some readers' confidence in the eyewitness value of the Succession Narrative, which has a similar concern, for its date too is far from certain.[36] To be sure, similar royal apologetics from other, nearby cultures seem often to have been composed near the end of the reigns they defend.[37] However, arguments such as this, with their heavy reliance on analogy rather than direct evidence, can never be definitive. In this case, all they really show is that apologies for a particular succession were often composed at some time other than that of the actual events they describe. That should hardly be surprising. A new king's rivals are unlikely to be impressed with mere stories. Real challenges require force, not propaganda, as Solomon plainly recognized in his treatment of Adonijah, Abiathar, Joab, and Shimei.[38] The problem addressed by such accounts, in Israel as elsewhere, is less political than psychological. Rather than protecting rulers whose power had been achieved through questionable means, they respond to his partisans' embarrassment at their hero's behavior. This may be the reason why so many of the Mesopotamian analogues were composed towards the end of their protagonists' careers, when virtually all enjoyed secure and prosperous positions. It is the judgment of history that provides their motivation, rather than immediate political concerns. As history's winners, with an empire and an army of their own, Solomon and his party hardly needed literary justification.

In fact, Solomon's legitimacy, and perhaps that of David's dynasty as a whole, continued to be problematic throughout the biblical period. After Solomon died, the country split, with the North continuing for centuries under non-Davidic rule. The Bible explains this schism as the outcome of an effort by Solomon's son to continue and even extend his father's policies (1 Kings 12:1–14). If this account is reliable, Northerners could justify their rejection of Jerusalem by pointing to Solomon's

---

numerical superiority ("The Boundary of Ephraim and Manasseh," pp. 229–31) and the latter as reflecting the transfer of the central shrine from Shechem (in Manasseh) to Bethel (in Ephraim) ("He Set Ephraim Before Manasseh," *Hebrew Union College Annual* 38 [1967] 135).

[36] Cf. notes 23 and 24 in this chapter.

[37] See Hayim Tadmor, "Autobiographical Apology in the Royal Assyrian Literature" in *History, Historiography and Interpretation, Studies in Biblical and Cuneiform Literatures*, ed. H. Tadmor and M. Weinfeld (Jerusalem: Magnes Press, 1983), especially pp. 37 and 54–56.

[38] Compare Solomon's treatment of Adonijah after coming to see his brother's behavior as a threat (1 Kings 2:23–25) with that accorded Abiathar, Joab, and Shimei as described in the same chapter.

questionable status, much as Saul's misconduct served to legitimate the appointment of David. Such a challenge would have created the need for a polemical response to accompany the more direct military reaction.

Nor did this issue die when the North fell to Assyria in the eighth century. Although the book of Chronicles was written long after that event, and even after the Babylonian conquest of Jerusalem brought the Davidic dynasty to a close over a hundred years later, it is still at pains to show that God's promise, which the book of Samuel had extended to David's descendants in general, applied to Solomon alone.[39] Whatever the circumstances motivating this during the postexilic period when Chronicles was written,[40] neither the polemic nor its postexilic setting can be easily denied.

If the apologetic character of these accounts makes it difficult to ascertain the actual process that brought Solomon to the throne, there need be no doubt about the complexity of those events nor the unexpected nature of their outcome, which provide the backdrop for the construction of these tales. Those issues plainly exercised ancient Israelites for a long period of time. The difficulty in determining the reason it would have been important at a time when Israel did not even enjoy political autonomy, much less a monarchy, merely reinforces the fact that this, like so many other polemics, existed for internal consumption, defusing supporters' embarrassment about their nation's past more than changing the minds of their opponents. Its purpose is to free David from the stain of having left his kingdom in chaos and, by implication, to suggest that his behavior had been legitimate, or at least as much so as that of Isaac and of Jacob.

The way this is presented in the Bible, with Solomon as yet another younger son whose success owes less to his own merit than to a complicated set of circumstances culminating in appointment by his father, is of broader than political interest. It is constructed so as to convey the sense of chosenness while leaving Solomon both personally and politically innocent—a younger son who bore no responsibility for the schemes that led to his success. The process of elimination, which tars each of his older brothers in succession, leaves Solomon as the most fit of David's sons, with the support of both his father and of God, whose role is tacitly

---

[39] See p. 144 above.

[40] Charles C. Torrey sees the competition posed to Jerusalem by other shrines as motivating Chronicles (*Ezra Studies* [1910; reprinted New York: Ktav Publishing House, 1970] p. 153); see also Otto Plöger, *Theocracy and Eschatology*, trans. S. Rudman (Oxford: Basil Blackwell, 1968) pp. 38–41. As the founding patron of the Jerusalem Temple, Solomon would surely have been a central figure in such a work.

maximized, even though He takes no direct part in the actual events. The story of Solomon's accession thus conforms in several notable ways to the larger pattern we have found elsewhere in the Bible. Better qualified than his older siblings, he is presented by biblical authors as an appropriate selection, even if not an initially obvious or even a patently meritorious candidate.

Having located a reasonable conceptual *Sitz im Leben* for the Bible's repeated stories of younger sons' displacing their older brothers does not exhaust this theme's ramifications for Israelite culture. For the underlying dynamic, in which God passes over an initial candidate, for whatever set of reasons, proves to be remarkably widespread in biblical lore. A similar configuration characterizes the portrayal of Samuel as having supplanted the line of Eli (1 Samuel 2).[41] David, too, the paradigm of royalty, is presented not merely as the founder of Israel's longest lived and divinely endorsed dynasty, but as having replaced Saul, God's original choice. This is a particularly telling example, since the book of Chronicles clearly demonstrates that things could have been presented quite differently. There, Saul's reign is largely ignored, leaving the impression that David was Israel's first king.[42] But the book of Samuel is quite clear that Saul had preceded David in that office, opening the door to those who might view David as a usurper.

Kingship itself is presented as a relative latecomer to Israel's social order, by pro- and antimonarchic sources alike. In this, the Bible stands apart from other Near Eastern cultures where governmental structures are given primordial or, at least, antediluvian status, as is best known from the Sumerian notion that kingship had been lowered from heaven (nam-lugal an-ta e_{11}-dè-a-ba) in some primeval period.[43] Biblical authors could and did sometimes see things similarly. The Bible does, after all, begin with creation, which serves as something of a prologue to the history of Israel which is its main concern. In Gerhard von Rad's words, "Presumptuous as it may sound, creation is part of the aetiology of Israel," locating her within a kind of primordial universal history.[44]

---

[41] See John T. Willis, "An Anti-Elide Narrative Tradition from a Prophetic Circle at the Ramah Sanctuary," *Journal of Biblical Literature* 90 (1971) 289–91.

[42] Although frequently mentioned in Chronicles, Saul is never identified there as Israel's king. 1 Chron 11:2 is taken over from 2 Sam 5:2. 13:3 only alludes to his once having ruled, while 10:14 and 12:23 refer to his kingdom's having been transferred to David without actually naming it.

[43] *The Sumerian King List* 1.41 (ed. Thorkild Jacobsen, Chicago: University of Chicago Press, 1939) pp. 76–77 (see also 1.1 on pp. 70–71).

[44] *Old Testament Theology* (New York: Harper & Brothers, 1962) vol. 1, p. 138.

For the most part, however, the status quo is set within history, and the existing order grounded in circumstances that are spelled out in great, if not always reliable detail.[45] It is, therefore, paradoxically appropriate that the Bible's predilection for rejecting initial arrangements emerges at the very beginnings of history, with creation itself presented as having needed modification. The continuing sinfulness of Adam and Eve's descendants, even after their expulsion from Eden, forced God to destroy everything He had so proudly made and return the world to its precreative, watery chaos, beginning again with Noah as a kind of second Adam.[46]

That effort, too, was doomed to failure when Noah, who is introduced as having been "righteous in his generation" (Gen 6:9), and his family turn out to be almost as poor a choice as those they were intended to replace. There are problems from the moment they leave the ark, with Noah's drunkenness followed by construction of the Tower of Babel, itself presented in a way that evokes motifs from the preceding flood story.[47] So once again God's plans were thwarted, forcing Him to scatter mankind and focus His attentions on only one people, itself not an entirely happy choice as the subsequent narratives make clear. In this respect, the biblical view parallels later rabbinic tradition, which held that Israel had been offered the Torah only after God was turned down by all the other nations.[48]

Beyond the implications of this for understanding the Bible's attitude towards human nature, it raises serious theological questions. After the flood, God promised Noah there would never again be such destruction throughout the world inasmuch as "mankind's ideas are wicked from his youth" (Gen 8:21). Left unsaid is the fact that it was to eradicate human sin that the flood had been undertaken in the first place (6:5). Despite God's efforts, nothing much seems to have changed, leaving the impression

---

[45] Cf. Peter Machinist, "The Question of Distinctiveness in Ancient Israel," in *Ah Assyria... , Studies in Assyrian History and Ancient Near Eastern Historiography Presented to Hayim Tadmor*, ed. Mordecai Cogan and Israel Eph'al (Scripta Hierosolymitana 33; Jerusalem: Magnes Press, 1991) pp. 208–10.

[46] For the flood as a new creation, see Jack M. Sasson, "The 'Tower of Babel' as a Clue to the Redactional Structuring of the Primeval History (Gen. 1–11:9)" in *The Bible World, Essays in Honor of Cyrus H. Gordon*, ed. Gary Rendsburg, Ruth Adler, Milton Arfa, and Nathan H. Winter (New York: Ktav Publishing House and The Institute of Hebrew Culture and Education of New York University, 1980) pp. 216–17.

[47] Jack M. Sasson, "The 'Tower of Babel,'" pp. 211–19; cf. also parallels with Eden (e.g., Gen 3:22 and 11:6 as motives for expulsion). Whatever the exact nature of Noah's sin (or that of his sons), its sinfulness is not in doubt.

[48] E.g., *Sifre* Deuteronomy §343 (ed. L. Finkelstein, New York: Jewish Theological Seminary of America, 1969, p. 396) and *Mechilta Bahodesh* §5 (ed. H. S. Horovitz, Jerusalem: Bamberger & Wahrman, 1960, p. 221).

that the flood itself had been an expensive failure for God, who seems to have come to terms with our propensity for sin, accepting humankind as we are—a fallible God learning to accommodate the fallibility of His creation.[49]

Throughout much of Israelite history the Bible presents God's initial choices as inadequate. The covenant with Abraham was supplemented by that through Moses, which was in turn subsumed by one with the family of David.[50] Indeed, it is this thematic structure that leaves the impression that Israel had been displaced by her own king as God's *bekōr*.[51] Nor is there any evidence that these choices had been based on the candidates' demonstrated worth. Abraham appears without introduction, just as Israel's eventual king was chosen without experience and her lawmaker without expertise.

This dynamic continued to be attractive long after the Hebrew Bible was completed. Forced to explain how they could be God's chosen people in the face of similar claims by the Jewish community, early Christians compared themselves to Isaac, the elect younger son who had displaced an entrenched but undeserving older brother (Galatians 4:22–31). The Jews, who were accustomed to thinking of themselves as weak but beloved, thus found the theological tables turned.[52]

Given the nature of this imagery, such a development may have been inevitable. As in many of the stories considered here, an initially dispossessed figure ceases to be so once he has been chosen by God and becomes instead the target, or at least an obstacle, for some other unfortunate character. Early Christianity saw Israel as Esau, holding a status that was neither appreciated nor deserved (Romans 9:10–13).[53] In one of history's crueler ironies, the Church retained this self-image, even after it achieved dominance. Where the Hebrew Bible sympathizes with Ishmael and Esau, Christian resentment of its older brother, due perhaps to the

---

[49] Dan Jacobson contrasts the Israelite satisfaction in connecting God with social change, which he identifies with "peripeteia," with the Egyptian concern with stability (*The Story of the Stories, The Chosen People and Its God* [New York: Harper & Row, 1982] p. 145).

[50] Cf. God's threat to replace the stiff-necked Israelites with the descendants of Moses (Exod 32:9–10 and Num 14:11–12).

[51] Ps 89:28; see pp. 28–29 above. Martin Buber makes a similar observation regarding the biblical presentation of humanity as the last of God's creations ("Abraham the Seer," *Judaism* 5 [1956] 293).

[52] Conversely, the rabbis portrayed Christian Rome as Esau, Jacob's more powerful, but undeserving brother.

[53] This image persisted, as in *Barnabbas* 13 (*PG* vol. 2, p. 766), where Ephraim and Manasseh are also invoked.

insecurity we all feel towards older siblings no matter how limited their success, has been manifest in a history whose results are all too familiar.[54]

It was not only the past with which biblical writers were dissatisfied. Rather than accepting the status quo, they looked forward to a time when justice would prevail and Israel's rightful place be restored. Their faith in an eschatological resolution and their certainty that justice would triumph in the end points to yet another reversal of the status quo. However, that raises a profound theological quandary. After all, God's endorsement may be reserved for a time yet to come, but this world, too, is of His making, including all the problems it contains.

In that context, it is important to remember that, no matter how much these tales depend on human actions, God's hand is always present. To be sure, the outcome is rarely announced as the result of direct divine intervention. The flood is, after all, something of a rarity, even in the Bible.[55] Most often, God exploits personality traits—the vanity of Joseph, the manipulativeness of Rebecca or Nathan, Sarah's protectiveness, and the like—for His own ends. Joseph admitted as much when he told his brothers, "You intended ill for me, but God planned it to be good" (Gen 50:20, cf. 45:5–8), and Adonijah made the same point in his acknowledgment that "the kingdom devolved and became my brother's because it was God's will" (1 Kings 2:15).[56] A similar conclusion applies to the actions of Jacob and Rebecca, which are presented as ensuring the fulfillment of God's oracle delivered prior to the twins' birth. Even Isaac's more subtle case does not differ fundamentally, since God had authorized the expulsion of Hagar and Ishmael in fulfillment of His promise to

---

[54] Pope John XXIII reversed the classic Christian identification of the Jews with Cain (e.g., Tertullian, *Adversus Judaeos* 5 [*PG* vol. 2, p. 607]; cf. Augustine, *Contra Faustus Manichaeum* 12.9 [*PL* vol. 42, p. 259] and *De Civitate Dei* 15.7 [*LCL* vol. 4, pp. 446–47]) when he asserted, "We realize that the mark of Cain stands upon our foreheads. Across the centuries our brother Abel has lain in the blood which we drew or shed the tears we caused by forgetting Thy Love" (F. E. Cartus, "Vatican II & the Jews," *Commentary* 39 [January, 1965] 21). More typical is John Paul II's reference to the Jews as "our elder brothers in the faith of Abraham" (letter to the president of the National Conference of Catholic Bishops, John L. May, printed in the *New York Times* on August 20, 1987, section II, p. 14; see also his remarks at a synagogue in Rome as reported on April 14, 1986, p. A4). These issues may underlie the omission of Gregory Baum's assertion that Romans 11 "does not justify calling the Jew the elder brother of the Christian or the Synagogue the elder sister of the Church" from the revised version of *The Jews and the Gospel, A Reexamination of the New Testament* (Westminster, MD: Newman Press, 1961) p. 252, republished as *Is the New Testament Anti-Semitic?* (Glen Rock, NJ: Paulist Press, 1965).

[55] Judah Goldin, "The Youngest Son or Where Does Genesis 38 Belong," *Journal of Biblical Literature* 96 (1977) 30, note 21; this appears close to the underlying point of 1 Kings 19:1–12.

[56] Contra Ernst Würthwein, *Die Erzählung von der Thronfolge Davids*, p. 15.

Abraham that it would be through Isaac "that your offspring will be called" (Gen 21:12, cf. 17:16, 19, 21). Jacob's choice of Rachel is also presented as the providential result of their "chance" meeting by a well, a propitious location in biblical typology.[57] The outcome of these stories cannot, therefore, be ascribed to human freedom alone.

Still, Jacob and Joseph were hardly innocents, nor did Sarah act in conscious response to revelation. The success of even passive figures, such as Ephraim and Solomon, is plainly attributed to parental decisions. For many of these stories, it is precisely through the machinations of human envy and desire that God's will is done. They draw attention to His power and ability to succeed despite, or because of, our failings and recalcitrance. In the words of sociologist Andrew Greeley, "God draws straight with crooked lines."[58]

But, as we have seen, God's lines are not always straight. Moreover, if the younger offspring who fill the Bible are God's tools, it is worth remembering that the older siblings, with whom its landscape is so littered, are also God's creatures. The complexities and moral ambiguities these stories describe owe a great deal to divine decisions. Whatever theological point may be illustrated by the Bible's predilection for unlikely heroes, therefore, also raises a serious question as to God's role and judgment. The murder of Abel was, after all, the outcome of a divine act, and it is at least odd that God could not have found agents whose behavior was more deserving and methods less convoluted than those presented in the Bible.

These difficulties are not resolved by appealing to some inevitable decline in human character, which confornted God with the impossible dilemma of finding a perfect line of descent. The Bible traces human sin to the time of Adam and Eve, and problems with royalty begin in the region of Saul. The prevalence of this pattern thus casts a shadow of doubt on the wisdom of a God whose ability to see into our hearts does not, apparently, include the ability to anticipate where those emotions will lead, a problem only exacerbated by the fact that it is He who created

---

[57] Cf. Robert Alter, *The Art of Biblical Narrative* (New York: Basic Books, 1981) pp. 52–58. Note the phrasing of Gen 29:5, according to which Jacob had just asked about his kinsman Laban when "lo (*wĕhinnēh*) Rachel, his daughter, came with the sheep"; similar implications are apparent in Ruth 2:4 and 4:1.

[58] *The Bible and Us, A Priest and a Rabbi Read Scripture Together*, with Jacob Neusner (New York: Warner Books, 1990) p. 99; contrast Kant's observation, "aus so krummen Holze, als woraus der Mensch gemacht ist, kann nichts ganz Gerades gezimmert werden" (in "Idee zu einer allgemeinen Geschichte in weltbürgenliche Absicht" in *Immanuel Kants Sämmtliche Werke in chronologischer Reihenfolge*, ed. G. Hartenstein [Leipzig: Leopold Voss, 1867] vol. 4, p. 149).

those hearts.[59] We must also wonder about the justice of a God whose choices seem so often of dubious merit and the methods of their success so questionable. To be sure, biblical authors note God's awareness of virtues we cannot see. But for many of these characters, it is their lack of virtue which seems the point. The claim that neither His methods nor His criteria need be our own[60] ultimately raises doubts about the nature of the universe in which we live. By so consistently allowing for the failure of God's initial efforts, the text challenges both His competence and His justice.

The structure of the younger-son motif, with its underlying uncertainty as to Israel's worth, thereby raises questions as well about the God who chose her in the first place. By populating so much of biblical narrative with figures who are seemingly undeserving of the positions they have been given, these tales collectively suggest the irrelevance of human merit and God's independence of the values one would expect to find at the heart of biblical literature. God works with these figures because He can and He must. He created them, and He chose them. As things turn out, neither God nor Israel is as perfect as they should be. Perhaps that is why they make such good partners.

---

[59] For a similar conclusion, see J. Cheryl Exum, "The Centre Cannot Hold: Thematic and Textual Instabilities in Judges," *Catholic Biblical Quarterly* 52 (1990) 410–31.

[60] E.g., Exod 33:19.

Selected Bibliography

Aberbach, Moses and Smolar, Leivy. "Aaron, Jeroboam, and the Golden Calves," *Journal of Biblical Literature* 86 (1967) 129–40.

Adler, Alfred. "Characteristics of the First, Second, Third Child," *Children, The Magazine for Parents* 3:5 (May 1928) 14, 52.

Adler, Alfred. *Understanding Human Nature.* Garden City, NY: Garden City Publishing Co., 1927.

Alt, Albrecht. *Essays on Old Testament History and Religion.* Garden City, NY: Doubleday, 1968.

Alter, Robert. *The Art of Biblical Narrative.* New York: Basic Books, 1981.

Alter, Robert. "Biblical Narrative," *Commentary* 61:5 (May 1976) 61–67.

Altus, William D. "Birth Order and Its Sequelae," *Science* 151 (1966) 44–49.

Amit, Yairah. "'*Hû' šā'ûl 1-YHWH,' Remizah Mehadeqqet, mi-Šiṭoteha shel ha-'Arikhah ha-Sifrutit,*" *Beth Mikra* 27 (1981/82) 38–43.

Andreas, Reichart. "Israel, the Firstborn of God: A Topic of Early Deuteronomic Theology." In *Proceedings of the Sixth World Congress of Jewish Studies,* vol. 1, pp. 341–49. Jerusalem: Jerusalem Academic Press, 1977.

Andriolo, Karin R. "A Structural Analysis of Genealogy and Worldview in the Old Testament," *American Anthropologist* 75 (1973) 1657–69.

Arfert, P. *Das Motiv von der Unterschobenen Braut in der internationalen Erzählungs-litteratur.* Schwerin: Bärensprungschen Hofbuchdruckerei, 1897.

Argyle, A. W. "πρωτότοκος πάσης κτίσεως (Colossians i.15)," *Expository Times* 66 (1954/55) 61–62.

Asheri, David. "Laws of Inheritance, Distribution of Land and Political Constitutions in Ancient Greece," *Historia* 12 (1963) 1–21.

Avishur, Yitzhak. "The 'Duties of the Son' in the 'Story of Aqhat' and Ezekiel's Prophecy on Idolatry," *Ugarit-Forschungen* 17 (1986) 49–60.

Babcock-Abrahams, Barbara. "'A Tolerated Margin of Mess': The Trickster and

His Tales Reconsidered," *Journal of the Folklore Institute* 11 (1974/75) 147–86.

Bächli, Otto. "Die Erwählung des Geringen im alten Testament," *Theologische Zeitschrift* 22 (1966) 385–95.

Bammel, E. "Die Bruderfolge im Hochpriestertum der herodianisch-römischen Zeit," *Zeitschrift des Deutschen Palästina-Vereins* 70 (1954) 147–53.

Bartlett, J. R. "The Brotherhood of Edom," *Journal for the Study of the Old Testament* 4 (1977) 2–27.

Bartlett, J. R. "The Edomite King-List of Genesis XXXVI.31–39 and I Chron. I.43–50," *Journal of Theological Studies* n.s. 16 (1965) 301–14.

Bartlett, J. R. "The Land of Seir and the Brotherhood of Edom," *Journal of Theological Studies* 20 (1969) 1–20.

Bartlett, J. R. "The Rise and Fall of the Kingdom of Edom," *Palestine Exploration Quarterly* 104 (1972) 26–37.

Bartlett, J. R. "The Use of the Word *rō'š* as a Title in the Old Testament," *Vetus Testamentum* 19 (1969) 1–10.

Bayliss, Miranda. "The Cult of Dead Kin in Assyria and Babylonia," *Iraq* 35 (1973) 115–25.

Beeston, A. F. L. "Epigraphic and Archaeological Gleanings from South Arabia," *Oriens Antiquus* 1 (1962) 41–52.

Beeston, A. F. L. "Kingship in Ancient South Arabia," *Journal of the Economic and Social History of the Orient* 15 (1972) 256–68.

Ben-Barak, Zafrira. "*Teqes Hakhtarat Yo'ash le-'or Teqes Hakhtarat Nabopolassar*." In *Mehqarim be-Toledot 'Am Yisra'el ve-'Eres Yisra'el* 5 (1980) 43–56.

Berlin, Adele. "Literary Exegesis of Biblical Narrative: Between Poetics and Hermeneutics." In *"Not in Heaven": Coherence and Complexity in Biblical Narrative*, ed. Jason P. Rosenblatt and Joseph Sitterson, Jr., pp. 120–28. Bloomington, IN: Indiana University Press, 1991.

Bernfeld, Shimon. "*Ha-Bekhorah be-Shivtei Yisra'el*," *Ha-Shiloah* 31 (1944) 1–9, 158–67, 341–47, 426–32.

Bess, Stephen H. "Systems of Land Tenure in Ancient Israel." Ph.D. dissertation, University of Michigan, 1963.

Bettelheim, Bruno. *The Uses of Enchantment, The Meaning and Importance of Fairy Tales*. New York: Alfred A. Knopf, 1976.

Blenkinsopp, Joseph. "Theme and Motif in the Succession History (2 Sam. XI 2ff) and the Yahwist Corpus," Supplement to *Vetus Testamentum* 15 (1965) 44–57.

Bloch, Marc. *Feudal Society*. Chicago: University of Chicago Press, 1961.

Braun, Roddy L. "The Message of Chronicles: Rally 'Round the Temple," *Concordia Theological Monthly* 42 (1971) 502–14.

Braun, Roddy L. "Solomonic Apologetic in Chronicles," *Journal of Biblical Literature* 92 (1973) 503–16.

Brin, Gershon. "*Bekhor Behemah Temey'ah*," *Beth Mikra* 21 (1975/76) 566–74.

Brin, Gershon. "*Bekhor le-'Em u-Vekhor le-'Av ba-Miqra'*." In *Sefer Ben-Zion Lurie, Meḥqarim ba-Miqra' uve-Toledot Yisra'el*, pp. 31–50. Jerusalem: Kiryat Sepher, 1979.

Brin, Gershon. "*Darkhei Ma'avar ha-Hegmoniyah ha-Mishpaḥatit veha-Qesher le-Sidrei ha-Bekhorah.*" In *Ha-Ṣvi Yisra'el, 'Asufat Meḥqarim ba-Miqra' Zekher Dr. Yisra'el Broide .z"l u-Veno Ṣvi Broide z"l*, ed. J. Licht and G. Brin, pp. 47–55. Tel Aviv: Tel Aviv University, School for Jewish Studies, 1976.

Brin, Gershon. "*Dinei Bekhorot ba-Miqra'*," *Tarbiz* 46 (1976/77) 1–7.

Brin, Gershon. "The Firstling of Unclean Animals," *Jewish Quarterly Review* 68 (1977) 1–15.

Brin, Gershon, "*Ha-Bekhor be-Yisra'el bi-Tequfat ha-Miqra'*." Ph.D. dissertation, Tel Aviv University, 1971.

Brin, Gershon. "*Le-Toledot ha-Nushah 'Hu' Yiheyeh Li le-Ven va'ani 'Eheyeh Lo le-'Av'*." In *Ha-Miqra' ve-Toledot Yisra'el. . .*, ed. B. Uffenheimer, pp. 57–64. Tel Aviv: Tel Aviv University, 1972.

Brin, Gershon. "*Ma'amado shel ha-Bekhor bi-Reshimot ha-Yaḥas*," *Beth Mikra* 24 (1978/79) 255–59.

Brin, Gershon. "*Parashat Bekhoratam shel Benei Ya'aqov*," *Tarbiz* 48 (1978/79) 1–8.

Brin, Gershon. "*Shetei Sugeyot be-Dinei Yerushah ba-Tequfah ha-Miqra'it— Meḥqar Hashva'ati*," *Dinei Yisra'el* 6 (1975) 231–49.

Brinkman, J. A. "A Note on the Middle Assyrian Laws," *Revue d'Assyriologie* 79 (1985) 88–89.

Brown, Arthur Mason. "The Concept of Inheritance in the Old Testament." Ph.D. dissertation, Columbia University, 1965.

Brugman, J., et al. *Essays on Oriental Laws of Succession*. Leiden: E. J. Brill, 1969.

Buber, Martin. *Kingship of God*. New York: Harper & Row, 1967.

Buccellati, G. "La 'carriera' di David e quella di Idrimi, re di Alalac," *Bibbia e Oriente* 4 (1962) 95–99.

Burney, C. F. "Christ as the APXH of Creation (Prov. viii 22, Col. i 15–18, Rev. iii 14.)," *Journal of Theological Studies* 27 (1925) 160–77.

Burns, John Barclay. "The Identity of Death's First-Born (Job xviii 13)," *Vetus Testamentum* 37 (1987) 362–64.

Callaway, Mary. *Sing, O Barren One, A Study in Comparative Midrash*. Atlanta, GA: Scholars Press, 1986.

Carmichael, Calum M. *The Laws of Deuteronomy*. Ithaca, NY: Cornell University Press, 1974.

Classen, C. Joachim. "Zur Herkunft der Sage von Romulus und Remus," *Historia* 12 (1963) 446–57.

Clements, Ronald E. *Abraham and David, Genesis XV and Its Meaning for Israelite Tradition*. Naperville, IL: Alec R. Allenson, Inc., 1967.

Cohen, Norman J. "Two That Are One—Sibling Rivalry in Genesis," *Judaism* 32 (1983) 331–42.

Colunga, Alberto. "La Ley de los Primogénitos y el Pentateuco," *Salmanticensis* 1 (1954) 450–55.

Conrad, Joachim. *Die junge Generation im alten Testament, Möglichkeiten und Grundzüge einer Beurteilung.* Aufsätze und Vorträge zur Theologie und Religionswissenschaft, vol. 47. Berlin: Evangelische Verlagsanstalt, 1970.

Conrad, Joachim. "Zum geschichtlichen Hintergrund der Darstellung von Davids Aufstieg," *Theologische Literaturzeitung* 97 (1972) 321–32.

Cooke, Gerald, "The Israelite King as Son of God," *Zeitschrift für die Alttestamentliche Wissenschaft* 73 (1961) 202–25.

Cover, Robert M. "Nomos and Narrative," *Harvard Law Review* 97 (1983) 4–68.

Crown, A. D. "A Reinterpretation of Judges IX in the Light of Its Humor," *Abr-Nahrain* 3 (1961/62) 90–98.

Cruveilhier, P. "Le Lévirat chez les hébreux et chez les assyriens," *Revue Biblique* 34 (1925) 524–46.

Dahl, Nils A. "Der Erstbegorene Satans und der Vater des Teufels (Polyk. 7, und Joh 8₄₄)." In *Apophoreta, Festschrift für Ernst Haenchen,* pp. 70–84. BZNW 30. Berlin: Alfred Töpelmann, 1964.

Daube, David. "*Consortium* in Roman and Hebrew Law," *Juridical Review* 62 (1950) 71–91.

Daube, David. "How Esau Sold His Birthright," *Cambridge Law Journal* 8 (1942) 70–75.

Daube, David. "Inheritance in Two Lukan Pericopes," *Zeitschrift der Savigny-Stiftung für Rechtsgeschichte* (Romanistische Abteilung) 72 (1955) 326–34.

Daube, David. "The Preponderance of Intestacy at Rome," *Tulane Law Review* 89 (1964/65) 253–62.

David, Martin. *Die Adoption im altbabylonischen Recht.* Leipzig: Theodor Weicher, 1927.

Davies, Eryl W. "Inheritance Rights and the Hebrew Levirate Marriage," *Vetus Testamentum* 31 (1981) 138–44, 257–68.

Davies, Eryl W. "The Meaning of *Pî Šᵉnayim* in Deuteronomy XXI 17," *Vetus Testamentum* 36 (1976) 341–47.

Donner, Herbert. "Adoption oder Legitimation? Erwägungen zur Adoption im alten Testament auf dem Hintergrund der altorientalischen Rechte," *Oriens Antiquus* 8 (1969) 87–119.

Draffkorn, Anne E. "*Ilāni/Elohim,*" *Journal of Biblical Literature* 76 (1957) 216–24.

Dundes Alan, ed. *The Study of Folklore.* Englewood Cliffs, NJ: Prentice-Hall, 1965.

Durand, Alfred. "Le Christ 'Premier-né'," *Recherches de Science Religieuse* 1 (1910) 56–66.

Ebeling, E. "Erbe, Erbrecht, Enterbung." In *Reallexikon der Assyriologie und Vorderasiatische Archäologie,* ed. E. Ebeling and B. Meissner, vol. 2, pp. 458–62. Berlin and Leipzig: Walter de Gruyter, 1938.

Ebeling, E. "Fratriarchat." In *Reallexikon der Assyriologie und Vorderasiatische*

Archäologie, ed. E. Weidner and W. von Soden, vol. 3, p. 100. Berlin: Walter de Gryter, 1957–71.

Eissfeldt, Otto. "Sohnespflichten im alten Orient," *Syria* 43 (1966) 39–47.

Eitrem, S. *Die göttlichen Zwillinge bei den Griechen*. Skrifter udgivne af Videnskabsselskalet. Christiania: Jacob Dybwad, 1902.

Emerton, J. A. "An Examination of a Recent Structuralist Interpretation of Genesis XXXVIII," *Vetus Testamentum* 26 (1976) 79–98.

Emerton, J. A. "Judah and Tamar," *Vetus Testamentum* 29 (1979) 403–15.

Ernest, Cécile and Angst, Jules. *Birth Order, Its Influence on Personality*. Berlin: Springer-Verlag, 1983.

Exum, J. Cheryl. "The Centre Cannot Hold: Thematic and Textual Instabilities in Judges," *Catholic Biblical Quarterly* 52 (1990) 410–31.

Farmer, Kathleen Anne. "The Trickster Genre in the Old Testament." Ph.D. dissertation, Southern Methodist University, 1978.

Feldman, Sandor S. "The Sin of Reuben, First-Born Son of Jacob," *Psychoanalysis and the Social Sciences* 4 (1955) 282–87.

Fichtner, Paula Sutter. *Protestantism and Primogeniture in Early Modern Germany*. New Haven, CT: Yale University Press, 1989.

Fishbane, Michael. *Text and Texture, Close Readings of Selected Biblical Texts*. New York: Schocken Books, 1979.

Flanagan, James W. "Court History or Succession Document, A Study of 2 Samuel 9–20 and 1 Kings 1–2," *Journal of Biblical Literature* 91 (1972) 172–81.

Fortes, Meyer. "The First Born," *The Journal of Child Psychology and Psychiatry and Allied Disciplines* 15 (1974) 81–104.

Frankfort, Henri. *Kingship and the Gods, A Study of Ancient Near Eastern Religion as the Integration of Society and Nature*. Chicago: University of Chicago Press, 1948.

Frazer, James George. *Folk-Lore in the Old Testament, Studies in Comparative Religion, Legend, and Law*. London: Macmillan and Co., 1919.

Fretheim, Terence E. "The Jacob Traditions, Theology and Hermeneutic," *Interpretation* 26 (1972) 419–36.

Frey, J.-B. "La signification du terme ΠΡΩΤΟΤΟΚΟΣ d'apres une inscription Juive," *Biblica* 11 (1930) 373–90.

Friedman, Mordecai A. "Tamar, A Symbol of Life: The 'Killer Wife' Superstition in the Bible and Jewish Tradition," *AJSreview* 15 (1990) 23–61.

Friedman, Richard Elliott. "Deception for Deception," *Bible Review* 2 (Spring 1986) 22–31, 68.

Garsiel, Moshe. *Malkhut David: Meḥqarim be-Historiyah ve-ʿIyyunim be-Historiographia*. Tel Aviv: Don Publishing House, 1975.

Gevaryahu, Chaim M. Y. "*Le-Beirur Ṭivam shel ha-Terafim ba-Tanakh (Lamah Ganevah Raḥel 'et ha-Terafim?)*," *Beth Mikra* 7:3 (1963) 81–86.

Gilula, Mordecai, "The Smiting of the First-Born—An Egyptian Myth?" *Tel Aviv* 4 (1977) 94–95.

Glück, J. J. "Merab or Michal," *Zeitschrift für die Alttestamentliche Wissenschaft* 77 (1965) 72–81.

Goldin, Judah. "The Youngest Son or Where Does Genesis 38 Belong." *Journal of Biblical Literature* 96 (1977) 27–44.

Goodnick, Benjamin. "The Saga of the Firstborn," *Dor le-Dor* 16 (Spring 1988) 170–78.

Goody, Jack. *Death, Property, and the Ancestors, A Study of the Mortuary Customs of the Lodagaa of West Africa*. Stanford, CA: Stanford University Press, 1962.

Goody, Jack. "Sideways or Downwards? Lateral and Vertical Succession, Inheritance and Descent in Africa and Eurasia," *Man* n.s. 5 (1970) 627–38.

Goody, Jack. *Succession to High Office*. Cambridge Papers in Social Anthropology 4. Cambridge: University Press, 1966.

Gordon, Cyrus H. "Fratriarchy in the Old Testament," *Journal of Biblical Literature* 54 (1935) 223–31.

Gordon, Cyrus H. Review of *Ancient Near Eastern Texts Relating to the Old Testament*, ed. James Pritchard, *Journal of Biblical Literature* 70 (1951) 159–63.

Gottwald, Norman K. *The Tribes of Yahweh, A Sociology of the Religion of Liberated Israel, 1250–1050* B.C.E. Maryknoll, NY: Orbis Books, 1979.

Greenberg, Moshe. "Another Look at Rachel's Theft of the Teraphim," *Journal of Biblical Literature* 81 (1962) 239–49.

Griffiths, J. Gwyn. *The Conflict of Horus and Seth, From Egyptian and Classical Sources*. Chicago: Argonaut, 1969.

Grønbaek, Jakob H. *Die Geschichte vom Aufstieg Davids (1 Sam. 15–2. Sam. 5), Tradition und Komposition*. Copenhagen: Prostant apud Munksgaard, 1971.

Gunn, D. M. "Narrative Patterns and Oral Tradition in Judges and Samuel," *Vetus Testamentum* 24 (1974) 286–317.

Habel, Norman C. "The Form and Significance of the Call Narratives," *Zeitschrift für die Alttestamentliche Wissenschaft* 77 (1965) 297–323.

Hagan, Harry. "Deception as Motif and Theme in 2 Sm 9–20; 1 Kgs 1–2," *Biblica* 60 (1979) 201–26.

Hamiel, H. Y. "'*Em Ya'aqov ve-'Eisav*," *Beth Mikra* 32 (1986/87) 332–44.

Harris, Irving D. *The Promised Seed, A Comparative Study of Eminent First and Later Sons*. New York: Free Press of Glencoe, 1964.

Harris, J. Rendel. *Boanerges*. Cambridge: University Press, 1913.

Harris, J. Rendel. *The Cult of the Heavenly Twins*. Cambridge: University Press, 1906.

Harris, J. Rendel. *The Dioscuri in the Christian Legends*. London: Cambridge University Press, 1903.

Hartland, E. Sidney. "Twins." In *Encyclopaedia of Religion and Ethics*, ed. James Hastings, vol. 12, pp. 491–500. New York: Charles Scribner's Sons, 1908–27.

Healy, John F. "The *Pietas* of an Ideal Son at Ugarit," *Ugarit-Forschungen* 11 (1979) 353–56.

Heider, George C. *The Cult of Molek, A Reassessment.* Sheffield, England: JSOT Press, 1985.

Heider, George C. "A Further Turn on Ezekiel's Baroque Twist in Ezek 20:25–6," *Journal of Biblical Literature* 107 (1988) 721–24.

Hempel, Johannes. "Eine Vorfrage zum Erstgeburtsopfer," *Zeitschrift für die Alttestamentliche Wissenschaft* 54 (1936) 311–31.

Hendel, Ronald S. *The Epic of the Patriarch, The Jacob Cycle and the Narrative Traditions of Canaan and Israel.* Atlanta, GA: Scholars Press, 1987.

Henige, David P. *The Chronology of Oral Tradition, Quest for a Chimera.* Oxford: Clarendon Press, 1974.

Henige, David P. "Comparative Chronology and the Ancient Near East: A Case for Symbiosis," *Bulletin of the American Schools of Oriental Research* 261 (1986) 57–68.

Henige, David P. "Oral Tradition and Chronology," *Journal of African History* 12 (1971) 371–89.

Henninger, Joseph. "Menschenopfer bei den Arabern," *Anthropos* 53 (1958) 721–805.

Henninger, Joseph. "Über Menschenopfer bei den vor-islamischen Arabern." In *Akten des Vierundzwanzigsten internationalen Orientalisten-Kongresses München*, ed. Herbert Franke, pp. 244–46. Wiesbaden: Deutsche Morgenländische Gesellschaft, 1959.

Henninger, Joseph. "Zum Erstgeborenenrecht bei den Semiten." In *Festschrift Werner Caskel*, ed. Erwin Gräf, pp. 162–83. Leiden: E. J. Brill, 1968.

Henninger, Joseph. "Zum Erstgeborenenrecht im alten Südarabien," *Ethnologische Zeitschrift Zürich* 2 (1972) 185–92.

Henninger, Joseph, Cazelles, Henri, and Feuillet, André. "Premiers-nés." In *Dictionnaire de la Bible*, Supplement vol. 8, pp. 461–512. Paris: Librairie Letouzey et Ané, 1972.

Hocherman, Yaakov. "*He'arot le-Kamah Miqra'ot be-Sefer Bereishit*," *Beth Mikra* 36 (1990/91) 20–28.

Hockel, Alfred. *Christus der Erstegborene, zur Geschichte der Exegese von Kol 1, 15.* Düsseldorf: Patmos-Verlag, 1965.

Huonder, Vitus. *Israel Sohn Gottes, zur Deutung eines alttestamentlichen Themas in der jüdischen Exegese des Mittelalters.* Orbis Biblicus et Orientalis 6. Freiburg, Switzerland: Universitätsverlag; Göttingen: Vandenhoeck & Ruprecht, 1975.

Ishida, Tamoo. "'The People of the Land' and the Political Crises in Judah," *Annual of the Japanese Biblical Institute* 1 (1975) 23–38.

Ishida, Tomoo. *The Royal Dynasties in Ancient Israel.* BZAW 142. Berlin: Walter de Gruyter, 1977.

Ishida, Tomoo. "Royal Succession in the Kingdoms of Israel and Judah with Special Reference to the People Under Arms as a Determining Factor in the Struggles for the Throne," Supplement to *Vetus Testamentum* 40 (1986) 96–106.

Ishida, Tomoo. "'Solomon Who is Greater Than David,' Solomon's Succession in 1 Kings I-II in the Light of the Inscription of Kilamuwa, King of Y'dy-Sam'al," Supplement to *Vetus Testamentum* 36 (1985) 145–53.

Ishida, Tomoo. "Solomon's Succession to the Throne of David—A Political Analysis." In *Studies in the Period of David and Solomon and Other Essays*, ed. T. Ishida, pp. 175–87. Winona Lake, IN: Eisenbrauns, 1982.

Jacobs, Joseph. *Studies in Biblical Archaeology*. London: David Nutt, 1894.

Johnson, Marshall D. *The Purpose of the Biblical Genealogies, With Special Reference to the Setting of the Genealogies of Jesus*. Cambridge: University Press, 1969.

Kaiser, Otto. "Den Erstegeborenen deiner Söhne sollst du mir geben." In *Denkender Glaube, Festschrift Carl Heinz Ratschow*, ed. Otto Kaiser, pp. 24–48. Berlin: Walter de Gruyter, 1976.

Kardimon, Samson. "Adoption as a Remedy for Infertility in the Period of the Patriarchs," *Journal of Semitic Studies* 3 (1958) 123–26.

Keim, C. Ray. "Primogeniture and Entail in Colonical Virginia," *The William and Mary Quarterly* (3d series) 25 (1968) 545–86.

Kenny, Courtney Stanhope. *The History of the Law of Primogeniture in England and Its Effect upon Landed Property*. pp. 24–48. Cambridge: J. Hall & Son, 1878.

Kingsbury, Edwin C. "He Set Ephraim Before Manasseh," *Hebrew Union College Annual* 38 (1967) 129–36.

Klíma, Josef. "Donationes mortis causa nach den akkadischen Rechtsurkunden aus Susa." In *Festschrift Johannes Friedrich*, ed. R. von Kienle et al., pp. 229–59. Heidelberg: Carl Winter Universitätsverlag, 1959.

Klíma, Josef. *Untersuchungen zum altbabylonischen Erbrecht*. Monographien des Archiv Orientálni 8. Prague: Orientalisches Institut, 1940.

Knauf, Ernst A. "Alter und Herkunft der edomitischen Königliste Gen 36, 31–39," *Zeitschrift für die Alttestamentliche Wissenschaft* 97 (1985) 245–53.

Koschaker, Paul. "Fratriarchat, Hausgemeinschaft und Mutterrecht in Keilschriftrechten," *Zeitschrift für Assyriologie* 41 (1933) 1–89.

Koschaker, Paul. "Zum Levirat nach hethitischem Recht," *Revue Hittite et Asianique* 2 (1933) 77–89.

Koskinen, Aarne A. *ARIKI, The First-Born, An Analysis of a Polynesian Chieftain Title*. FF Communications 181; Helsinki: Suomalainen Tiedeakatemia, Academia Scientiarum Fennica, 1960.

Kramer, Samuel N. "Schooldays: A Sumerian Composition Relating to the Education of a Scribe," *Journal of the American Oriental Society* 69 (1949) 199–214.

Kuntzmann, Raymond. *Le symbolisme des jumeaux au Proche-Orient ancien, Naissance, fonction et évolution d'un symbole*. Paris: Beauchesne, 1983.

Lack, Rémi, S. M. M. "Les origines de *elyon*, le tres-haut, dan la tradition culturelle d'Israel," *Catholic Biblical Quarterly* 24 (1962) 44–64.

Langlamet, F. "Pour ou contre Salomon? Le Rédaction prosalomonienne de I Rois, I–II," *Revue Biblique* 83 (1976) 321–79, 481–528.

Laughlin, John C. H. "The 'Strange Fire' of Nadab and Abihu," *Journal of Biblical Literature* 95 (1976) 559–65.

Laurence, Perceval M. *The Law and Custom of Primogeniture*. Cambridge: J. Hall & Son, 1878.

Lawton, Robert B. "1 Samuel 18: David, Merob, and Michal," *Catholic Biblical Quarterly* 51 (1989) 423–25.

Leman, Kevin. *The Birth Order Book, Why You Are the Way You Are*. Old Tappan, NJ: Fleming H. Revell, Co., 1984.

Levine, Lawrence W. "'Some Go Up and Some Go Down': The Meaning of the Slave Trickster." In *The Hofstadter Aegis, A Memorial*, ed. Stanley Elkins and Eric McKitrick, pp. 94–124. New York: Alfred A. Knopf, 1974.

Liverani, Mario. "L'histoire de Joas," *Vetus Testamentum* 24 (1974) 438–53.

Liverani, Mario. "Partire sul carro, per il deserto," *Annali dell'istituto Orientali di Napoli* 37 (1972) 403–15.

Lust, J. "Ex., XX, 4–26 une Parodie de l'histoire religieuse d'Israel," *Ephemerides theologicae lovanienses* 43 (1967) 488–527.

Maag, Victor. "Jakob-Esau-Edom," *Theologische Zeitschrift* 13 (1957) 418–29.

Machinist, Peter. "The Epic of Tukulti-Ninurta I, A Study in Middle Assyrian Literature." Ph.D. dissertation, Yale University, 1978.

Machinist, Peter. "The Question of Distinctiveness in Ancient Israel, An Essay." In *Ah Assyria..., Studies in Assyrian History and Ancient Near Eastern Historiography Presented to Hayim Tadmor*, ed. Mordechai Cogan and Israel Eph'al, pp. 196–212. Scripta Hierosolymitana 33. Jerusalem: Magnes Press, 1991.

Maine, Henry Sumner. *Ancient Law*. 10th ed. Boston: Beacon Press, 1963; first published in 1884.

Maine, Henry Sumner. *Lectures on the Early History of Institutions*. London: John Murray, 1875.

Marchel, W. *Abba, Père! La Prière du Christ et des Chrétiens*. Rev. ed. Rome: Pontifical Biblical Institute, 1971.

Mattha, Girgis. "Rights and Duties of the Eldest Son According to the Native Egyptian Laws of the Third Century B.C.," *Bulletin of the Faculty of Arts*, University of Cairo 12:2 (December 1950) 113–18.

Mazar, Benjamin. "The Historical Background of the Book of Genesis," *Journal of Near Eastern Studies* 28 (1969) 73–83.

McCarter, P. Kyle, Jr. "The Apology of David," *Journal of Biblical Literature* 99 (1980) 489–504.

McCarter, P. Kyle, Jr. "Plots, True or False, The Succession Narrative as Court Apologetic," *Intrpretation* 35 (1981) 355–67.

McComiskey, Thomas Edward. "The Status of the Secondary Wife: Its Develop-

ment in Ancient Near Eastern Law, A Study and Comprehensive Index."
Ph.D. dissertation, Brandeis University, 1965.

Mendelsohn, Isaac. "On the Preferential Status of the Eldest Son," *Bulletin of
the American Schools of Oriental Research* 156 (1959) 38–40.

Mendelsohn, Isaac. "A Ugaritic Parallel to the Adoption of Ephraim and
Manasseh," *Israel Exploration Journal* 9 (1959) 180–83.

van der Merwe, B. J. "Joseph as Successor of Jacob." In *Studia Biblica et Semitica
Theodoro Christiano Vriezen*, pp. 221–32. Wageningen: H. Veenman Zonen,
1966.

Michaelis, Wilhelm. "Der Beitrag der Septuaginta zur Bedeutungsgeschichte von
ΠΡΩΤΟΤΟΚΟΣ." In *Sprachgeschichte und Wortbedeutung, Festschrift
Albert Debrunner*, pp. 313–20. Bern: Francke Verlag, 1954.

Michaelis, Wilhelm. "Die biblische Vorstellung von Christus als dem Erstgeborenen,"
Zeitschrift für systematische Theologie 23 (1954) 137–57.

Miller, Alan W. "Claude Lévi-Strauss and Genesis 37–Exodus 20." In *Shiv'im:
Essays and Studies in Honor of Ira Eisenstein*, ed. Ronald A. Brauner,
pp. 21–52. Philadelphia: Reconstructionist Rabbinical College; New York:
Ktav Publishing House, 1977.

Miscall, Peter D. "The Jacob and Joseph Stories as Analogies," *Journal for the
Study of the Old Testament* 6 (1978) 28–40.

Mommsen, Th. "Die Remuslegende," *Hermes* 16 (1881) 1–23.

Moret, M. A. "Le privilège du fils aîné, en Egypte et en Mésopotamie au IIIe
Millénaire," *Comptes Rendus de l'Academie des Inscriptions et Belles Letters*
(1933) 82–94.

Mosca, Paul G. "Child Sacrifice in Canaanite and Israelite Religion, A Study in
Mulk and מלך." Ph.D. dissertation, Harvard University, 1975.

Mosca, Paul G. "Ugarit and Daniel 7: A Missing Link," *Biblica* 67 (1986) 496–517.

Mühl, Max. "Der Mythos vom eingeborenen Sohn," *Archiv für Kulturgeschichte*
37 (1955) 1–15.

Ne'eman, P. "*Haqamat Melekh ve-Horashat ha-Melukhah be-Yisra'el*," *Beth
Mikra* 15 (1970) 189–201.

Ne'eman, Pinḥas. "*Shevu'at David u-Ṣeva'ato (He'arot la-Sippur ha-Miqra'i 'al
'Aliyato shel Shelomoh la-Melukhah*," *Beth Mikra* 10:2–3 (1965)
70–76.

Neisser, Edith G. *The Eldest Child*. New York: Harper & Brothers, 1957.

Niditch, Susan. *Underdogs and Tricksters, A Prelude to Biblical Folklore*. San
Francisco: Harper & Row, 1987.

North, C. R. "The Religious Aspects of Hebrew Kingship," *Zeitschrift für die
Alttestamentliche Wissenschaft* 9 (1932) 8–38.

Nübel, Hans-Ulrich. *Davids Aufstieg in der frühe israelitischer Geschichtsschreibung*.
Bonn: Rheinische Friedrich-Wilhelms-Universität, 1959.

Oden, Robert A., Jr. "Method in the Study of Near Eastern Myths," *Religion* 9
(1973) 182–96.

Oller, Gary Howard. "The Autobiography of Idrimi: A New Text Edition with

Philological and Historical Commentary." Ph.D. dissertation, University of Pennsylvania, 1977.

Paradise, Jonathan S. "Nuzi Inheritance Practices." Ph.D. dissertation, University of Pennsylvania, 1972.

Pettinato, Giovanni. "Gli Archivi Reali di Tell Mardikh-Ebla Riflessioni e Prospettive," *Revista Biblica* 25 (1977) 225–43.

Pognon, H. "Lexicographie Assyrienne," *Revue d'Assyriologie* 9 (1912) 125–41.

Puukko, A. F. "Die Leviratsehe in den altorientalischen Gesetzen," *Archiv Orientâlni* 17:2 (1949) 296–99.

Qariv, Avraham. *Shivʿat ʾAmudei ha-Tanakh,ʾIshim ve-ʾIdeʾot be-Sefer ha-Sefarim.* Tel Aviv: Am Oved, 1968.

Radin, Paul. *The Trickster, A Study in American Indian Mythology*, with commentaries by Karl Kerényi and C. G. Jung. London: Routledge and Kegan Paul, 1956.

Rank, Otto. *The Double, A Psychoanalytic Study,* Trans. Harry Tucker, Jr. Chapel Hill, NC: University of North Carolina Press, 1971.

Ranke, Kurt. *Die Zwei Brüder, Eine Studie zu vergleichenden Märchenforschung.* FF Communications 114. Helsinki: Suomalainen Tiedeakatemia, Academia Scientiarum Fennica, 1934.

Reisenberger, Azila Talit. "*Harbah ʾArbeh,*" *Beth Mikra* 36 (1990/91) 80–83.

Rendsburg, Gary A. "David and His Circle in Genesis XXXVIII," *Vetus Testamentum* 36 (1986) 438–46.

Reventlow, Henning Graf. *Opfere deinen Sohn, Eine Auslegung von Genesis 22.* Neukirchen-Vluyn: Neukirchener Verlag des Erziehungsvereins, 1968.

Ricketts, Mac Linscott. "The North American Indian Trickster," *History of Religions* 51 (1965/66) 327–50.

Rockley, Evelyn Cecil. *Primogeniture, A Short History of Its Development in Various Countries and Its Practical Effects.* London: John Murray, 1895.

Rosenblatt, Paul C. and Skoogberg, Elizabeth L, "Birth Order in Cross-Cultural Perspective," *Developmental Psychology* 10 (1974) 48–54.

Rubin, Nisan. "*Le-Mashmaʿuto ha-Ḥevratit shel ha-Bekhor ba-Miqraʾ,*" *Beth Mikra* 33 (1987/88) 155–70.

Rundgren, Frithiof, "Parallelen zu Akk. *šinēpūm* '2/3,'" *Journal of Cuneiform Studies* 9 (1955) 29–30.

Sarna, Nahum M. "The Anticipatory Use of Information as a Literary Feature of the Genesis Narratives." In *The Creation of Sacred Literature, Composition and Redaction of the Biblical Text*, ed. Richard E. Friedman, pp. 76–82. Berkeley, CA: University of California Press, 1981.

Sarna, Nahum M. "The Mythological Background of Job 18," *Journal of Biblical Literature* 82 (1963) 315–18.

Sasson, Jack M. "A Genealogical 'Convention' in Biblical Chronography?" *Zeitschrift für die Alttestamentliche Wissenschaft* 90 (1978) 171–85.

Savran, George W. *Telling and Retelling in Biblical Narrative.* Bloomington, IN: Indiana University Press, 1988.

Schlisske, Werner. *Gottessöhne und Gottessohn im alten Testament, Phasen der Entmythisierung im alten Testament.* Stuttgart: W. Kohlhammer, 1973.

Schneidau, Herbert N. *Sacred Discontent, The Bible and Western Tradition.* Baton Rouge, LA: Louisiana State University Press, 1976.

Seidl, Erwin. *Einführung in die ägyptische Rechtsgeschichte bis zum Ende des Neuen Reiches.* 2d ed. Ägyptologische Forschungen 10. Glückstadt: J. J. Augustin, 1951.

Seidl, Erwin. "La Preminente Posizione Successoria del Figlio Maggiore nel Diritto dei Papiri," *Istituto Lombardo* (Rend. Lett.) 99 (1967) 185–92.

Sethe, Kurt. "Ein Prozessurteil aus dem alten Reich," *Zeitschrift für Ägyptische Sprache und Altertumskunde* 61 (1926) 67–79.

Seux, M.-J. *Épithètes Royales Akkadiennes et Sumériennes.* Paris: Letouzey et Ané, 1967.

Shammas, Carole, Salmon, Marylynn, and Dahlin, Michel. *Inheritance in America from Colonial Times to the Present.* New Brunswick, NJ: Rutgers University Press, 1987.

Skaist, Aaron. "The Ancestor Cult and Succession in Mesopotamia." In *Death in Mesopotamia*, XXVIᵉ Rencontre assyriologique internationale, ed. Bendt Alster, pp. 123–28. Copenhagen: Akademisk Forlag, 1980.

Smith, Morton. "A Note on Burning Babies," *Journal of the American Oriental Society* 95 (1975) 477–79.

Stager, Lawrence E. "The Archaeology of the Family in Ancient Israel," *Bulletin of the American Schools of Oriental Research* 260 (1985) 1–35.

Stager, Lawrence E. "The Rite of Child Sacrifice at Carthage." In *New Light on Ancient Carthage*, ed. John Griffiths Pedley, pp. 1–11. Ann Arbor, MI: University of Michigan Press, 1980.

Stager, Lawrence E. and Wolff, Samuel R. "Child Sacrifice at Carthage: Religious Rite or Population Control?" *Biblical Archaeology Review* 10:1 (January-February 1984) 30–51.

Steinmetz, Devora. *From Father to Son, Kinship, Conflict, and Continuity in Genesis.* Louisville, KY: Westminster/John Knox Press, 1991.

Sternberg, Meir. *The Poetics of Biblical Narrative, Ideological Literature and the Drama of Reading.* Bloomington, IN: Indiana University Press, 1985.

Stevenson, J. H. "The Law of the Throne—Tanistry and the Introduction of the Law of Primogeniture: A Note on the Succession of the Kings of Scotland from Kenneth MacAlpin to Robert Bruce," *The Scottish Historical Review* 25 (1927) 1–12.

Sutton-Smith, Brian and Rosenberg, B. G. *The Sibling.* New York: Holt, Rinehart and Winston, 1970.

Szubin, H. Z. and Porten, Bezalel. "Testamentary Succession at Elephantine," *Bulletin of the American Schools of Oriental Research* 252 (1983) 35–45.

Tabor, James. "Firstborn of Many Brothers: A Pauline Notion of Apotheosis." In *Society of Biblical Literature 1984 Seminar Papers*, ed. Kent H. Richards, pp. 295–303. Chico, CA: Scholars Press, 1984.

Tadmor, Hayim. "Autobiographical Apology in the Royal Assyrian Literature." In *History, Historiography and Interpretation, Studies in Biblical and Cuneiform Literatures*, ed. H. Tadmor and M. Weinfeld, pp. 36–57. Jerusalem: Magnes Press, 1983.

Tadmor, Hayim. " 'The People' and the Kingship in Ancient Israel: The Role of Political Institutions in the Biblical Period," *Journal of World History* 11 (1968) 46–68.

Tallqvist, Knut Leonard. *Akkadische Götterepitheta*. StOr 7. Helsinki: Societas Orientalis Fennica, 1938.

Tatar, Maria. *The Hard Facts of the Grimms' Fairy Tales*. Princeton, NJ: Princeton University Press, 1987.

Thirsk, Joan. "The European Debate on Customs of Inheritance, 1500–1700." In *Family and Inheritance, Rural Society in Western Europe, 1200–1800*, eds. Jack Goody, Joan Thirsk, and E. P. Thompson, pp. 177–91. Cambridge: Cambridge University Press, 1976.

Thirsk, Joan. "Younger Sons in the Seventeenth Century," *History* n.s. 54 (1969) 358–77.

Thornton, T. C. G. "Charismatic Kingship is Israel and Judah," *Journal of Theological Studies* 14 (1963) 1–11.

Thornton, T. C. G. "Solomonic Apologetic in Samuel and Kings," *Church Quarterly Review* 169 (1968) 159–66.

Thureau-Dangin, F. "Notes Assyriologiques," *Revue d'Assyriologie* 10 (1913) 93–100.

Tigay, Jeffrey H. *The Evolution of the Gilgamesh Epic*. Philadelphia: University of Pennsylvania Press, 1982.

Tsevat, Mattitiahu. "*bᵉkhôr*." In *Theological Dictionary of the Old Testament*, ed. G. Johannes Botterweck and Helmer Ringgren, vol. 2, pp. 121–27. Grand Rapids, MI: William B. Eerdmans Publishing Company, 1977.

Tsevat, Mattitiahu. "Die Namengebung Samuels und die Substitutionstheorie," *Zeitschrift für die Alttestamentliche Wissenschaft* 99 (1987) 250–54.

Turner, Victor W. *The Ritual Process, Structure and Anti-Structure*. Chicago: Aldine Publishing Co., 1969.

Tymms, Ralph. *Doubles in Literary Psychology*. Cambridge: Bowes & Bowes, 1949.

Unterman, Jeremiah. "Inheritance and Succession in Ancient Israel." B.A. thesis, Rutgers University, 1968.

de Vaux, Roland. *Studies in Old Testament Sacrifice*. Cardiff: University of Wales Press, 1964.

Veijola, T. "Salomo—der erstgeborene Bathsebas," Supplement to *Vetus Testamentum* 30 (1979) 230–50.

Vinogradoff, Paul. *Outlines of Historical Jurisprudence*. London: Oxford University Press, 1920.

Ward, Donald. *The Divine Twins, An Indo-European Myth in Germanic Tradition*. Folklore Studies 19. Berkeley, CA: University of California Press, 1968.

Wasserstein, Abraham. "*Gilguleha shel 'Iggeret Shabbeta'it be-Ha'ataqot she-'einam Benei Berit,*" *Zion* 37 (1972) 239–43.

Waterman, Leroy. "Jacob the Forgotten Supplanter," *American Journal of Semitic Languages* 55 (1938) 25–43.

Watson, Paul. "A Note on the 'Double Portion' of Deuteronomy 21:17 and II Kings 2:9," *Restoration Quarterly* 8 (1965) 70–75.

Weinfeld, Moshe. "Burning Babies in Ancient Israel," *Ugarit-Forschungen* 10 (1978) 411–13.

Weinfeld, Moshe. "The Covenant of Grant in the Old Testament and in the Ancient Near East," *Journal of the American Oriental Society* 90 (1970) 184–203.

Weinfeld, Moshe. "The Worship of Molech and of the Queen of Heaven and Its Background," *Ugarit-Forschungen* 4 (1972) 133–54.

Weir, Cecil J. Mullo. *A Lexicon of Accadian Prayers in the Rituals of Expiation.* London: Oxford University Press, Humphrey Milford, 1934.

Weiser, Artur. "Die Legitimation des Königs David, Zur Eigenart und Entstehung der sogen. Geschichte von Davids Aufstieg," *Vetus Testamentum* 16 (1966) 325–54.

Wilhelm, Gernot. "Ta/erdennu, Ta/urtannu, Ta/urtānu, *Ugarit-Forschungen* 2 (1970) 277–82.

Williams, James G. "The Beautiful and the Barren: Conventions in Biblical Type-Scenes," *Journal for the Study of the Old Testament* 17 (1980) 107–19.

Wilson, Robert R. *Genealogy and History in the Biblical World.* New Haven, CT: Yale University Press, 1977.

Wolf, Herbert Martin. "The Apology of Ḫattušiliš Compared with Other Political Self-Justifications of the Ancient Near East." Ph.D. dissertation, Brandeis University, 1967.

Wolff, Hans Walter. "The Kerygma of the Yahwist," *Interpretation* 20 (1966) 131–58.

Würthwein, Ernst. *Die Erzählung von der Thronfolge Davids—theologische oder politische Geschichtesschreibung?* Zurich: Theologischer Verlag, 1974.

Wyatt, Nicolas. "The Expression *B^ekôr Māwet* in Job XVIII 13 and Its Mythological Background," *Vetus Testamentum* 40 (1990) 207–16.

Zakovitch, Yair. "*Sippur Bavu'ah—Meimad Nosaf le-Ha'arakhat Demuyot ba-Sippur ha-Miqra'i,*" *Tarbiz* 54 (1984/85) 165–76.

Zalevsky, Shaul. '*Aliyat Shelomo li-Melukhah—Pirqei 'Iyyun be-Sefer Melakhim uve-Sefer Divrei ha-Yamim.* Jerusalem: J. Marcus, 1981.

Zalevksy, Shaul. "*Ha-Ma'avaq 'al ha-Melukhah bein 'Adoniyahu le-Shelomoh',*" *Beth Mikra* 20 (1975) 490–510.

Zimmerli, Walther. "Erstgeborene und Leviten: Ein Beitrag zur exilisch-nachexilischen Theologie." In *Near Eastern Studies in Honor of William Foxwell Albright*, ed. Hans Goedicke, pp. 459–69. Baltimore, MD: The Johns Hopkins University Press, 1971.

Index of Biblical and
Other Sources

Subject Index